The Collected Short Works of Thorstein Veblen

Volume II

Thorstein Veblen

VERNON PRESS

www.vernonpress.com

In the Americas:
Vernon Press
1000 N West Street,
Suite 1200, Wilmington,
Delaware 19801
United States

In the rest of the world
Vernon Press
C/Sancti Espiritu 17,
Malaga, 29006
Spain

ISBN 978-1-62273-215-9

Contents

Publisher's Note

This three-volume collection contains Veblen's publications in academic journals and other scholarly press. The articles are organized under major chapters covering Veblen's pioneering thoughts on social organization; economic theory; social theory; institutions, social organization and economic performance; contemporary policies and social movements; social applications of evolutionary reasoning. The original outlets and years of publication are listed below.

- On the Nature of Capital II: Investment, Intangible Assets, and the Pecuniary Magnate (The Quarterly Journal of Economics, 1908)
- Böhm-Bawerk's Definition Of Capital And The Source Of Wages (Quarterly Journal of Economics, 1892)
- Gustav Schmoller's Economics (Quarterly Journal of Economics, 1901)
- The Use Of Loan Credit In Modern Business (The Decennial Publications Of The University Of Chicago, 1903)
- Credit and Prices (The Journal of Political Economy, 1905)
- The Overproduction Fallacy (The Quarterly Journal of Economics, 1892)

SOCIAL THEORY

- The Barbarian Status of Women (American Journal of Sociology, 1899)
- The Economic Theory of Women's Dress (Popular Science Monthly, 1894)
- The Beginnings of Ownership (American Journal of Sociology, 1898)
- The Instinct of Workmanship and the Irksomeness of Labor (American Journal of Sociology, 1898)

INSTITUTIONS, SOCIAL ORGANIZATION AND ECONOMIC PERFORMANCE

- Christian Morals and the Competitive System (International Journal of Ethics, 1910)
- The Intellectual Pre-Eminence of Jews in Modern Europe (Political Science Quarterly, 1919)
- The Opportunity of Japan (The Journal of Race Development, 1915)

VOLUME III

COMMENTARY ON CONTEMPORARY POLICIES AND SOCIAL
MOVEMENTS

- The Industrial System and the Captains of Industry (DIAL. A Fort-
  nightly, 1919)
- The Captains of Finance and the Engineers (DIAL. A Fortnightly,
  1919)
- The Country Town (The Freeman, 1923)
- The Army of the Commonweal (Journal of Political Economy, 1894)
- The Price of Wheat Since 1867 (Journal of Political Economy, 1892)
- The Food Supply And The Price Of Wheat (The Journal of Political
  Economy, 1893)
- The Later Railway Combinations (The Journal of Political Economy,
  1901)
- On the General Principles of a Policy of Reconstruction (Journal of
  the National Institute of Social Sciences, 1918)

PHILOSOPHY

- Kant's Critique of Judgment (The Journal of Speculative Philosophy,
  1884)

SOCIAL APPLICATIONS OF EVOLUTIONARY REASONING

- The Evolution of the Scientific Point of View (The University of Cali-
  fornia Chronicle, 1908)
- The Place of Science in Modern Civilisation (American Journal of
  Sociology, 1906)
- The Mutation Theory and the Blond Race (The Journal of Race De-
  velopment, 1913)
- The Blond Race and the Aryan Culture (University of Missouri Bulle-
  tin, 1913)
- An Early Experiment in Trusts (The Journal of Political Economy,
  1904)
- As to a Proposed Inquiry into Baltic and Cretan Antiquities (The
  American Journal of Sociology, 1910)

REFLECTIONS

ON ECONOMIC THEORY

(continued)

Chapter 1

Why Is Economics Not An Evolutionary Science?

M. G. de La Pouge recently said, "Anthropology is destined to revolution-
ise the political and the social sciences as radically as bacteriology has
revolutionised the science of medicine1[1].

In so far as he speaks of economics, the eminent anthropologist is not
alone in his conviction that the science stands in need of rehabilitation.
His words convey a rebuke and an admonition, and in both respects he
speaks the sense of many scientists in his own and related lines of inquiry.
It may be taken as the consensus of those men who are doing the serious
work of modern anthropology, ethnology, and psychology, as well as of
those in the biological sciences proper, that economics is helplessly behind the times, and unable to handle its subject matter in a way to entitle
it to standing as a modern science.

The other political and social sciences come in for their share of this ob-
loquy, and perhaps on equally cogent grounds. Nor are the economists
themselves buoyantly indifferent to the rebuke. Probably no economist
today has either the hardihood or the inclination to say that the science
has now reached a definitive formulation, either in the detail of results or
as regards the fundamental features of theory. The nearest recent approach to such a position on the part of an economist of accredited standing is perhaps to be found in Professor Marshall's Cambridge address of a
year and a half ago[2].

But these utterances are so far from the jaunty confidence shown by the
classical economists of half a century ago that what most forcibly strikes
the reader of Professor Marshall's address is the exceeding modesty and
the uncalled for humility of the spokesman for the "old generation." With
the economists who are most attentively looked to for guidance, uncertainty as to the definitive value of what has been and is being done, and as
to what we may, with effect, take to next, is so common as to suggest that
indecision is a meritorious work.

Even the Historical School, who made their innovation with so much
home grown applause some time back, have been unable to settle down
contentedly to the pace which they set themselves. The men of the sciences that are proud to own themselves "modern" find fault with the econo-

---

[1] The Fundamental Laws of Anthropo-sociology," Journal of Political Economy,
December, 1897, p. 54. The same paper, in substance, appears in the Rivista Italiana
di Sociologia for November, 1897.

[2] The Old Generation of Economists and the New", Quarterly Journal of Economics,
January, 1897, p. 133.

mists for being still content to occupy themselves with repairing a structure and doctrines and maxims resting on natural rights, utilitarianism, and administrative expediency.

This aspersion is not altogether merited, but is near enough to the mark to carry a sting. These modern sciences are evolutionary sciences, and their adepts contemplate that characteristic of their work with some complacency. Economics is not an evolutionary science - by the confession of its spokesmen; and the economists turn their eyes with something of envy and some sense of baffled emulation to these rivals that make broad their phylacteries with the legend, "Up to date." Precisely wherein the social and political sciences, including economics, fall short of being evolutionary sciences, is not so plain. At least, it has not been satisfactorily pointed out by their critics. Their successful rivals in this matter - the sciences that deal with human nature among the rest - claim as their substantial distinction that they are realistic: they deal with facts. But economics, too, is realistic in this sense: it deals with facts, often in the most painstaking way, and latterly with an increasingly strenuous insistence on the sole efficacy of data. But this "realism" does not make economics an evolutionary science. The insistence on data could scarcely be carried to a higher pitch than it was carried by the first generation of the Historical School; and yet no economics is farther from being an evolutionary science than the received economics of the Historical School.

The whole broad range of erudition and research that engaged the energies of that school commonly falls short of being science, in that, when consistent, they have contented themselves with an enumeration of data and a narrative account of industrial development, and have not presumed to offer a theory of anything or to elaborate their results into a consistent body of knowledge. Any evolutionary science, on the other hand, is a close-knit body of theory. It is a theory of a process, of an unfolding sequence. But here, again, economics seems to meet the test in a fair measure, without satisfying its critics that its credentials are good. It must be admitted, e.g., that J. S. Mill's doctrines of production, distribution, and exchange, are a theory of certain economic processes, and that he deals in a consistent and effective fashion with the sequences of fact that make up his subject matter. So, also, Cairnes's discussion of normal value, of the rate of wages, and of international trade, are excellent instances of a theoretical handling of economic processes of sequence and the orderly unfolding development of fact. But an attempt to cite Mill and Cairnes as exponents of an evolutionary economics will produce no better effect than perplexity, and not a great deal of that.

Very much of monetary theory might be cited to the same purpose and with the like effect. Something similar is true even of late writers who have avowed some penchant for the evolutionary point of view; as, e.g., Professor Hadley, - to cite a work of unquestioned merit and unusual reach. Measurably, he keeps the word of promise to the ear; but any one who may cite his Economics as having brought political economy into line as an evolutionary science will convince neither himself nor his interlocutor.

Something to the like effect may fairly be said of the published work of that later English strain of economists represented by

Professors Cunningham and Ashley, and Mr. Cannan, to name but a few of the more eminent figures in the group. Of the achievements of the classical economists, recent and living, the science may justly be proud; but they fall short of the evolutionist's standard of adequacy, not in failing to offer a theory of a process or of a developmental relation, but through conceiving their theory in terms alien to the evolutionist's habits of thought. The difference between the evolutionary and the pre-evolutionary sciences lies not in the insistence on facts. There was a great and fruitful activity in the natural sciences in collecting a collating facts before these sciences took on the character which marks them as evolutionary. Nor does the difference lie in the absence of efforts to formulate and explain schemes of process, sequence, growth, and development in the pre-evolutionary days. Efforts of this kind abounded, in number and diversity; and many schemes of development of great subtlety and beauty, gained a vogue both as theories of organic and inorganic development and as schemes of the life history of nations and societies. It will not even hold true that our elders overlooked the presence of cause and effect in formulating their theories and reducing their data to a body of knowledge. But the terms which were accepted as the definitive terms of knowledge were in some degree different in the early days from what they are now.

The terms of thought in which the investigators of some two or three generations back definitively formulated their knowledge of facts, in their last analyses, were different in kind from the terms in which the modern evolutionist is content to formulate his results. The analysis does not run back to the same ground, or appeal to the same standard of finality or adequacy, in the one case as in the other. The difference is a difference of spiritual attitude or point of view in the two contrasted generations of scientists. To put the matter in other words, it is a difference in the basis of valuation of the facts for the scientific purpose, or in the interest from which the facts are appreciated. With the earlier as with the later generation the basis of valuation of the facts handled is, in matters of detail, the causal relation which is apprehended to subsist between them.

This is true to the greatest extent for the natural sciences. But in their handling of the more comprehensive schemes of sequence and relation - in their definitive formulation of the results - the two generations differ. The modern scientist is unwilling to depart from the test of causal relation or quantitative sequence. When he asks the question, Why? he insists on an answer in terms of cause and effect. He wants to reduce his solution of all problems to terms of the conservation of energy or the persistence of quantity. This is his last recourse. And this last recourse has in our time been made available for the handling of schemes of development and theories of a comprehensive process by the notion of a cumulative causation. The great deserts of the evolutionist leaders - if they have great deserts as leaders - lie, on the one hand, in their refusal to go back of the colorless sequence of phenomena and seek higher ground for their ultimate syntheses, and, on the other hand, in their having shown how this colorless impersonal sequence of cause and effect can be made use of for theory proper, by virtue of its cumulative character.

For the earlier natural scientists, as for the classical economists, this ground of cause and effect is not definitive. Their sense of truth and substantiality is not satisfied with a formulation of mechanical sequence. The ultimate term in their systematisation of knowledge is a "natural law." This natural law is felt to exercise some sort of a coercive surveillance over the sequence of events, and to give a spiritual stability and consistence to the causal relation at any given juncture. To meet the high classical requirement, a sequence - and a developmental process especially - must be apprehended in terms of a consistent propensity tending to some spiritually legitimate end. When facts and events have been reduce to these terms of fundamental truth and have been made to square with the requirements of definitive normality, the investigator rests his case. Any causal sequence which is apprehended to traverse the imputed propensity in events is a "disturbing factor."

Logical congruity with the apprehended propensity is, in this view, adequate ground of procedure in building up a scheme of knowledge or of development. The objective point of the efforts of the scientists working under the guidance of this classical tradition, is to formulate knowledge in terms of absolute truth; and this absolute truth is a spiritual fact. It means a coincident of facts with the deliverances of an enlightened and deliberate common sense. The development and the attenuation of this preconception of normality or of a propensity in events might be traced in detail from primitive animism down through the elaborate discipline of faith and metaphysics, overruling providence, order of nature, natural rights, natural law, underlying principles. But all that may be necessary here is to point out that, by descent and by psychological content, this constraining normality is of a spiritual coherence to the facts dealt with. The question of interest is how this preconception of normality has fared at the hands of modern science, and how it has come to be superseded in the intellectual primacy by the latter day preconception of a non-spiritual sequence.

This question is of interest because its answer may throw light on the question as to what chance there is for the indefinite persistence of this archaic habit of thought in the methods of economic science. Under primitive conditions, men stand in immediate personal contact with the material facts of the environment; and the force and discretion of the individual in shaping the facts of the environment count obviously, and to all appearance solely, in working out the conditions of life. There is little of impersonal or mechanical sequence visible to primitive men in their everyday life; and what there is of this kind in the processes of brute nature about them is in large part inexplicable and passes for inscrutable. It is accepted as malignant or beneficent, and is construed in the terms of personality that are familiar to all men at first hand, - the terms know to all men by first hand knowledge of their own acts. The inscrutable movements of the seasons and of the natural forces are apprehended as actions guided by discretion, will power, or propensity looking to an end, much as human actions are. The processes of inanimate nature are agencies whose habits of life are to be learned, and who are to be coerced, outwitted, circumvented, and turned to account, much as the beasts are.

At the same time the community is small, and the human contact of the individual is not wide. Neither the industrial life nor the non-industrial social life forces upon men's attention the ruthless impersonal sweep of events that no man can withstand or deflect, such as becomes visible in the more complex and comprehensive life process of the larger community of the later day. There is nothing decisive to hinder men's knowledge of facts and events being formulated in terms of personality - in terms of habit and propensity and will power. As time goes on and as the situation departs from this archaic character, - where it does depart from it, - the circumstances which condition men's systematisation of facts change in such a way as to throw the impersonal character of the sequence of events more and more into the foreground. The penalties for failure to apprehend facts in dispassionate terms fall surer and swifter. The sweep of events is force home more consistently on men's minds.

The guiding hand of a spiritual agency or a propensity in events becomes less readily traceable as men's knowledge of things grows ampler and more searching. In modern times, and particularly in the industrial countries, this coercive guidance of men's habits of thought in the realistic direction has been especially pronounced; and the effect shows itself in a somewhat reluctant but cumulative departure from the archaic point of view. The departure is most visible and has gone farthest in those homely branches of knowledge that have to do immediately with modern mechanical processes, such as engineering designs and technological contrivances generally. Of the sciences, those have wandered farthest on this way (of integration of disintegration, according as one may choose to view it) that have to do with mechanical sequence and process; and those have best and longest retained the archaic point of view intact which - like the moral, social, or spiritual sciences - have to do with process and sequence that is less tangible, less traceable by the use of the senses, and that therefore less immediately forces upon the attention the phenomenon of sequence as contrasted with that of propensity.

There is no abrupt transition from the pre-evolutionary to the post evolutionary standpoint. Even in those natural sciences which deal with the processes of life and the evolutionary sequence of events the concept of dispassionate cumulative causation has often and effectively been helped out by the notion that there is in all this some sort of a meliorative trend that exercises a constraining guidance over the course of cause and effects. The faith in this meliorative trend as a concept useful to the science has gradually weakened, and it has repeatedly been disavowed; but it can scarcely be said to have yet disappeared from the field. The process of change in the point of view, or in the terms of definitive formulation of knowledge, is a gradual one; and all the sciences have shared, though in an unequal degree, in the change that is going forward.

Economics is not an exception to the rule, but it still shows too many reminiscences of the "natural" and the "normal," of "verities" and tendencies," of "controlling principles" and "disturbing causes" to be classed as

an evolutionary science. The history of the science shows a long and devious course of disintegrating animism, - from the days of the scholastic
writers, who discussed usury from the point of view of its relation to the
divine suzerainty, to the Physiocrats, who rested their case on an "*ordre
naturel*" and a "*loi naturelle*" that decides what is substantially true and, in
a general way, guides the course of events by the constraint of logical congruence. There has been something of a change from Adam Smith, whose
recourse in perplexity was to the guidance of "an unseen hand," to Mill
and Cairnes, who formulated the laws of "natural" wages and "normal"
value, and the former of whom was so well content with his work as to say,
"Happily, there is nothing in the laws of Value which remains for the present or any future writer to clear up; the theory of the subject is complete[3]
.

But the difference between the earlier and the later point of view is a difference of degree rather than of kind. The standpoint of the classical
economists, in their higher or definitive syntheses and generalisations,
may not inaptly be called the standpoint of ceremonial adequacy. The ultimate laws and principles which they formulated were laws of the normal
or the natural, according to preconception regarding the ends to which, in
the nature of things, all things tend. In effect, this preconception imputes
to things a tendency to work out what the instructed common sense of the
time accepts as the adequate or worthy end of human effort. It is a projec-
tion of the accepted ideal of conduct. This ideal of conduct is made to
serve as a canon of truth, to the extent that the investigator contents himself with an appeal to its legitimation for premises that run back of the
facts with which he is immediately dealing, for the "controlling principles"
that are conceived intangibly to underlie the process discussed, and for
the "tendencies" that run beyond the situation as it lies before him. As
instances of the use of this ceremonial canon of knowledge may be cited
the "conjectural history" that plays so large a part in the classical treatment of economic institutions, such as the normalized accounts of the
beginnings of barter in the transactions of the putative hunter, fisherman,
and boat-builder, or the man with the plane and the two planks, or the two
men with the basket of apples and the basket of nuts[4] .

Of a similar import is the characterisation of money as "the great wheel
of circulation[5] or as "the medium of exchange." Money is here discussed
in terms of the end which, "in the normal case," it should work out according to the given writer's ideal of economic life, rather than in terms of
causal relation.

With later writers especially, this terminology is no doubt to be commonly taken as a convenient use of metaphor, in which the concept of
normality and propensity to an end has reached an extreme attenuation.

---

[3] Political Economy, Book III, chap. i.

[4] Marshall, Principles of Economics (2nd.), Book V, chap. ii, p. 395, note.

[5] Adam Smith, Wealth of Nations (Bohn ed.), Book II, chap. ii, p. 289.

But it is precisely in this use of figurative terms for the formulation of theory that the classical normality still lives in its attenuated life in modern economics; and it is this facile recourse to inscrutable figures of speech as the ultimate terms of theory that has saved the economists from being dragooned into the ranks of modern science. The metaphors are effective, both in their homiletical use and as a labor-saving device, - more effective than their user designs them to be. By their use the theorist is enabled serenely to enjoin himself from following out an elusive train of causal sequence. He is also enabled, without misgivings, to construct a theory of such an institution as money or wages or land-ownership without descending to a consideration of the living items concerned, except for convenient corroboration of his normalised scheme of symptoms.

By this method the theory of an institution or a phase of life may be stated in conventionalised terms of the apparatus whereby life is carried on, the apparatus being invested with a tendency to an equilibrium at the normal, and the theory being a formulation of the conditions under which this putative equilibrium supervenes. In this way we have come into the usufruct of a cost of production theory of value which is pungently reminiscent of the time when Nature abhorred a vacuum. The ways and means and the mechanical structure of industry are formulated in a conventionalised nomenclature, and the observed motions of this mechanical apparatus are then reduced to a normalised scheme of relations.

The scheme so arrived at is spiritually binding on the behavior of the phenomena contemplated. With this normalised scheme as a guide, the permutations of a given segment of the apparatus are worked out according to the values assigned the several items and features comprised in the calculation; and a ceremonially consistent formula is constructed to cover that much of the industrial field. This is the deductive method. The formula is then tested by comparison with observed permutations, by the polariscopic use of the "normal case"; and the results arrived at are thus authenticated by induction. Features of the process that do not lend themselves to interpretation in the terms of the formula are abnormal cases and are due to disturbing causes. In all this the agencies or forces causally at work in the economic life process are neatly avoided. The outcome of the method, at its best, is a body of logically consistent propositions concerning the normal relations of things - a system of economic taxonomy.

At its worst, it is a body of maxims for the conduct of business and a polemical discussion of disputed points of policy .In all this, economic science is living over again in its turn the experiences which the natural sciences passed through some time back. In the natural sciences the work of the taxonomist was and continues to be of great value, but the scientists grew restless under the regime of symmetry and system making. They took to asking why, and so shifted their inquiries from the structure of the coral reefs to the structure and habits of life of the polyp that lives in and by them. In the science of plants, systematic botany has not ceased to be of service; but the stress of investigation and discussion among the botanists today falls on the biological value of any given feature of structure, function, or tissue rather than on its taxonomic bearing.

All the talk about cytoplasm, centrosomes, and karyokinetic process, means that the inquiry now looks consistently to the life process, and aims to explain it in terms of cumulative causation. What may be done in economic science of the taxonomic kind is show at its best in Cairnes's work, where the method is well conceived and the results effectively formulated and applied. Cairnes handles the theory of the normal case in economic life with a master hand. In his discussion the metaphysics of propensity and tendencies no long avowedly rules the formulation of theory, nor is the inscrutable meliorative trend of a harmony of interests confidently appealed as an engine of definitive use in giving legitimacy to the economic situation at the given time. There is less of an exercise of faith in Cairnes's economic discussions than in those of the writers that went before him.

The definitive terms of the formulation are still the terms of normality and natural law, but the metaphysics underlying this appeal to normality is so far removed from the ancient ground of the beneficent "order of nature" as to have become at least nominally impersonal and to proceed without a constant regard to the humanitarian bearing of the "tendencies" which it formulates. The metaphysics has been attenuated to something approaching in colorlessness the naturalist's conception of natural law. It is a natural law which, in the guise of "controlling principles," exercises a constraining surveillance over the trend of thing; but it is no longer conceived to exercise its constraint in the interest of certain ulterior human purposes. The element of beneficence has been well-nigh eliminated, and the system is formulated in terms of the system itself. Economics as it left Cairnes's hand, so far as this theoretical work is concerned, comes near being taxonomy for taxonomy's sake.

No equally capable writer has come as near making economics the ideal "dismal" science as Cairnes in his discussion of pure theory. In the days of the early classical writers economics had a vital interest for the laymen of the time, because it formulated the common sense metaphysics of the time in its application to a department of human life. But in the hands of the later classical writers the science lost much of its charm in this regard. It was not longer a definition and authentication of the deliverances of current common sense as to what ought to come to pass; and it, therefore, in large measure lost the support of the people out of doors, who were unable to take an interest in what did not concern them; and it was also out of touch with that realistic or evolutionary habit of mind which got under way about the middle of the century in the natural sciences. It was neither vitally metaphysical nor matter of fact, and it found comfort with very few outside of its own ranks.

Only for those who by the fortunate accident of birth or education have been able to conserve the taxonomic animus has the science during the last third of a century continued to be of absorbing interest. The result has been that from the time when the taxonomic structure stood forth as a completed whole in its symmetry and stability the economists themselves, beginning with Cairnes, have been growing restive under its discipline of stability, and have made many efforts, more or less sustained, to galvanise it into movement. At the hands of the writers of the classical line these excursions have chiefly aimed at a more complete and comprehensive taxonomic scheme of permutations; while the historical departure threw away the taxonomic ideal without getting rid of the preconceptions on which it is based; and the later Austrian group struck out on a theory of process, but presently came to a full stop because the process about which they busied themselves was not, in their apprehension of it, a cumulative or unfolding sequence. But what does all this signify? If we are getting restless under the taxonomy of a monocotyledonous wage doctrine and a cryptogamic theory of interest, with involute, loculicidal, tomentous and moniliform variants, what is the cytoplasm, centrosome, or karyokinetic process to which we may turn, and in which we may find surcease from the metaphysics of normality and controlling principles?

What are we going to do about it? The question is rather, What are we doing about it? There is the economic life process still in great measure awaiting theoretical formulation. The active material in which the economic process goes on is the human material of the industrial community. For the purpose of economic science the process of cumulative change that is to be accounted for is the sequence of change in the methods of doing thing, - the methods of dealing with the material means of life. What has been done in the way of inquiry into this economic life process? The ways and means of turning material objects and circumstances to account lie before the investigator at any given point of time in the form of mechanical contrivances and arrangements for compassing certain mechanical ends. It has therefore been easy to accept these ways and means as items of inert matter having a given mechanical structure and thereby serving the material ends of man.

As such, they have been scheduled and graded by the economists under the head of capital, this capital being conceived as a mass of material objects serviceable for human use. This is well enough for the purposes of taxonomy; but it is not an effective method of conceiving the matter for the purpose of a theory of the developmental process. For the latter purpose, when taken as items in a process of cumulative change or as items in the scheme of life, these productive goods are facts of human knowledge, skill, and predilection; that is to say, they are, substantially, prevalent habits of thought, and it is as such that they enter into the process of industrial development. The physical properties of the materials accessible to man are constants: it is the human agent that changes, - his insight and his appreciation of what these things can be used for is what develops. The accumulation of goods already on hand conditions his handling and utilisation of the materials offered, but even on this side - the "limitation of industry by capital" - the limitation imposed is on what men can do and on the methods of doing it. The changes that take place in the mechanical contrivances are an expression of changes in the human factor.

Changes in the material facts breed further change only through the human factor. It is in the human material that the continuity of development is to be looked for; and it is here, therefore, that the motor forces of the process of economic development must be studied if they are to be studied in action at all. Economic action must be subject matter of the science if the science is to fall into line as an evolutionary science. Nothing new has been said in all this. But the fact is all the more significant for being a familiar fact. It is a fact recognised by common consent throughout much of the later economic discussion, and this current recognition of the fact is a long step towards centering discussion and inquiry upon it. If economics is to follow the lead or the analogy of the other sciences that have to do with a life process, the way is plain so far as regards the general direction in which the move will be made.

The economists of the classical trend have made no serious attempt to depart from the standpoint of taxonomy and make their science a genetic account of the economic life process. As has just been said, much the same is true for the Historical School. The latter have attempted an account of developmental sequence, but they have followed the lines of pre Darwinian speculations on development rather than lines which modern science would recognise as evolutionary. They have given a narrative survey of phenomena, not a genetic account of an unfolding process. In this work they have, no doubt, achieved results of permanent value; but the results achieved are scarcely to be classed as economic theory. On the other hand, the Austrians and their precursors and their co-adjutors in the value discussion have taken up a detached portion of economic theory, and have inquired with great nicety into the process by which the phenomena within their limited field are worked out. The entire discussion of marginal utility and subjective value as the outcome of a valuation process must be taken as a genetic study of this range of facts. But here, again, nothing further has come of the inquiry, so far as regards a rehabilitation of economic theory as a whole.

Accepting Menger as their spokesman on this head, it must be said that the Austrians have on the whole showed themselves unable to break with the classical tradition that economics is a taxonomic science. The reason for the Austrian failure seems to lie in a faulty conception of human nature, - faulty for the present purpose, however adequate it may be for any other. In all the received formulations of economic theory, whether at the hands of English economists or those of the Continent, the human material with which the inquiry is concerned is conceived in hedonistic terms; that is to say, in terms of a passive and substantially inert and immutably given human nature. The psychological and anthropological preconceptions of the economists have been those which were accepted by the psychological and social sciences some generations ago. The hedonistic conception of man is that of a lightning calculator of pleasures and pains who oscillates like a homogeneous globule of desire of happiness under the impulse of stimuli that shift him about the area, but leave him intact. He has neither antecedent nor consequent.

He is an isolated definitive human datum, in stable equilibrium except for the buffets of the impinging forces that displace him in one direction or another. Self-imposed in elemental space, he spins symmetrically about his own spiritual axis until the parallelogram of forces bears down upon him, whereupon he follows the line of the resultant. When the force of the

impact is spent, he comes to rest, a self-contained globule of desire as before. Spiritually, the hedonistic man is not a prime mover. He is not the
seat of a process of living, except in the sense that he is subject to a series
of permutations enforce upon him by circumstances external and lien to
him. The later psychology, re-enforced by modern anthropological research, gives a different conception of human nature. According to this
conception, it is the characteristic of man to do something, not simply to
suffer pleasures and pains through the impact of suitable forces. He is not
simply a bundle of desires that are to be saturated by being placed in the
path of the forces of the environment, but rather a coherent structure of
propensities and habits which seeks realisation and expression in an unfolding activity.

According to this view, human activity, and economic activity among the
rest, is not apprehended as something incidental to the process of saturat-
ing given desires. The activity is itself the substantial fact of the process,
and the desires under whose guidance the action takes place are circumstances of temperament which determine the specific direction in which
the activity will unfold itself in the given case. These circumstances of
temperament are ultimate and definitive for the individual who acts under
them, so far as regards his attitude as agent in the particular action in
which he is engaged. But, in the view of the science, they are elements of
the existing frame of mind of the agent, and are the outcome of his antecedents and his life up to the point at which he stands. They are the products of his hereditary traits and his past experience, cumulatively wrought
out under a given body of traditions conventionalities, and material circumstances; and they afford the point of departure for the next step in the
process. The economic life history of the individual is a cumulative process of adaptation of means to ends that cumulatively change as the process goes on, both the agent and his environment being at any point the
outcome of the last process. His methods of life today are enforce upon
him by his habits of life carried over from yesterday and by the circumstances left as the mechanical residue of the life of yesterday.

What is true of the individual in this respect is true of the group in which
he lives. All economic change is a change in the economic community, - a
change in the community's methods of turning material things to account. The change is always in the last resort a change in habits of
thought. This is true even of changes in the mechanical processes of industry. A given contrivance for effecting certain material ends becomes a
circumstance which affects the further growth of habits of thought - habitual methods of procedure - and so becomes a point of departure for
further development of the methods of compassing the ends sought and
for the further variation of ends that are sought to be compassed. In all
this flux there is not definitively adequate method of life and no definitive
or absolutely worthy end of action, so far as concerns the science which
sets out to formulate a theory of the process of economic life. What remains as a hard and fast residue is the fact of activity directed to an objective end. Economic action is teleological, in the sense that men always and
everywhere seek to do something. What, in specific detail, they seek, is not

to be answered except by a scrutiny of the details of their activity; but, so long as we have to do with their life as members of the economic community, there remains the generic fact that their life is an unfolding activity of a teleological kind.

It may or may not be a teleological process in the sense that it tends or should tend to any end that is conceived to be worthy or adequate by the inquirer or by the consensus of inquirers. Whether it is or is not, is question with which the present inquiry is not concerned; and it is also a question of which an evolutionary economics need take no account. The question of a tendency in events can evidently not come up except on the ground of some preconception or prepossession on the part of the person looking for the tendency. In order to search for a tendency, we must be possessed of some notion of a definitive end to be sought, or some notion as to what is the legitimate trend of events. The notion of a legitimate trend in a course of events is an extra evolutionary preconception, and lies outside the scope of an inquiry into the causal sequence in any process.

The evolutionary point of view, therefore, leaves no place for a formulation of natural laws in terms of definitive normality, whether in economics or in any other branch of inquiry. Neither does it leave room for that other question of normality, What should be the end of the developmental process under discussion? The economic life history of any community is its life history in so far as it is shaped by men's interest in the material means of life. This economic interest has counted for much in shaping the cultural growth of all communities. Primarily and mot obviously, it has guided the formation, the cumulative growth, of that range of conventionalities and methods of life that are currently recognized as economic institutions; but the same interest has also pervaded the community's life and its cultural growth at points where the resulting structural features are not chiefly and most immediately of an economic bearing. The economic interest goes with men through life, and it goes with the race throughout its process of cultural development. It affects the cultural structure at all points, so that all institutions may be said to be in some measure economic institutions.

This is necessarily the case, since the base of action - the point of departure - as any step in the process is the entire organic complex of habits of thought that have been shaped by the past process. The economic interest does not act in isolation, for it is but one of several vaguely isolable interests on which the complex of teleological activity carried out by the individual proceeds. The individual is but a single agent in each case; and he enters into each successive action as a whole, although the specific end sought in a given action may be sought avowedly on the basis of a particular interest; as e.g., the economic, aesthetic, sexual, humanitarian, devotional interests. Since each of these passably isolable interests is a propensity of the organic agent man, with his complex of habits of thought, the expression of each is affected by habits of life formed under the guidance of all the rest. There is, therefore, no neatly isolable range of cultural phenomena that can be rigorously set apart under the head of economic institutions, although a category of "economic institutions" maybe of service as a convenient caption, comprising those institutions in which the economic interest most immediately and consistently finds expression, and which most immediately and with the least limitation are of an economic bearing.

From what has been said it appears that an evolutionary economics must be the theory of a process of cultural growth as determined by the economic interest, a theory of a cumulative sequence of economic institutions stated in terms of the process itself. Except for the want of space to do here what should be done in some detail if it is done at all, many efforts by the later economists in this direction might be cited to show the trend of economic discussion in this direction. There is not a little evidence to this effect, and much of the work done must be rated as effective work for this purpose. Much of the work of the Historical School, for instance, and that of its later exponents especially, is too noteworthy to be passed over in silence, even with all due regard to the limitations space.

We are now ready to return to the question why economics is not an evolutionary science. It is necessarily the aim of such an economics to trace the cumulative working out of the economic interest in the cultural sequence. It must be a theory of the economic life process of the race or the community. The economists have accepted the hedonistic preconceptions concerning human nature and human action, and the conception of the economic interest which a hedonistic psychology gives does not afford material for a theory of the development of human nature. Under hedonism the economic interest is not conceived in terms of action. It is therefore not readily apprehended or appreciated in terms of a cumulative growth of habits of thought, and does not provoke, even if it did lend itself to, treatment by the evolutionary method. At the same time the anthropological preconceptions current in that common sense apprehension of human nature to which economists have habitually turned has not enforced the formulation of human nature in terms of a cumulative growth of habits of life. These received anthropological preconceptions are such as have made possible the normalized conjectural accounts of primitive barter with which all economic readers are familiar, and the no less normalized conventional derivation of landed property and its rent, or the sociologico-philosophical discussion of the "function" of this or that class in the life of society or of the nation.

The premises and the point of view required for an evolutionary economics have been wanting. The economists have not had the materials for such a science ready to their hand, and the provocation to strike out in such a direction has been absent. Even if it has been possible at any time to turn to the evolutionary line of speculation in economics, the possibility of a departure is not enough to bring it about. So long as the habitual view taken of a given range of facts is of the taxonomic kind and the material lends itself to treatment by that method, the taxonomic method is the easiest, gives the most gratifying immediate results, and best fits into the accepted body of knowledge of the range of facts in question. This has been the situation in economics. The other sciences of its group have likewise been a body of taxonomic discipline, and departures from the accredited method have lain under the odium of being meretricious innovations. The well-worn paths are easy to follow and lead into good company. Advance along them visibly furthers the accredited work which the science has in hand. Divergence from the paths means tentative work, which is necessarily slow and fragmentary and of uncertain value. It is only when the methods of the science and the syntheses resulting from their use come to be out of line with habits of thought that prevail in other matters that the scientist grows restive under the guidance of the received methods and standpoints, and seeks a way out.

Like other men, the economist is an individual with but one intelligence. He is a creature of habits and propensities given through the antecedents, hereditary and cultural, of which he is an outcome; and the habits of thought formed in any one line of experience affect his thinking in any other. Methods of observation and of handling facts that are familiar through habitual use in the general range of knowledge, gradually assert themselves in any given special range of knowledge. They may be accepted slowly and with reluctance where their acceptance involves innovation; but, if they have the continued backing of the general body of experience, it is only a question of time when they shall come into dominance in the special field. The intellectual attitude and the method of correlation enforced upon us in the apprehension and assimilation of facts in the more elementary ranges of knowledge that have to do with brute facts assert themselves also when the attention is directed to those phenomena of the life process with which economics has to do; and the range of facts which are habitually handled by other methods than that in traditional vogue in economics has now become so large and so insistently present at every turn that we are left restless, if the new body of facts cannot be handled according to the method of mental procedure which is in this way becoming habitual.

In the general body of knowledge in modern times the facts are apprehended in terms of causal sequence. This is especially true of that knowledge of brute facts which is shaped by the exigencies of the modern mechanical industry. To men thoroughly imbued with this matter of fact habit of mind the laws and theorems of economics, and of the other sciences that treat of the normal course of things, have a character of "unreality" and futility that bars out any serious interest in their discussion. The laws and theorems are "unreal" to them because they are not to be apprehended in the terms which these men make use of in handling the facts with which they are perforce habitually occupied. The same matter of fact spiritual attitude and mode of procedure have now made their way well up into the higher levels of scientific knowledge, even in the sciences which deal in a more elementary way with the same human material that makes the subject matter of economics, and the economists themselves are beginning to feel the unreality of their theorems about "normal" cases.

Provided the practical exigencies of modern industrial life continue of the same character as they now are, and so continue to enforce the impersonal method of knowledge, it is only a question of time when that (substantially animistic) habit of mind which proceeds on the notion of a definitive normality shall be displaced in the field of economic inquiry by that (substantially materialistic) habit of mind which seeks a comprehension of facts in terms of a cumulative sequence. The later method of apprehending and assimilating facts and handling them for the purposes of knowledge may be better or worse, more or less worthy or adequate, than the earlier; it may be of greater or less ceremonial or aesthetic effect; we may be move to regret the incursion of underbred habits of though into the scholar's domain. But all that is beside the present point. Under the stress of modern technological exigencies, men's everyday habits of thought are falling into the lines that in the sciences constitute the evolutionary method; and knowledge which proceeds on a higher, more archaic plain is becoming alien and meaningless to them. The social and political sciences must follow the drift, for they are already caught in it.

Chapter 2

Industrial and Pecuniary Employments

For purposes of economic theory, the various activities of men and things about which economists busy themselves were classified by the early writers according to a scheme which has remained substantially unchanged, if not unquestioned, since their time. This scheme is the classical three-fold division of the factors of production under Land, Labor, and Capital. The theoretical aim of the economists in discussing these factors and the activities for which they stand has not remained the same throughout the course of economic discussion, and the three-fold division has not always lent itself with facility to new points of view and new Purposes of theory, but the writers who have shaped later theory have, on the whole, not laid violent hands on the sacred formula.

These facts must inspire the utmost reserve and circumspection in any one who is moved to propose even a subsidiary distinction of another kind between economic activities or agents. The terminology and the conceptual furniture of economics are complex and parti-colored enough without gratuitous innovation. It is accordingly not the aim of this paper to set aside the time-honored classification of factors, or even to formulate an iconoclastic amendment, but rather to indicate how and why this classification has proved inadequate for certain purposes of theory which were not contemplated by the men who elaborated it. To this end a bit of preface may be in place as regards the anus which led to its formulation and the uses which the three-fold classification originally served.

The economists of the late eighteenth and early nineteenth centuries were believers in a Providential order, or an order of Nature. How they came by this belief need not occupy us here; neither need we raise a question as to whether their conviction of its truth was well or ill grounded. The Providential order or order of Nature is conceived to work in an effective and just way toward the end to which it tends; and in the economic field this objective end is the material welfare of mankind. The science of that time set itself the task of interpreting the facts with which it dealt, in terms of this natural order. The material circumstances which condition men's life fall within the scope of this natural order of the universe, and as members of the universal scheme of things men fall under the constraining guidance of the laws of Nature, who does all things well. As regards their purely theoretical work, the early economists are occupied with bringing the facts of economic life under natural laws conceived somewhat after the manner indicated; and when the facts handled have been fully interpreted in the light of this fundamental postulate the theoretical work of the scientist is felt to have been successfully done. The economic laws aimed at and formulated tinder the guidance of this preconception are laws of what takes place "naturally" or "normally," and it is of the essence of things so conceived that in the natural or normal course there is no wasted or misdirected effort. The standpoint is given by the material interest of mankind, or, more concretely, of the community or "society" in which the economist is placed; the resulting economic theory is formulated as an analysis of the "natural" course of the life of the community, the ultimate theoretical postulate of which might, not unfairly, be stated as in some sort a law of the conservation of economic energy.

When the course of things runs off naturally or normally, in accord with the exigencies of human welfare and the constraining laws of nature, economic income and outgo balance one another. The natural forces at play in the economic field may increase indefinitely through accretions brought in under man's dominion and through the natural increase of mankind, and, indeed, it is of the nature of things that an orderly progress of this kind should take place; but within the economic organism, as within the larger organism of the universe, there prevails an equivalence of expenditure and returns, an equilibrium of flux and reflux, which is not broken over in the normal course of things. So it is, by implication, assumed that the product which results from any given industrial process or operation is, in some sense or in some unspecified respect, the equivalent of the expenditure of forces, or of the effort, or what not, that has gone into the process out of which the product emerges.

This theorem of equivalence is the postulate which lies at the root of the classical theory of distribution, but it manifestly does not admit of proof - or of disproof - either, for that matter; since neither the economic forces which go into the process nor the product which emerges are, in the economic respect, of such a tangible character as to admit of quantitative determination. They are in fact incommensurable magnitudes. To this last remark the answer may conceivably present itself that the equivalence in question is an equivalence in utility or in exchange value, and that the quantitative determination of the various items in terms of exchange value or of utility is, theoretically, not impossible; but when it is called to mind that the forces or factors which go to the production of a given product take their utility or exchange value from that of the product, it will easily be seen that the expedient will not serve.

The equivalence between the aggregate factors of production in any given case and their product remains a dogmatic postulate whose validity cannot be demonstrated in any terms that will not reduce the whole proposition to an aimless fatuity, or to metaphysical grounds which have now been given up. The point of view from which the early, and even the later classical, economists discussed economic life was that of "the society" taken as a collective whole and conceived as an organic unit. Economic theory sought out and formulated the laws of the normal life of the social organism -, as it is conceived to work out in that natural course whereby the material welfare of society is attained. The details of economic life are construed, for purposes of general theory, in terms of their subservience to the aims imputed to the collective life process. Those features of detail which will bear construction as links in the process whereby the collective welfare is furthered, are magnified and brought into the foreground, while such features as will not bear this construction are treated as minor disturbances. Such a procedure is manifestly legitimate and expedient in a theoretical inquiry whose aim is to determine the laws of health of the social organism and the normal functions of this organism in a state of health.

The social organism is, in this theory, handled as an individual endowed with a consistent life purpose and something of an intelligent apprehension of what means will serve the ends which it seeks. With these collective ends the interests of the individual members are conceived to be fundamentally at one; and, while men may not see that their own individual interests coincide with those of the social organism, yet, since men are members of the comprehensive organism of nature and consequently subject to beneficent natural law, the ulterior trend of unrestrained individual action is, on the whole, in the right direction.

The details of individual economic conduct and its consequences are of interest to such a general theory chiefly as they further or disturb the beneficent "natural" course. But if the aims and methods of individual conduct were of minor importance in such an economic theory, that is not the case as regards individual rights. The early political economy was not simply a formulation of the natural course of economic phenomena, but it embodied an insistence on what is called "natural liberty." Whether this insistence on natural liberty is to be traced to utilitarianism or to a less specific faith in natural rights, the outcome for the purpose in hand is substantially the same. To avoid going too far afield, it may serve the turn to say that the law of economic equivalence, or conservation of economic energy, was, in early economics, backed by this second corollary of the order of nature., the closely related postulate of natural rights.

The classical doctrine of distribution rests on both of these, and it is consequently not only a doctrine of what must normally take place as regards the course of life of society at large, but it also formulates what ought of right to take place as regards the remuneration for work and the distribution of wealth among men.

Under the resulting natural-economic law of equivalence and equity, it is held that the several participants or factors in the economic process severally get the equivalent of the productive force which they expend. They severally get as much as they produce; and conversely, in the normal case they severally produce as much as they get. In the earlier formulations, as, for example, in the authoritative formulation of Adam Smith, there is no clear or consistent pronouncement as regards the terms in which this equivalence between production and remuneration runs. With the later, classical economists, who had the benefit of a developed utilitarian philosophy, it seems to be somewhat consistently conceived in terms of an ill-defined serviceability. With some later writers it is an equivalence of exchange values; but as this latter reduces itself to tautology, it need scarcely be taken seriously.

When we are told in the later political economy that the several agents or factors in production normally earn what they get, it is perhaps fairly to be construed as a claim that the economic service rendered the community by any one of the agents in production equals the service received by the agent in return. In terms of serviceability, then, if not in terms of productive force[1] the individual agent, or at least the class or group of agents to which the individual belongs, normally gets as much as he contributes and contributes as much as he gets. This applies to all those employments or occupations which are ordinarily carried on in any community, throughout the aggregate of men's dealings with the material means of life. All activity which touches industry comes in under this law of equivalence and equity.

Now, to a theorist whose aim is to find the laws governing the economic life of a social organism, and who for this purpose conceives the economic community as a unit, the features of economic life which are of particular consequence are those which show the correlation of efforts and the solidarity of interests. For this purpose, such activities and such interests as do not fit into the scheme of solidarity contemplated are of minor importance, and are rather to be explained away or construed into subservience to the scheme of solidarity than to be incorporated at their face value into the theoretical structure. Of this nature are what are here to be spoken of under the term "pecuniary employments," and the fortune which these pecuniary employments have met at the hands of classical economic theory is such as is outlined in the last sentence .In a theory proceeding on the premise of economic solidarity, the important bearing of any activity that is taken up and accounted for, is its bearing upon the furtherance of the collective life process. Viewed from the standpoint of the collective interest, the economic process is rated primarily as a process for the provision of the aggregate material means of life. As a late representative of the classical school expresses it:"

Production, in fact, embraces every economic operation except consumption[2] .It is this aggregate productivity, and the bearing of all details upon the aggregate productivity, that constantly occupies the attention of the classical economists. What partially diverts their attention from this central and ubiquitous interest, is their persistent lapse into natural-rights morality. The result is that acquisition is treated as a sub-head under production, and effort directed to acquisition is construed in terms of production. The pecuniary activities of men, efforts directed to acquisition and operations incident to the acquisition or tenure of wealth, are treated as incidental to the distribution to each of his particular proportion in the production of goods. Pecuniary activities, in short, are handled as incidental features of the process of social production and consumption, as details incident to the method whereby the social interests are served. Instead of being dealt with as the controlling factor about which the modern economic process turns. Apart from the metaphysical tenets indicated above as influencing them, there are, of course, reasons of economic his-

---

[1] Some late writers, as, e.g., J. B. Clark, apparently must be held to conceive the equivalence in terms of productive force rather than of serviceability; or, perhaps, in terms of serviceability on one side of the equation and productive force on the other.

[2] J. B. Clark, The Distribution of Wealth, p. 20

tory for the procedure of the early economists in so relegating the pecuniary activities to the background of economic theory. In the days of Adam Smith, for instance, economic life still bore much of the character of what Professor Schmoller calls Stadt-wirtschaft.

This was the case to some extent in practice, but still more decidedly in tradition. To a greater extent than has since been the case, households produced goods for their own consumption, without the intervention of sale; and handicraftsmen still produced for consumption by their customers, without the intervention of a market. In a considerable measure, the conditions which the Austrian marginal-utility theory supposes, of a producing seller and a consuming buyer, actually prevailed. It may not be true that in Adam Smith's time the business operations, the bargain and sale of goods, were, in general, obviously subservient to their production and consumption, but it comes nearer being true at that time than at any time since then. And the tradition having once been put into form and authenticated by Adam Smith, that such was the place of pecuniary transactions in economic theory, this tradition has lasted on in the face of later and further changes.

Under the shadow of this tradition the pecuniary employments are still dealt with as auxiliary to the process of production, and the gains from such employments are still explained as being due to a productive effect imputed to them. According to ancient prescription, then, all normal, legitimate economic activities carried on in a well regulated community serve a materially useful end, and so far as they are lucrative they are so by virtue of and in proportion to a productive effect imputed to them. But in the situation as it exists at any time there are activities and classes of persons which are indispensable to the community, or which are at least unavoidably present in modern economic life, and which draw some income from the aggregate product, at the same time that these activities are not patently productive of goods and can not well be classed as industrial, in any but a highly sophisticated sense. Some of these activities, which are concerned with economic matters but are not patently of an industrial character, are integral features of modern economic life, and must therefore be classed as normal; for the existing situation, apart from a few minor discrepancies, is particularly normal in the apprehension of present-day economists.

Now, the law of economic equivalence and equity says that those who normally receive in income must perforce serve some productive end; and, since the existing organization of society is conceived to be eminently normal, it becomes imperative to find some ground on which to impute industrial productivity to those classes and employments which do not at first view appear to be industrial at all. Hence there is commonly visible in the classical political economy, ancient and modern, a strong inclination to make the schedule of industrially productive employments very comprehensive; so that a good deal of ingenuity has been spent in economically justifying their presence by specifying the productive effect of such non-industrial factors as the courts, the army, the police, the clergy, the schoolmaster, the physician, the opera singer. But these non-economic employments are not so much to the point in the present inquiry; the point being employments which are unmistakably economic, but not industrial in the naive sense of the word industry, and which yield an income. Adam Smith analysed the process of industry in which he found the community of his time engaged, and found the three classes of agents or factors: Land, Labor, and Capital (stock).

The productive factors engaged being thus determined, the norm of natural-economic equivalence and equity already referred to above. indicated what would be the natural sharers in the product. Later economists have shown great reserve about departing from this three-fold division of factors, with its correlated three-fold division of sharers of remuneration; apparently because they have retained an instinctive, indefeasible trust in the law of economic equivalence which underlies it. But circumstances have compelled the tentative intrusion of a fourth class of agent and income. The undertaker and his income presently came to be so large and ubiquitous figures in economic life that their presence could not be overlooked by the most normalising economist.

The undertaker's activity has been interpolated in the scheme of productive factors, as a peculiar and fundamentally distinctive kind of labor, with the function of coordinating - and directing industrial processes. Similarly, his income has been interpolated in the scheme of distribution, as a peculiar kind of wages, proportioned to the heightened productivity given the industrial process by his work[3] .His work is discussed in expositions of the theory of production. In discussions of his functions and his income the point of the argument is, how and in what degree does his activity increase the output of goods, or how and in what degree does it save wealth to the community. Beyond his effect in enhancing the effective volume of the aggregate wealth the undertaker receives but scant attention, apparently for the reason that so soon as that point has been disposed of the presence of the undertaker and his income has been reconciled with the tacitly accepted natural law of equivalence between productive service and remuneration.

The normal balance has been established, and the undertaker's function has been justified and subsumed under the ancient law that Nature does all things well and equitably. This holds true of the political economy of our grandfathers. But this aim and method of handling the phenomena of life for theoretical ends, of course, did not go out of vogue abruptly in the days of our grandfathers[4] .There is a large sufficiency of the like aim and animus in the theoretical discussions of a later time; but specifically to cite

---

[3] The undertaker gets an income; therefore be must produce goods. But human activity directed to the production of goods is labor; therefore the undertaker is a particular kind of laborer. There is, of course, some dissent from this position.

[4] The change which has supervened as regards the habitual resort to a natural law of equivalence is in large part a change with respect to the degree of immediacy and "reality" imputed to this law, and to a still greater extent a change in the degree of overtness with which it is avowed.

and analyse the evidence of its presence would be laborious, nor would it conduce to the general peace of mind. Some motion towards a further revision of the scheme is to be seen in the attention which has latterly been given to the function and the profits of that peculiar class of undertakers whom we call speculators. But even on this head the argument is apt to turn on the question of how the services which the speculator is conceived to render the community are to be construed into an equivalent of his gains[5].

The difficulty of interpretation encountered at this point is considerable, partly because it is not quite plain whether the speculators as a class come out of their transactions with a net gain or with a net loss. A systematic net loss, or a nonprofits balance, would, on the theory of equivalence, mean that the class which gets this loss or doubtful gain is of no service to the community; yet we are, out of the past, committed to the view that the speculator is useful - indeed economically indispensable - and shall therefore have his reward. In the discussions given to the speculator and his function some thought is commonly given to the question of the "legitimacy" of the speculator's traffic. The legitimate speculator is held to earn his gain by services of an economic kind rendered the community. The recourse to this epithet, "legitimate," is chiefly of interest as showing that the tacit postulate of a natural order is still in force. Legitimate are such speculative dealings as are, by the theorist, conceived to serve the ends of the community, while illegitimate speculation is that which is conceived to be disserviceable to the community.

The theoretical difficulty about the speculator and his gains (or losses) is that the speculator *ex professo* is quite without interest in or connection with any given industrial enterprise or any industrial plant. He is, industrially speaking, without visible means of support. He may stake his risks on the gain or on the loss of the community with equal chances of success, and he may shift from one side to the other without winking. The speculator may be treated as an extreme case of undertaker, who deals exclusively with the business side of economic life rather than with the industrial side. But he differs in this respect from the common run of business men in degree rather than in kind. His traffic is a pecuniary traffic, and it touches industry only remotely and uncertainly; while the business man as commonly conceived is more or less immediately interested in the successful operation of some concrete industrial plant.

But since the undertaker first broke into economic theory, some change has also taken place as regards the immediacy of the relations of the common run of undertakers to the mechanical facts of the industries in which they are interested. Half a century ago it was still possible to construe the average business manager in industry as an agent occupied with

---

[5] See, e.g., a paper by H. C. Emery in the Papers and Proceedings of the Twelfth Annual Meeting of the American Economic Association, on "The Place of the Speculator in the Theory of Distribution," and more particularly the discussion following the paper.

the superintendence of the mechanical processes involved in the production of goods or services. But in the later development the connection between the business manager and the mechanical processes has, on an average, grown more remote; so much so, that his superintendence of the plant or of the processes is frequently visible only to the scientific imagination. That activity by virtue of which the undertaker is classed as such makes him a business man, not a mechanic or foreman of the shop.

His superintendence is a superintendence of the pecuniary affairs of the concern, rather than of the industrial plant; especially is this true in the higher development of the modern captain of industry. As regards the nature of the employment which characterises the undertaker, it is possible to distinguish him from the men who are mechanically engaged in the production of goods, and to say that his employment is of a business or pecuniary kind, while theirs is of an industrial or mechanical kind. It is not possible to draw a similar distinction between the undertaker who is in charge of a given industrial concern, and the business man who is in business but is not interested in the production of goods or services. As regards the character of employment, then, the line falls not between legitimate and illegitimate pecuniary transactions, but between business and industry.

The distinction between business and industry has, of course, been possible - from the beginning of economic theory, and, indeed, the distinction has from time to time temporarily been made in the contrast frequently pointed out between the proximate interest of the business man and the ulterior interest of society at large. What appears to have hindered the reception of the distinction into economic doctrine, is the constraining presence of a belief in an order of Nature and the habit of conceiving the economic community as an organism. The point of view given by these postulates has made such a distinction between employments not only useless, but even disserviceable for the ends to which theory has been directed. But the fact has come to be gradually more and more patent that there are constantly, normally present in modern economic life an important range of activities and classes of persons who work for an income but of whom it cannot be said that they, either proximately or remotely, apply themselves to the production of goods.

Their services, proximate or remote, to society are often of quite a problematical character. They are ubiquitous, and it will scarcely do to say that they are anomalous, for they are of ancient prescription, they are within the law and within the pale of popular morals. Of these strictly economic activities that are lucrative without necessarily being serviceable to the community, the greater part are to be classed as "business." Perhaps the largest and most obvious illustration of these legitimate business employments is afforded by the speculators in securities. By way of further illustration may be mentioned the extensive and varied business of real-estate men (land-agents) engaged in the purchase and sale of property for speculative gain or for a commission; so, also, the closely related business of promoters and boomers of other than real-estate ventures; as also attorneys, brokers, bankers, and the like, although the work performed by

these latter will more obviously bear interpretation in terms of social serviceability. The traffic of these business men shades off insensibly from
that of the bona fide speculator who has no ulterior end of industrial efficiency to serve, to that of the captain of industry or entrepreneur as conventionally set forth in the economic manuals.

The characteristic in which these business employments resemble one
another, and in which they differ from the mechanical occupations as well
as from other non-economic employments, is that they are concerned
primarily with the phenomena of value - with exchange or market values
and with purchase and sale - and only indirectly and secondarily, if at all,
with mechanical processes. What holds the interest and guides and shifts
the attention of men within these employments is the main chance. These
activities begin and end within what may broadly be called "the higgling of
the market." Of the industrial employments, in the stricter sense, it may be
said, on the other hand, that they begin and end outside the higgling of
the market. Their proximate aim and effect is the shaping and guiding of
material things and processes. Broadly, they may be said to be primarily
occupied with the phenomena of material serviceability, rather than with
those of exchange value. They are taken up with phenomena which make
the subject matter of Physics and the other material sciences.

The business man enters the economic life process from the pecuniary
side, and so far as he works an effect in industry he works it through the
pecuniary dispositions which he makes. He takes thought most immediately of men's convictions regarding market values; and his efforts as a
business man are directed to the apprehension, and commonly also to the
influencing of men's beliefs regarding market values. The objective point
of business is the diversion of purchase and sale into some particular
channel, commonly involving a diversion from other channels. The laborer and the man engaged in directing industrial processes, on the other
hand, enter the economic process from the material side; in their characteristic work they take thought most immediately of mechanical effects,
and their attention is directed to turning men and things to account for
the compassing of some material end.

The ulterior aim, and the ulterior effect, of these industrial employments
may be some pecuniary result; work of this class commonly results in an
enhancement, or at least an alteration, of market values. Conversely, business activity may, and in a majority of cases it perhaps does, effect an enhancement of the aggregate material wealth of the community, or the aggregate serviceability of the means at hand; but such an industrial outcome is by no means bound to follow from the nature of the business
man's work. From what has just been said it appears that, if we retain the
classical division of economic theory into Production, Distribution, and
Consumption, the pecuniary employments do not properly fall under the
first of these divisions, Production, if that term is to retain the meaning
commonly assigned to it. In an earlier and less specialised organisation of
economic life, particularly, the undertaker frequently performs the work of
a foreman or a technological expert, as well as the work of business management. Hence in most discussions of his work and his theoretical rela-

tions his occupation is treated as a composite one. The technological side of his composite occupation has even given a name to his gains (wages of superintendence), as if the undertaker were primarily a master-workman. The distinction at this point has been drawn between classes of persons instead of between classes of employments; with the result that the evident necessity of discussing his technological employment under production has given countenance to the endeavor to dispose of the undertaker's business activity under the same head. This endeavor has, of course, not wholly succeeded. In the later development, the specialisation of work in the economic field has at this point progressed so far, and the undertaker now in many cases comes so near being occupied with business affairs alone, to the exclusion of technological direction and supervision, that, with this object lesson before us, we no longer have the same difficulty in drawing a distinction between business and industrial employments. And even in the earlier days of the doctrines, when the aim was to dispose of the undertaker's work under the theoretical head of Production, the business side of his work persistently obtruded itself for discussion in the books and chapters given to Distribution and Exchange.

The course taken by the later theoretical discussion of the entrepreneur, leaves no question but that the characteristic fact about his work is that he is a business man, occupied with pecuniary affairs. Such pecuniary employments, of which the purely fiscal or financiering forms of business are typical, are nearly all and nearly throughout, conditioned by the institution of property or ownership - an institution which, as John Stuart Mill remarks, belongs entirely within the theoretical realm of Distribution. Ownership, no doubt, has its effect upon productive industry, and, indeed, its effect upon industry is very large, both in scope and range, even if we should not be prepared to go the length of saying that it fundamentally conditions all industry; but ownership is not itself primarily or immediately a contrivance for production. Ownership directly touches the results of industry, and only indirectly the methods and processes of industry. If the institution of property be compared with such another feature of our culture, for instance, as the domestication of plants or the smelting of iron, the meaning of what has just been said may seem clearer.

So much then of the business man's activity as is conditioned by the institution of property, is not to be classed, in economic theory, as productive or industrial activity at all. Its objective point is an alteration of the distribution of wealth. His business is, essentially, to sell and buy - sell in order to buy cheaper, buy in order to sell dearer[6] .It may or may not, indirectly, and in a sense incidentally, result in enhanced production. The business man may be equally successful in his enterprise, and he may be equally well remunerated, whether his activity does or does not enrich the community. Immediately and directly, so long as it is confined to the pecuniary or business sphere, his activity is incapable of enriching or impoverishing the community as a whole except, after the fashion conceived by

---

[6] Cf. e.g., Marx, Capital, especially bk. i, ch. iv.

the mercantilists, through his dealings with men of other communities. The circulation and distribution of goods incidental to the business man's traffic is commonly, though not always or in the nature of the case, serviceable to the community; but the distribution of goods is a mechanical, not a pecuniary transaction, and it is not the objective point of business nor its invariable outcome. From the point of view of business, the distribution or circulation of goods is a means of gain, not an end sought. It is true, industry is closely conditioned by business.

In a modern community, the business man finally decides what may be done in industry, or at least in the greater number and the more conspicuous branches of industry. This is particularly true of those branches that are currently thought of as peculiarly modem. Under existing circumstances of ownership, the discretion in economic matters, industrial or otherwise, ultimately rests in the hands of the business men. It is their business to have to do with property, and property means the discretionary control of wealth. In point of character, scope and growth, industrial processes and plants adapt themselves to the exigencies of the market, wherever there is a developed market, and the exigencies of the market are pecuniary exigencies. The business man, through his pecuniary dispositions, enforces his choice of what industrial processes shall be in use. He can, of course, not create or initiate methods or aims for industry; if he does so he steps out of the business sphere *into the material domain of industry. But he can decide whether and which of the known processes and industrial arts shall be practiced, and to what extent. Industry must be conducted to suit the business man in his quest for gain; which is not the same as saying that it must be conducted to suit the needs or the convenience of the community at large.

Ever since the institution of property was definitely installed, and in proportion as purchase and sale has been practiced, some approach has been made to a comprehensive system of control of industry by pecuniary transactions and for pecuniary ends, and the industrial organisation is nearer such a consummation now than it ever has been. For the great body of modern industry the final term of the sequence is not the production of the goods but their sale; the endeavor is not so much to fit the goods for use as for sale. It is well known that there are many lines of industry in which the cost of marketing the goods equals the cost of making and transporting them.

Any industrial venture which falls short in meeting the pecuniary exigencies of the market declines and yields ground to others that meet them with better effect. Hence shrewd business management is a requisite to success in any industry that is carried on within the scope of the market. Pecuniary failure carries with it industrial failure, whatever may be the cause to which the pecuniary failure is due - whether it be inferiority of the goods produced, lack of salesmanlike tact, popular prejudice, scanty or ill-devised advertising, excessive truthfulness, or what not. In this way industrial results are closely dependent upon the presence of business ability; but the cause of this dependence of industry upon business in a given case is to be sought in the fact that other rival ventures have the backing of shrewd business management, rather than in any help which business management in the aggregate affords to the aggregate industry of the community.

Shrewd and farsighted business management is a requisite of survival in the competitive pecuniary struggle in which the several industrial concerns are engaged, because shrewd and farsighted business management abounds and is employed by all the competitors. The ground of survival in the selective process is fitness for pecuniary gain, not fitness for serviceability at large. Pecuniary management is of an emulative character and gives, primarily, relative success only. If the change were equitably distributed, an increase or decrease of the aggregate or average business ability in the community need not immediately affect the industrial efficiency or the material welfare of the community. The like can not be said with respect to the aggregate or average industrial capacity of the men at work. The latter are, on the whole, occupied with production of goods; the business men, on the other hand, are occupied with the acquisition of them.

Theoreticians who are given to looking beneath the facts and to contemplating the profounder philosophical meaning of life speak of the function of the undertaker as being the guidance and coordination of industrial processes with a view to economies of production. No doubt, the remoter effect of business transactions often is such coordination and economy, and, no doubt also, the undertaker has such economy in view and is stimulated to his maneuvers of combination by the knowledge that certain economies of this kind are feasible and will inure to his gain if the proper business arrangements can be effected. But it is practicable to class even this indirect furthering of industry by the undertaker as a permissive guidance only. The men in industry must first create the mechanical possibility of such new and more economical methods and arrangements, before the undertaker sees the chance, makes the necessary business arrangements, and gives directions that the more effective working arrangements be adopted.

It is notorious and it is a matter upon which men dilate, that the wide and comprehensive consolidations and coordinations of industry, which often add so greatly to its effectiveness, take place at the initiative of the business men who are in control. It should be added that the fact of their being in control precludes such coordination from being effected except by their advice and consent. And it should also be added, in order to a passably complete account of the undertaker's function, that he not only can and does effect economising coordinations of a large scope, but he also can and does at times inhibit the process of consolidation and coordination. It happens so frequently that it might fairly be said to be the common run that business interests and undertaker's maneuvers delay consolidation, combination, coordination for some appreciable time after they have become patently advisable on industrial grounds. The industrial advisability or practicability is not the decisive point. Industrial advisability must wait on the eventual convergence of jarring pecuniary interests and on the strategical moves of business men playing for position.

Which of these two offices of the business man in modern industry, the furthering or the inhibitory, has the more serious or more far-reaching consequences is, on the whole, somewhat problematical. The furtherance of coordination by the modern captain of industry bulks large in our vision, in great part because the process of widening coordination is of a cumulative character. After a given step in coordination and combination has been taken, the next step takes place on the basis of the resulting situation. Industry, that is to say the working force engaged in industry, has a chance to develop new and larger possibilities to be taken further advantage of. In this way each successive move in the enhancement of the efficiency of industrial processes, or in the widening of coordination in industrial processes, pushes the captain of industry to a further concession, making possible a still farther industrial growth. But as regards the undertaker's inhibitory dealings with industrial coordination the visible outcome is not so striking.

The visible outcome is simply that nothing of the kind then takes place in the premises. The potential cumulative sequence is cut off at the start, and so it does not figure in our appraisement of the disadvantage incurred. The loss does not commonly take the more obtrusive form of an absolute retreat, but only that of a failure to advance where the industrial situation admits of an advance. It is, of course, impracticable to foot up and compare gain and loss in such a case, where the losses, being of the nature of inhibited growth, cannot be ascertained. But since the industrial serviceability of the captain of industry is, on the whole, of a problematical complexion, it should be advisable for a cautious economic theory not to rest its discussion of him on his serviceability[7] .

---

[7] It is not hereby intended to depreciate the services rendered the community by the captain of industry in his management of business. Such services are no doubt rendered and are also no doubt of substantial value. Still less is it the intention to decry the pecuniary incentive as a motive to thrift and diligence. It may well be that the pecuniary traffic which we call business is the most effective method of conducting the industrial policy of the community; not only the most effective that has been contrived, but perhaps the best that can be contrived. But that is a matter of surmise and opinion. In a matter of opinion on a point that can not be verified, a reasonable course is to say that the majority are presumably in the right. But all that is beside the point. However probable or reasonable such a view may be, it can find no lodgment in modern scientific theory, except as a corollary of secondary importance. Nor can scientific theory build upon the ground it may be conceived to afford. Policy may so build, but science can not. Scientific theory is a formulation of the laws of phenomena in terms of the efficient forces at work in the sequence of phenomena. So long as (under the old dispensation of the order of nature) the animistically conceived natural laws, with their God-given objective end, were considered to exercise a constraining guidance over the course of events whereof they were claimed to be laws, so long it was legitimate scientific procedure for economists to formulate their theory in terms of these laws of the natural course; because so long they were speaking in terms of what was, to them, the efficient forces at work. But so soon as these natural laws were reduced to the plane of colorless empirical generalization as to what commonly happens, while the efficient forces at

It appears, then, as all economists are no doubt aware, that there is in modern society a considerable range of activities, which are not only normally present, but which constitute the vital core of our economic system; which are not directly concerned with production, but which are nevertheless lucrative. Indeed, the group comprises most of the highly remunerative employments in modern economic life. The gains from these employments must plainly be accounted for on other grounds than their productivity, since they need have no productivity.

But it is not only as regards the pecuniary employments that productivity and remuneration are constitutionally out of touch. It seems plain, from what has already been said, that the like is true for the remuneration gained in the industrial employments. Most wages, particularly those paid in the industrial employments proper, as contrasted with those paid for domestic or personal service, are paid on account of pecuniary serviceability to the employer, not on grounds of material serviceability to mankind at large. The product is valued, sought and paid for on account of and in some proportion to its vendibility, not for more recondite reasons of ulterior human welfare at large. It results that there is no warrant, in general theory, for claiming that the work of highly paid persons (more particularly that of highly paid business men) is of greater substantial use to the community than that of the less highly paid.

---

work are conceived to be of quite another cast, so soon must theory abandon the ground of the natural course, sterile for modern scientific purposes, and shift to the ground of the causal sequence, where alone it will have to do with the forces at work as they are conceived in our time. The generalisations regarding the normal course, as "normal" has been defined in economics since J. S. Mill, are not of the nature of theory, but only rule-of-thumb. And the talk about the "function" of this and that factor of production, etc., in terms of the collective life purpose, goes to the same limbo; since the collective life purpose is no longer avowedly conceived to cut any figure in the every-day guidance of economic activities or the shaping of economic results. The doctrine of the social-economic function of the undertaker may for the present purpose be illustrated by a supposititious parallel from Physics. - It is an easy generalisation, which will scarcely be questioned, that, in practice, pendulums commonly vibrate in a plane approximately parallel with the nearest wall of the clock-case in which they are placed. The normality of this parallelism is fortified by the further observation that the vibrations are also commonly in a plane parallel with the nearest wall of the room; and when it is further called to mind that the balance which serves the purpose of a pendulum in watches similarly vibrates in a plane parallel with the walls of its case, the absolute normality of the whole arrangement is placed beyond question. It is true, the parallelism is not claimed to be related to the working of the pendulum, except as a matter of fortuitous convenience; but it should be manifest from the generality of the occurrence that in the normal case, in the absence of disturbing causes, and in the long run, all pendulums will "naturally" tend to swing in a plane faultlessly parallel with the nearest wall. The use which has been made of the "organic concept." in economics and in social science at large, is fairly comparable with this supposititious argument concerning the pendulum.

At the same time, the reverse could, of course, also not be claimed. Wages, resting on a pecuniary basis, afford no consistent indication of the relative productivity of the recipients, except in comparisons between persons or classes whose products are identical except in amount, - that is to say, where a resort to wages as an index of productivity would be of notice anyway[8] .

A result of the acceptance of the theoretical distinction here attempted between industrial and pecuniary employments and an effective recognition of the pecuniary basis of the modern economic organisation would be to dissociate the two ideas of productivity and remuneration. In mathematical language, remuneration could no longer be conceived and handled as a "function" of productivity,- unless productivity be taken to mean pecuniary serviceability to the person who pays the remuneration. In modern life remuneration is, in the last analysis, uniformly obtained by virtue of an agreement between individuals who commonly proceed on their own interest in point of pecuniary gain.

The remuneration may, therefore, be said to be a "function" of the pecuniary service rendered the person who grants the remuneration; but what is pecuniarily serviceable to the individual who exercises the discretion in the matter need not be productive of material gain to the community as a whole. Nor does the algebraic sum of individual pecuniary gains measure the aggregate serviceability of the activities for which the gains are got.

In a community organized, as modern communities are, on a pecuniary basis, the discretion in economic matters rests with the individuals, in severalty; and the aggregate of discrete individual interests nowise expresses the collective interest. Expressions constantly recur in economic discussions which imply that the transactions discussed are carried out for the sake of the collective good or at the initiative of the social organism, or that "society" rewards so and so for their services. Such expressions are commonly of the nature of figures of speech and are serviceable for homiletical rather than for scientific use. They serve to express their user's faith in a beneficent order of nature, rather than to convey or to formulate information in regard to facts. Of course, it is still possible consistently to hold that there is a natural equivalence between work and its reward, that remuneration is naturally, or normally, or in the long run, proportioned to the material service rendered the community by the recipient; but that proposition will hold true only if "natural" or "normal" be taken in such a sense as to admit of our saying that the natural does not coincide with the actual; and it must be recognised that such a doctrine of the "natural" ap-

---

8 Since the ground of payment of wages is the vendibility of the product, and since the ground of a difference in wages is the different vendibility of the product acquired through the purchase of the labor for which the wages are paid, it follows that wherever the difference in vendibility rests on a difference in the magnitude of the product alone, there wages should be somewhat in proportion to the magnitude of the product.

portionment of wealth or of income disregards the efficient facts of the case.

Apart from effects of this kind in the way of equitable arrangements traceable to grounds of sentiment, the only recourse which modern science would afford the champion of a doctrine of natural distribution, in the sense indicated, would be a doctrine of natural selection; according to which all disserviceable or unproductive, wasteful employments would, perforce, be weeded out as being incompatible with the continued life of any community that tolerated them. But such a selective elimination of unserviceable or wasteful employments would presume the following two conditions, neither of which need prevail:

(1) It must be assumed that the disposable margin between the aggregate productivity of industry and the aggregate necessary consumption is so narrow as to admit of no appreciable waste of energy or of goods;

(2) it must be assumed that no deterioration of the condition of society in the economic respect does or can "naturally" take place. As to the former of these two assumptions, it is to be said that in a very poor community, and under exceptionally hard economic circumstances, the margin of production may be as narrow as the theory would require. Something approaching this state of things may be found, for instance, among some Eskimo tribes. But in a modern industrial community - where the margin of admissible waste probably always exceeds fifty per cent. of the output of goods - the facts make no approach to the hypothesis.

The second assumed condition is, of course, the old-fashioned assumption of a beneficent, providential order or meliorative trend in human affairs. As such, it needs no argument at this day. Instances are not far to seek of communities in which economic deterioration has taken place while the system of distribution, both of income and of accumulated wealth, has remained on a pecuniary basis. To return to the main drift of the argument. The pecuniary employments have to do with wealth in point of ownership, with market values, with transactions of exchange, purchase and sale, bargaining for the purpose of pecuniary gain. These employments make up the characteristic occupations of business men, and the gains of business are derived from successful endeavors of the pecuniary kind. These business employments are the characteristic activity (constitute the "function") of what are in theory called undertakers. The dispositions which undertakers, qua business men, make are pecuniary dispositions - whatever industrial sequel they may or may not have - and are carried out with a view to pecuniary gain.

The wealth of which they have the discretionary disposal may or may not be in the form of "production goods"; but in whatever form the wealth in question is conceived to exist, it is handled by the undertakers in terms of values and is disposed of by them in the pecuniary respect. When, as may happen, the undertaker steps down from the pecuniary plane and directs the mechanical handling and functioning of "production goods," he becomes for the time a foreman. The undertaker, if his business venture is of the industrial kind, of course takes cognizance of the aptness of a given industrial method or process for his purpose, and he has to choose between different industrial processes in which to invest his values; but his work as undertaker, simply, is the investment and shifting of the values under his hand from the less to the more gainful point of investment. When the investment takes the form of material means of industry, or industrial plant, the sequel of a given business transaction is commonly some particular use of such means; and when such industrial use follows, it commonly takes place at the hands of other men than the undertaker, although it takes place within limits imposed by the pecuniary exigencies of which the undertaker takes cognizance.

Wealth turned to account in the way of investment or business management may or may not, in consequence, be turned to account, materially, for industrial effect. Wealth, values, so employed for pecuniary ends is capital in the business sense of the word[9] .Wealth, material means of industry, physically employed for industrial ends is capital in the industrial sense. Theory, therefore, would require that care be taken to distinguish between capital as a pecuniary category, and capital as an industrial category, if the term capital is retained to cover the two concepts[10] .The distinction here made substantially coincides with a distinction which many late writers have arrived at from a different point of approach and have, with varying success, made use of under different terms[11] .

A further corollary touching capital may be pointed out. The gains derived from the handling of capital in the pecuniary respect have no immediate relation, stand in no necessary relation of proportion, to the productive effect compassed by the industrial use of the material means over which the undertaker may dispose; although the gains have a relation of dependence to the effects achieved in point of vendibility. But vendibility need not, even approximately, coincide with serviceability, except serviceability be construed in terms of marginal utility or some related conception, in which case the outcome is a tautology. Where, as in the case commonly assumed by economists as typical, the investing undertaker seeks his gain through the production and sale of some useful article, it is commonly also assumed that his effort is directed to the most economical production of as large and serviceable a product as may be, or at least it is

---

[9] All wealth so used is capital, but it does not follow that all pecuniary capital is social wealth.

[10] In current theory the term capital is used in these two senses; while in business usage it is employed pretty consistently in the former sense alone. The current ambiguity in the term capital has often been adverted to by economists, and there may be need of a revision of the terminology at this point; but this paper is not concerned with that question.

[11] Professor Fetter, in a recent paper (Quarterly Journal of Economics, November, 1900) is, perhaps, the writer who has gone the farthest in this direction in the definition of the capital concept. Professor Fetter wishes to confine the term capital to pecuniary capital, or rather to such pecuniary capital as is based on the ownership of material goods. The wisdom of such a terminological expedient is, of course, not in question here.

assumed that such production is the outcome of his endeavors in the natural course of things. This account of the aim and outcome of business enterprise may be natural, but it does not describe the facts. The facts being, of course, that the undertaker in such a case seeks to produce economically as vendible a product as may be. In the common run vendibility depends in great part on the serviceability of the goods, but it depends also on several other circumstances; and to that highly variable, but nearly always considerable extent to which vendibility depends on other circumstances than the material serviceability of the goods, the pecuniary management of capital must be held not to serve the ends of production.

Neither immediately, in his purely pecuniary traffic, nor indirectly, in the business guidance of industry through his pecuniary traffic, therefore, can the undertaker's dealings with his pecuniary capital be accounted a productive occupation, nor can the gains of capital be taken to mark or to measure the productivity due to the investment. The "cost of production" of goods in the case contemplated is to an appreciable, but indeterminable, extent a cost of production of vendibility - an outcome which is often of doubtful service to the body of consumers, and which often counts in the aggregate as waste. The material serviceability of the means employed in industry, that is to say the functioning of industrial capital in the service of the community at large, stands in no necessary or consistent relation to the gainfulness of capital in the pecuniary respect.

Productivity can accordingly not be predicated of pecuniary capital. It follows that productivity theories of interest should be as difficult to maintain as productivity theories of the gains of the pecuniary employments, the two resting on the same grounds. It is, further, to be remarked that pecuniary capital and industrial capital do not coincide in respect of the concrete things comprised under each. From this and from the considerations already indicated above, it follows that the magnitude of pecuniary capital may vary independently of variations in the magnitude of industrial capital - not indefinitely, perhaps, but within a range which, in its nature, is indeterminate. Pecuniary capital is a matter of market values, while industrial capital is, in the last analysis, a matter of mechanical efficiency, or rather of mechanical effects not reducible to a common measure or a collective magnitude. So far as the latter may be spoken of as a homogenous aggregate - itself a doubtful point at best - the two categories of capital are disparate magnitudes, which can be mediated only through a process of valuation conditioned by other circumstances besides the mechanical efficiency of the material means valued.

Market values being a psychological outcome, it follows that pecuniary capital, an aggregate of market values, may vary in magnitude with a freedom which gives the whole an air of caprice, - such as psychological phenomena, particularly the psychological phenomena of crowds, frequently present, and such as becomes strikingly noticeable in times of panic or of speculative inflation. On the other hand, industrial capital, being a matter of mechanical contrivances and adaptation, cannot similarly vary through a revision of valuations. If it is taken as an aggregate, it is a physical magnitude, and as such it does not alter its complexion or its mechanical efficiency in response to the greater or less degree of appreciation with which it is viewed.

Capital pecuniarily considered rests on a basis of subjective value; capital industrially considered rests on material circumstances reducible to objective terms of mechanical, chemical and physiological effect. The point has frequently been noted that it is impossible to get at the aggregate social (industrial) capital by adding up the several items of individual (pecuniary) capital. A reason for this, apart from variations in the market values of given material means of production, is that pecuniary capital comprises not only material things but also conventional facts, psychological phenomena not related in any rigid way to material means of production, - as e.g., good will, fashions, customs, prestige, effrontery, personal credit. Whatever ownership touches, and whatever affords ground for pecuniary discretion, may be turned to account for pecuniary gain and may therefore be comprised in the aggregate of pecuniary capital.

Ownership, the basis of pecuniary capital, being itself a conventional fact, that is to say a matter of habits of thought, it is intelligible that phenomena of convention and opinion should figure in an inventory of pecuniary capital; whereas, industrial capital being of a mechanical character, conventional circumstances do not affect it - except as the future production of material means to replace the existing outfit may be guided by convention - and items having but a conventional existence are, therefore, not comprised in its aggregate. The disparity between pecuniary and industrial capital, therefore, is something more than a matter of an arbitrarily chosen point of view, as some recent discussions of the capital concept would have us believe; just as the difference between the pecuniary and the industrial employments, which are occupied with the one or the other category of capital, means something more than the same thing under different aspects.

But the distinction here attempted has a farther bearing, beyond the possible correction of a given point in the theory of distribution. Modern economic science is to an increasing extent concerning itself with the question of what men do and bow and why they do it, as contrasted with the older question of how Nature, working through human nature, maintains a favorable balance in the output of goods. Neither the practical questions of our generation, nor the pressing theoretical questions of the science, run on the adequacy or equity of the share that goes to any class in the normal case. The questions are rather such realistic ones as these: Why do we, now and again, have hard times and unemployment in the midst of excellent resources, high efficiency and plenty of unmet wants? Why is one-half our consumable product contrived for consumption that yields no material benefit?

Why are large coordinations of industry, which greatly reduce cost of production, a cause of perplexity and alarm? Why is the family disintegrating among the industrial classes, at the same time that the wherewithal to maintain it is easier to compass? Why are large and increasing portions of the community penniless in spite of a scale of remuneration which is very appreciably above the subsistence minimum? Why is there a widespread disaffection among the intelligent workmen who ought to know better? These and the like questions, being questions of fact, are not to be answered on the grounds of normal equivalence. Perhaps it might better be said that they have so often been answered on those grounds, without any approach to disposing of them, that the outlook for help in that direction has ceased to have a serious meaning. These are, to borrow Professor Clark's phrase, questions to be answered on dynamic, not on static grounds. They are questions of conduct and sentiment, and so far as their solution is looked for at the bands of economists it must be looked for along the line of the bearing which economic life has upon the growth of sentiment and canons of conduct.

That is to say, they are questions of the bearing of economic life upon the cultural changes that are going forward. For the present it is the vogue to hold that economic life, broadly, conditions the rest of social organization or the constitution of society. This vogue of the proposition will serve as excuse from going into an examination of the grounds on which it may be justified, as it is scarcely necessary to persuade any economist that it has substantial merits even if he may not accept it in an unqualified form. What the Marxists have named the "Materialistic Conception of History" is assented to with less and less qualification by those who make the growth of culture their subject of inquiry. This materialistic conception says that institutions are shaped by economic conditions; but, as it left the hands of the Marxists, and as it still functions in the hands of many who knew not Marx, it has very little to say regarding the efficient force, the channels, or the methods by which the economic situation is conceived to have its effect upon institutions.

What answer the early Marxists gave to this question, of how the economic situation shapes institutions, was to the effect that the causal connection lies through a selfish, calculating class interest. But, while class interest may count for much in the outcome, this answer is plainly not a competent one, since, for one thing, institutions by no means change with the alacrity which the sole efficiency of a reasoned class interest would require. Without discrediting the claim that class interest counts for something in the shaping of institutions, and to avoid getting entangled in preliminaries, it may be said that institutions are of the nature of prevalent habits of thought, and that therefore the force which shapes institutions is the force or forces which shape the habits of thought prevalent in the community.

But habits of thought are the outcome of habits of life. Whether it is intentionally directed to the education of the individual or not, the discipline of daily life acts to alter or reinforce the received habits of thought, and so acts to alter or fortify the received institutions under which men live. And the direction in which, on the whole, the alteration proceeds is conditioned by the trend of the discipline of daily life. The point here immediately at issue is the divergent trend of this discipline in those occupations which are prevailingly of an industrial character, as contrasted with those which are prevailingly of a pecuniary character. So far as regards the different cultural outcome to be looked for on the basis of the present economic situation as contrasted with the past, therefore, the question immediately in hand is as to the greater or less degree in which occupations are differentiated into industrial and pecuniary in the present as compared with the past.

The characteristic feature which is currently held to differentiate the existing economic situation from that out of which the present has developed, or out of which it is emerging, is the prevalence of the machine industry with the consequent larger and more highly specialised organisation of the market and of the industrial force and plant. As has been pointed out above, and as is well enough known from the current discussions of the economists, industrial life is organised on a pecuniary basis and managed from the pecuniary side. This, of course, is true in a degree both of the present and of the nearer past, back at least as far as the Middle Ages. But the larger scope of organisations in modern industry means that the pecuniary management has been gradually passing into the hands of a relatively decreasing class, whose contact with the industrial classes proper grows continually less immediate. The distinction between employments above spoken of is in an increasing degree coming to coincide with a differentiation of occupations and of economic classes. Some degree of such specialisation and differentiation there has, of course, been, one might almost say, always. But in our time, in many branches of industry, the specialisation has been carried so far that large bodies of the working population have but an incidental contact with the business side of the enterprise, while a minority have little if any other concern with the enterprise than its pecuniary management. This was not true, e. g., at the time when the undertaker was still salesman, purchasing agent, business manager, foreman of the shop, and master workman. Still less was it true in the days of the self-sufficing manor or household, or in the days of the closed town industry.

Neither is it true in our time of what we call the backward or old-fashioned industries. These latter have not been and are not organised on a large scale, with a consistent division of labor between the owners and business managers on the one side and the operative employees on the other. Our standing illustrations of this less highly organised class of industries are the surviving handicrafts and the common run of farming as carried on by relatively small proprietors. In that earlier phase of economic life, out of which the modern situation has gradually grown, all the men engaged had to be constantly on their guard, in a pecuniary sense, and were constantly disciplined in the husbanding of their means and in the driving of bargains, - as is still true, e. g., of the American farmer. The like was formerly true also of the consumer, in his purchases, to a greater extent than at present. A good share of the daily attention of those who were engaged in the handicrafts was still perforce given to the pecuniary or business side of their trade.

But for that great body of industry which is conventionally recognised as eminently modern, specialisation of function has gone so far as, in great measure, to exempt the operative employees from taking thought of pecuniary matters. Now, as to the bearing of all this upon cultural changes that are in progress or in the outlook. Leaving the "backward," relatively unspecialised, industries on one side, as being of an equivocal character for the point in hand and as not differing characteristically from the corresponding industries in the past so far as regards their disciplinary value; modern occupations may, for the sake of the argument, be broadly distinguished, as economic employments have been distinguished above, into business and industrial.

The modern industrial and the modern business occupations are fairly comparable as regards the degree of intelligence required in both, if it be borne in mind that the former occupations comprise the highly trained technological experts and engineers as well as the highly skilled mechanics. The two classes of occupations differ in that the men in the pecuniary occupations work within the lines and under the guidance of the great institution of ownership, with its ramifications of custom, prerogative, and legal right; whereas those in the industrial occupations are, in their work, relatively free from the constraint of this conventional norm of truth and validity. It is, of course, not true that the work of the latter class lies outside the reach of the institution of ownership; but it is true that, in the beat and strain of the work, when the agent's powers and attention are fully taken up with the work which he has in hand, that of which he has perforce to take cognisance is not conventional law, but the conditions impersonally imposed by the nature of material things.

This is the meaning of the current commonplace that the required close and continuous application of the operative in mechanical industry bars him out of all chance for an all-around development of the cultural graces and amenities. It is the periods of close attention and hard work that seem to count for most in the formation of habits of thought. An a priori argument as to what cultural effects should naturally follow from such a difference in discipline between occupations, past and present, would probably not be convincing, as a priori arguments from half-authenticated premises commonly are not. And the experiments along this line which later economic developments have so far exhibited have been neither neat enough, comprehensive enough, nor long continued enough to give definite results. Still, there is something to be said under this latter head, even if this something may turn out to be somewhat familiar. It is, e.g., a commonplace of current vulgar discussions of existing economic questions, that the classes engaged in the modern mechanical or factory industries are improvident and apparently incompetent to take care of the pecuniary details of their own life. In this indictment may well be included not only factory hands, but the general class of highly skilled mechanics, inventors, technological experts.

The rule does not hold in any hard and fast way, but there seems to be a substantial ground of truth in the indictment in this general form. This will be evident on comparison of the present factory population with the class of handicraftsmen of the older culture whom they have displaced, as also on comparison with the farming population of the present time, especially the small proprietors of this and other countries. The inferiority which is currently conceded to the modern industrial classes in this respect is not due to scantier opportunities for saving, whether they are compared with the earlier handicraftsmen or with the modern farmer or peasant. This phenomenon is commonly discussed in terms which impute to the improvident industrial classes something in the way of total depravity, and there is much preaching of thrift and steady habits. But the preaching of thrift and self-help, unremitting as it is, is not producing an appreciable effect. The trouble seems to run deeper than exhortation can reach. It seems to be of the nature of habit rather than of reasoned conviction. Other causes may be present and may be competent partially to explain the improvidence of these classes; but the inquiry is at least a pertinent one; how far the absence of property and thrift among them may be traceable to the relative absence of pecuniary training in the discipline of their daily life.

If, as the general lie of the subject would indicate, this peculiar pecuniary situation of the industrial classes is in any degree due to comprehensive disciplinary causes, there is material in it for an interesting economic inquiry. The surmise that the trouble with the industrial class is something of this character is strengthened by another feature of modern vulgar life, to which attention is directed as a further, and, for the present, a concluding illustration of the character of the questions that are touched by the distinction here spoken for. The most insidious and most alarming malady, as well as the most perplexing and unprecedented, that threatens the modern social and political structure is what is vaguely called socialism. The point of danger to the social structure, and at the same time the substantial core of the socialistic disaffection, is a growing disloyalty to the institution of property, aided and abetted as it is by a similarly growing lack of deference and affection for other conventional features of social structure. The classes affected by socialistic vagaries are not consistently averse to a competent organisation and control of society, particularly not in the economic respect, but they are averse to organisation and control on conventional lines.

The sense of solidarity does not seem to be either defective or in abeyance, but the ground of solidarity is new and unexpected. What their constructive ideals may be need not concern nor detain us; they are vague and inconsistent and for the most part negative. Their disaffection has been set down to discontent with their lot by comparison with others, and to a mistaken view of their own interests; and much and futile effort has been spent in showing them the error of their ways of think, e.g. But what the experience of the past suggests that we should expect under the guidance of such motives and reasoning as these would be a demand for a redistribution of property, a reconstitution of the conventions of ownership on such new lines as the apprehended interests of these classes would seem to dictate. But such is not the trend of socialistic thinking, which contemplates rather the elimination of the institution of property. To the socialists property or ownership does not seem inevitable or inherent in the nature of things; to those who criticise and admonish them it commonly does.

Compare them in this respect with other classes who have been moved by hardship or discontent, whether well or ill advised, to put forth denunciations and demands for radical economic changes; as e. g., the American farmers in their several movements, of grangerism, populism, and the like. These have been loud enough in their denunciations and complaints, and they have been accused of being socialistic in their demand for a virtual redistribution of property. They have not felt the justice of the accusation, however, and it is to be noted that their demands have consistently run on a rehabilitation of property on some new basis of distribution, and have been uniformly put forth with the avowed purpose of bettering the claimants in point of ownership. Ownership, property "honestly" acquired, has been sacred to the rural malcontents, here and elsewhere; what they have aspired to do has been to remedy what they have conceived to be certain abuses under the institution, without questioning the institution itself.

Not so with the socialists, either in this country or elsewhere. Now, the spread of socialistic sentiment shows a curious tendency to affect those classes particularly who are habitually employed in the specialised industrial occupations, and are thereby in great part exempt from the intellectual discipline of pecuniary management. Among these men, who by the circumstances of their daily life are brought to do their serious and habitual thinking in other than pecuniary terms, it looks as if the ownership preconception were becoming obsolescent through disuse. It is the industrial population, in the modern sense, and particularly the more intelligent and skilled men employed in the mechanical industries, that are most seriously and widely affected.

With exceptions both ways, but with a generality that is not to be denied, the socialistic disaffection spreads through the industrial towns, chiefly and most potently among the better classes of operatives in the mechanical employments; whereas the relative] indigent and unintelligent regions and classes, which the differentiation between pecuniary and industrial occupations has not reached, are relatively free from it. In like manner the upper and middle classes, whose employments are of a pecuniary character, if any, are also not seriously affected; and when avowed socialistic sentiment is met with among these upper and middle classes it commonly turns out to be merely a humanitarian aspiration for a more "equitable" redistribution of wealth - a readjustment of ownership under some new and improved method of control - not a contemplation of the traceless disappearance of ownership. Socialism, in the sense in which the word connotes a subversion of the economic foundations of modern culture, appears to be found only sporadically and uncertainly outside the limits, in time and space, of the discipline exercised by the modern mechanical, non-pecuniary occupations.

This state of the case need of course not be due solely to the disciplinary effects of the industrial employments, nor even solely to effects traceable to those employments whether in the way of disciplinary results, selective development, or what not. Other factors, particularly factors of an ethnic character, seem to cooperate to the result indicated; but, so far as evidence bearing on the point is yet in hand and has been analysed, it indicates that this differentiation of occupations is a necessary requisite to the growth of a consistent 'body of socialistic sentiment; and the indication is also that wherever this differentiation prevails in such a degree of accentuation and affects such considerable and compact bodies of people as to afford ground for a consistent growth of common sentiment, a result is some form of iconoclastic socialism. The differentiation ay of course have a selective as well as a disciplinary effect upon the population affected, and an off-hand separation of these two modes of influence can of course not be made.

In any case, the two modes of influence seem to converge to the outcome indicated; and, for the present purpose of illustration simply, the tracing out of the two strands of sequence in the case neither can nor need be undertaken. By force of this differentiation, in one way and another, the industrial classes are learning to think in terms of material cause and effect, to the neglect of prescription and conventional grounds of validity; just as, in a faintly incipient way, the economists are also learning to do in their discussion of the life of these classes. The resulting decay of the popular sense of conventional validity of course extends to other matters than the pecuniary conventions alone, with the outcome that the socialistically affected industrial classes are pretty uniformly affected with an effortless iconoclasm in other directions as well. For the discipline to which their work and habits of life subject them gives not so much a training away from the pecuniary conventions, specifically, as a positive and somewhat unmitigated training in methods of observation and inference proceeding on grounds alien to all conventional validity. But the practical experiment going on in the specialisation of discipline, in the respect contemplated, appears still to be near its beginning, and the growth of aberrant views and habits of thought due to the peculiar disciplinary trend of this late and unprecedented specialisation of occupations has not yet had time to work itself clear. The effects of the like one-sided discipline are similarly visible in the highly irregular, conventionally indefensible attitude of the industrial classes in the current labor and wage disputes, not of an avowedly socialistic aim.

So also as regards the departure from the ancient norm in such non-economic, or secondarily economic matters as the family relation and responsibility, where the disintegration of conventionalities in the industrial towns is said to threaten the foundations of domestic life and morality; and again as regards the growing inability of men trained to materialistic, industrial habits of thought to appreciate, or even to apprehend, the meaning of religious appeals and consolations that proceed on the old-fashioned conventional or metaphysical grounds of validity. But these and other like directions in which the cultural effects of the modern specialisation of occupations, whether in industry or in business, may be traceable can not be followed up here.

Chapter 3

On The Nature Of Capital

I .THE PRODUCTIVITY OF CAPITAL GOODS[1]

The knowledge of ways and means is a communal product. Access to the common stock of technological knowledge is necessary to the production of a livelihood. With the advance of the industrial arts the possession of material equipment has become a requisite to the effective use of this common stock of knowledge and skill, .Hence the grant advantage of owning capital goods, and hence the dominant position of the owner-employer in modern economic life.

It has been usual in expositions of economic theory to speak of capital as an array of "productive goods." What is immediately had in mind in this expression, as well as in the equivalent "capital goods," is the industrial equipment, primarily the mechanical appliances employed in the processes of industry. When the productive efficiency of these and of other, subsidiary classes of capital goods is subjected to further analysis, it is not unusual to trace it back to the productive labor of the workmen, the labor of the individual workman being the ultimate productive factor in the commonly accepted systems of theory. The current theories of production, as also those of distribution, are drawn in individualistic terms, particularly when these theories are based on hedonistic premises, as they commonly are.

Now, whatever may or may not be true for human conduct in some other bearing, in the economic respect man has never lived an isolated, self-sufficient life as an individual, either actually or potentially. Humanly speaking, such a thing is impossible. Neither an individual person nor a single household, nor a single line of descent, can maintain its life in isolation. Economically speaking, this is the characteristic trait of humanity that separates mankind from the other animals. The life-history of the race has been a life-history of human communities, of more or less considerable size, with more or less of group solidarity, and with more or less of cultural continuity over successive generations. The phenomena of human life occur only in this form. This continuity, congruity, or coherence of the group, is of an immaterial character. It is a matter of knowledge, usage, habits of life and habits of thought, not a matter of mechanical continuity or contact, or even of consanguinity. Wherever a human community is met with, as, e.g., among any of the peoples of the lower cultures, it is found in possession of something in the way of a body of technological knowledge, - knowledge serviceable and requisite to the quest of a liveli-

---

[1] Subtitle originally was omitted. See: Quarterly Journal of Economics, Vol. 23, Issue 1 (Nov., 1908), p. 104.

hood, comprising at least such elementary acquirements as language, the use of fire, of a cutting edge, of a pointed stick, of some tool for piercing, of some form of cord, thong, or fibre, together with some skill in the making of knots and lashings. Co-ordinate with this knowledge of ways and means, there is also uniformly present some matter-of-fact knowledge of the physical behavior of the materials with which men have to deal in the quest of a livelihood, beyond what any one individual has learned or can learn by his own experience alone.

This information and proficiency in the ways and means of life vests in the group at large; and, apart from accretions borrowed from other groups, it is the product of the given group, though not produced by any single generation. It may be called the immaterial equipment, or, by a license of speech, the intangible assets[2] of the community; and, in the early days at least, this is far and away the most important and consequential category of the community's assets or equipment. Without access to such a common stock of immaterial equipment no individual and no fraction of the community can make a living, much less make an advance. Such a stock of knowledge and practice is perhaps held loosely and informally; but it is held as a common stock, pervasively, by the group as a body, in its corporate capacity, as one might say; and it is transmitted and augmented in and by the group, however loose and haphazard the transmission may be conceived to be, not by individuals and in single lines of inheritance.

The requisite knowledge and proficiency of ways and means is a product, perhaps a by-product, of the life of the community at large; and it can also be maintained and retained only by the community at large. Whatever may be true for the unsearchable prehistoric phases of the life-history of the race, it appears to be true for the most primitive human groups and phases of which there is available information that the mass of technological knowledge possessed by any community, and necessary to its maintenance and to the maintenance of each of its members or subgroups, is too large a burden for any one individual or any single line of descent to carry. This holds true, of course, all the more rigorously and consistently, the more advanced the "state of the industrial arts" may be. But it seems to hold true with a generality that is fairly startling that whenever a given cultural community is broken up or suffers a serious diminution of members, its technological heritage deteriorates and dwindles, even tho it may have been apparently meagre enough before.

On the other hand, it seems to hold true with a similar uniformity that, when an individual member or a fraction of a community on what we call a lower stage of economic development is drawn away and trained and

---

[2] "Assets" is, of course, not to be taken literally in this connection. The term properly covers a pecuniary concept, not an industrial (technological) one, and it connotes ownership as well as value; and it will be used in this literal sense when in a later article ownership and investment come into the discussion. In the present connection it is used figuratively, for want of a better term, to convey the connotation of value and serviceability without thereby implying ownership.

instructed in the ways of a larger and more efficient technology, and is then thrown back into his home community, such an individual or fraction proves unable to make head against the technological bent of the community at large or even to create a serious diversion. Slight, perhaps transient, and gradually effective technological consequences may result from such an experiment; but they become effective by diffusion and assimilation through the body of the community, not in any marked degree in the way of an exceptional efficiency on the part of the individual or fraction which has been subjected to exceptional training. And inheritance in technological matters runs not in the channels of consanguinity, but in those of tradition and habituation, which are necessarily as wide as the scheme of life of the community.

Even in a relatively small and primitive community the mass of detail comprised in its knowledge and practice of ways and means is large, - too large for any one individual or household to become competently expert in it all; and its ramifications are extensive and diverse at the same time that all these ramifications bear, directly or indirectly, on the life and work of each member of the community. Neither the standard and routine of living nor the daily work of any individual in the community would remain the same after the introduction of an appreciable change, for good or ill, in any branch of the community's equipment of technological expedients. If the community grows larger, to the dimensions of a modern civilized people, and this immaterial equipment grows proportionately great and various, then it will become increasingly difficult to trace the connection between any given change in technological detail and the fortunes of any given obscure member of the community. But it is at least safe to say that an increase in the volume and complexity of the body of technological knowledge and practise does not progressively emancipate the life and work of the individual from its dominion.

The complement of technological knowledge so held, used, and transmitted in the life of the community is, of course, made up out of the experience of individuals. Experience, experimentation, habit, knowledge, initiative, are phenomena of individual life, and it is necessarily from this source that the community's common stock is all derived. The possibility of its growth lies in the feasibility of accumulating knowledge gained by individual experience and initiative, and therefore it lies in the feasibility of one individual's learning front the experience of another. But the initiative and technological enterprise of individuals, such, e.g., as shows itself in inventions and discoveries of more and better ways and means, proceeds on and enlarges the accumulated wisdom of the past. Individual initiative has no chance except on the ground afforded by the common stock, and the achievements of such initiative are of no effect except as accretions to the common stock. And the invention or discovery so achieved always embodies so much of what is already given that the creative contribution of the inventor or discoverer is trivial by comparison. In any known phase of culture this common stock of intangible, technological equipment is relatively large and complex, - i.e., relatively to the capacity of any individual member to create or to use it; and the history of its growth and use is the history of the development of material civilization. It is a knowledge of ways and means, and is embodied in the material contrivances and processes by means of which the members of the community make their living.

Only by such means does technological efficiency go into effect. These "material contrivances" ("capital goods," material equipment) are such things as tools, vessels, vehicles, raw materials, buildings, ditches, and the like, including the land in use; but they include also, and through the greater part of the early development chiefly, the useful minerals, plants, and animals. To say that these minerals, plants, and animals are useful - in other words, that they are economic goods - means that they have been brought within the sweep of the community's knowledge of ways and means. In the relatively early stages of primitive culture the useful plants and minerals are, no doubt, made use of in a wild state, as, e.g., fish and timber have continued to be used. Yet in so far as they are useful they are unmistakably to be counted in among the material equipment ("tangible assets") of the community.

The case is well illustrated by the relation of the Plains Indians to the buffalo, and by the north-west coast Indians to the salmon, on the one hand, and by the use of a wild flora by such communities as the Coahuila Indians, the Australian blacks, or the Andamanese, on the other hand. But with the current of time, experience, and initiative, domesticated (that is to say improved) plants and animals come to take the first place. We have then such "technological expedients" in the first rank as the many species and varieties of domestic animals, and more particularly still the various grains, fruits, root crops, and the like, virtually all of which were created by man for human use; or perhaps a more scrupulously veracious account would say that they were in the main created by the women through long ages of workmanlike selection and cultivation.

These things, of course, are useful because men have learned their use, and their use, so far as it has been learned, has been learned by protracted and voluminous experience and experimentation, proceeding at each step on the accumulated achievements of the past. Other things, which may in time, come to exceed these in usefulness are still useless, economically non-existent, on the early levels of culture, because of what men in that time have not yet learned. While this immaterial equipment of industry, the intangible assets of the community, have apparently always been relatively very considerable and are always mainly in the keeping of the community at large, the material equipment, the tangible assets, on the other hand, have, in the early stages (say the earlier 90 per cent.) of the life-history of human culture, been relatively slight, and have apparently been held somewhat loosely by individuals or household groups. This material equipment is relatively very slight in the earlier phases of technological development, and the tenure by which it is held is apparently vague and uncertain. At a relatively primitive phase of the development, and under ordinary conditions of climate and surroundings, the possession of the concrete articles ("capital goods") needed to turn the commonplace knowledge of ways and means to account is a matter of slight consequence, - contrary to the view commonly spoken for by the economists of the classical line.

Given the commonplace technological knowledge and the commonplace training, - and these are given by common notoriety and the habituation of daily life, - the acquisition, construction, or usufruct of the slender material equipment needed arranges itself almost as a matter of course, more particularly where this material equipment does not include a stock of domestic animals or a plantation of domesticated trees and vegetables. Under given circumstances a relatively primitive technological scheme may involve some large items of material equipment, as the buffalo pens (piskun) of the Blackfoot Indians or the salmon weirs of the river Indians of the north-west coast. Such items of material equipment are then likely to be held and worked collectively, either by the community at large or by subgroups of a considerable size.

Under ordinary, more generally prevalent conditions it appears that even after a relatively great advance has been made in the cultivation of crops the requisite industrial equipment is not a matter for serious concern, particularly so aside from the tilled ground and the cultivated trees, as is indicated by the singularly loose and inconsequential notions of ownership prevalent among peoples occupying such a stage of culture. A primitive stage of communism is not known. But, as the common stock of technological knowledge increases in volume, range, and efficiency, the material equipment whereby this knowledge of ways and means is put into effect grows greater, more considerable relatively to the capacity of the individual. And so soon, or in so far, as the technological development falls into such shape as to require a relatively large unit of material equipment for the effective pursuit of industry, or such as otherwise to make the possession of the requisite material equipment a matter of consequence, so as seriously to handicap the individuals who are without these material means, and to place the current possessors of such equipment at a marked advantage, then the strong arm intervenes, property rights apparently begin to fall into definite shape, the principles of ownership gather force and consistency, and men begin to accumulate capital goods and take measures to make them secure.

An appreciable advance in the industrial arts is commonly followed or accompanied by an increase of population. The difficulty of procuring a livelihood may be no greater after such an increase: it may even be less; but there results a relative curtailment of the available area and raw materials, and commonly also an increased accessibility of the several portions of the community. A wide-reaching control becomes easier. At the same, time a larger unit of material equipment is needed for the effective pursuit of industry. As this situation develops, it becomes worth while - that is to say, it becomes feasible - for the individual with the strong arm to engross, or "corner," the usufruct of the commonplace knowledge of ways and means by taking over such of the requisite material as may be relatively scarce and relatively indispensable for procuring a livelihood under the current state of the industrial arts[3] .

Circumstances of space and numbers prevent escape from the now technological situation. The commonplace knowledge of ways and means cannot be turned to account, under the new conditions, without a material equipment adapted to the then current state of the industrial arts; and such a suitable material equipment is no longer a slight matter to be compassed by workmanlike initiative and application. *Beati possidentes.* The emphasis of the technological situation, as one might say, may fall now on one line of material items, now on another, according as the exigencies of climate, topography, flora and fauna, density of population, and the like, may decide. So also, under the rule of the game exigencies, the early growth of property lights and of the principles (habits of thought) of ownership may settle on one or another line of material items, according as one or another affords the strategic advantage for engrossing the current technological efficiency of the community.

Should the technological situation, the state of the industrial arts, be such as to throw the strategic emphasis on manual labor, on workmanlike skill and application, and if at the same time the growth of population has made land relatively scarce, or hostile contact with other communities has made it impracticable for members of the community to range freely over outlying tracts, then it would be expected that the growth of ownership should take the direction primarily of slavery, or of some equivalent form of servitude, so effecting a naive and direct monopolistic control of the current knowledge of ways and means[4] .

Whereas if the development has taken such a turn, and the community is so placed as to make the quest of a livelihood a matter of the natural increase of flocks and herds, then it should reasonably be expected that these items of equipment will be the chief and primary subject of property rights. In point of fact, it appears that a pastoral culture commonly involves also some degree of servitude, along with the ownership of flocks and herds. Under different circumstances the mechanical appliances of industry, or the tillable land, might come into the position of strategic advantage, and might come in for the foremost place in men's consideration as objects of ownership. The evidence afforded by the known (relatively) primitive cultures and communities seems to indicate that slaves and cattle have in this way come into the primacy as objects of ownership at an earlier period in the growth of material civilization than land or the mechanical appliances. And it seems similarly evident - more so, indeed - that land has on the whole preceded the mechanical equipment as the stronghold of ownership and the means of engrossing the community's

---

[3] Motives of exploit and emulation, no doubt, play a serious part in bringing on the practise of ownership and in establishing the principles on which it rests; but this play of motives and the concomitant growth of institutions cannot be taken up here. Cf. Theory of the Leisure Class, chaps. i, ii, iii.

[4] Cf. H. Niebuer, Slavery as an Industrial System, chap. iv., sect. 12.

industrial efficiency. It is not until a late period in the life-history of material civilization that ownership of the industrial equipment, in the narrower sense in which that phrase is commonly employed, comes to be the dominant and typical method of engrossing the immaterial equipment.

Indeed, it is a consummation which has been reached only a very few times even partially, and only once with such a degree of finality as to leave the fact indisputable. If it may be said, loosely, that mastery through the ownership of slaves, cattle, or land comes on in force only after the economic development has run through some nine-tenths of its course hitherto, then it may be said likewise that some ninety-nine one-hundredths of this course of development bad been completed before the ownership of the mechanical equipment came into undisputed primacy as the basis of pecuniary dominion. So late an innovation, indeed; is this modern institution of "capitalism," - the predominant ownership of industrial capital as we know it, - and yet so intimate a fact is it in our familiar scheme of life, that we have some difficulty in seeing it in perspective at all, and we find ourselves hesitating between denying its existence, on the one hand, and affirming it to be a fact of nature antecedent to all human institutions, on the other hand.

In so speaking of the ownership of industrial equipment as being an institution for cornering the community's intangible assets, there is conveyed an unavoidably implied, tho unintended, note of condemnation. Such an implication of merit or demerit is an untoward circumstance in any theoretical inquiry. Any sentimental bias, whether of approval or disapproval, aroused by such an implied censure, must unavoidably hamper the dispassionate pursuit of the argument. To mitigate the effect of this jarring note as far as may be, therefore, it will be expedient to turn back for a moment to other more primitive and remoter forms of the institution, - as slavery and landed wealth, - and so reach the modern facts of industrial capital by a roundabout and gradual approach. These ancient institutions of ownership, slavery and landed wealth, are matters of history.

Considered as dominant factors in the community's scheme of life, their record is completed; and it needs no argument to enforce the proposition that it is a record of economic dominion by the owners of the slaves or the land, as the case may be. The effect of slavery in its best day, and of landed wealth in mediaeval and early modern times, was to make the community's industrial efficiency serve the needs of the slave-owners in the one case and of the land-owners in the other. The effect of these institutions in this respect is not questioned now, except in such sporadic and apologetical fashion as need not detain the argument. But the fact that such was the direct and immediate effect of these institutions of ownership in their time by no means involves the instant condemnation of the institutions in question. It is quite possible to argue that slavery and landed wealth, each in its due time and due cultural setting, have served the amelioration of the lot of man and the advance of human culture. What these arguments may be that aim to show the merits of slavery and landed wealth as a means of cultural advance does not concern the present inquiry, neither do the merits of the case in which the arguments are offered. The matter is referred to here to call to mind that any similar theoretical outcome of an analysis of the productivity of "capital goods" need not be admitted to touch the merits of the case in controversy between the socialistic critics of capitalism and the spokesmen of law and order.

The nature of landed wealth, in point of economic theory, especially as regards its productivity, has been sifted with the most jealous precautions and the most tenacious logic during the past century; and any economic student can easily review the course of the argument whereby that line of economic theory has been run to earth. It is only necessary here to shift the point of view slightly to bring the whole argument concerning the rent of land to bear on the present question. Rent is of the nature of a differential gain, resting on a differential advantage in point of productivity of the industry employed upon or about it. This differential advantage attaching to a given parcel of land may be a differential as against another parcel or as against industry applied apart from land. The differential advantage attaching to agricultural land - e.g., as against industry at large - rests on certain broad peculiarities of the technological situation.

Among them are such peculiarities as these: the human species, or the fraction of it concerned in the case, is numerous, relatively to the extent of its habitat; the methods of getting a living, as hitherto elaborated, the ways and means of life, make use of certain crop plants and certain domestic animals. Apart from such conditions, taken for granted in arguments concerning agricultural rent, there could manifestly be no differential advantage attaching to land and no production of rent. With increased command of methods of transportation, the agricultural lands of England, e.g., and of Europe at large, declined in value, not because these lands became less fertile, but because an equivalent result could more advantageously be got by a new method. So, again, the flint- and amber-bearing regions that are now Danish and Swedish territory about the waters at the entrance to the Baltic were in the neolithic culture of northern Europe the most favored and valuable lands within that cultural region.

But, with the coming of the metals and the relative decline of the amber trade, they began to fall behind in the scale of productivity and preference. So also in later time, with the rise of "industry" and the growth of the technology of communication, urban property has gained, as contrasted with rural property, and land placed in an advantageous position relatively to shipping and railroads has acquired a value and a "productiveness" which could not be claimed for it apart from these modern technological expedients. The argument of the single-tax advocates and other economists as to the "unearned increment" is sufficiently familiar, but its ulterior implications have not commonly been recognized. The unearned increment, it is held, is produced by the growth of the community in numbers and in the industrial arts. The contention seems to be sound, and is commonly accepted; but it has commonly been overlooked that the argument involves the ulterior conclusion that all land values and land productivity, including the "original and indestructible powers of the soil," are a function of the "state of the industrial arts."

It is only within the given technological situation, the current scheme of ways and means, that any parcel of land has such productive powers as it has. It is, in other words, useful only because, and in so far, and in such manner, as men have learned to make use of it. This is what brings it into the category of "land," economically speaking. And the preferential position of the landlord as a claimant of the "net product" consists in his legal right to decide whether, how far, and on what terms men shall put this technological scheme into effect in those features of it which involve the use of his parcel of land. All this argument concerning the unearned increment may be carried over, with scarcely a change of phrase, to the case of "capital goods." The Danish flint supply was of first-rate economic consequence, for a thousand years or so, during the stone age; and the polished-flint utensils of that time were then "capital goods" of inestimable importance to civilization, and were possessed of a "productivity" so serious that the life of mankind in that world may be said to have been balanced on the fine-ground edge of those magnificent polished-flint axes.

All that lasted through its technological era. The flint supply and the mechanical expedients and "capital goods," whereby it was turned to account, were valuable and productive then, but neither before nor after that time. Under a changed technological situation the capital goods of that time have become museum exhibits, and their place in human economy has been taken by technological expedients which embody another "state of the industrial arts," the outcome of later and different phases of human experience. Like the polished-flint axe, the metal utensils which gradually displaced it and its like in the economy of the Occidental culture were the product of long experience and the gradual learning of ways and means.

The steel axe, as well as the flint axe, embodies the same ancient technological expedient of a cutting edge, as well as the use of a helve and the efficiency due to the weight of the tool. And in the case of the one or the other, when seen in historical perspective and looked at from the point of view of the community at large, the knowledge of ways and means embodied in the utensils was the serious and consequential matter. The construction or acquisition of the concrete "capital goods" was simply an easy consequence. It "cost nothing but labor," as Thomas Mun would say. Yet it might be argued that each concrete article of "capital goods" was the product of some one man's labor, and, as such, its productivity, when put to use, was but the indirect, ulterior, deferred productiveness of the maker's labor. But the maker's productivity in the ease was but a function of the immaterial technological equipment at his command, and that in its turn was the slow spiritual distillate of the community's time-long experience and initiative.

To the individual producer or owner, to whom the community's accumulated stock of immaterial equipment was open by common notoriety, the cost of the concrete material goods would be the effort involved in making or getting them and in making good his claim to them. To his neighbor who had made or acquired no such parcel of "productive goods," but to whom the resources of the community, material and immaterial, were open on the same easy terms, the matter would look very much the same. He would have no grievance, nor would he have occasion to seek one. Yet, as a resource in the maintenance of the community's life and a factor in the advance of material civilization, the whole matter would have a different meaning. So long, or rather in so far, as the "capital goods" required to meet the technological demands of the time were slight enough to be compassed by the common man with reasonable diligence and proficiency, so long the draft upon the common stock of immaterial assets by any one would be no hindrance to any other, and no differential advantage or disadvantage would emerge.

The economic situation would answer passably to the classical theory of a free competitive system, - "the simple and obvious system of natural liberty," which rests on the presumption of equal opportunity. In a roughly approximate way, such a situation supervened in the industrial life of western Europe on the transition from mediaeval to modern times, when handicraft and "industrial" enterprise superseded landed wealth as the chief economic factor. Within the "industrial system," as distinct from the privileged non-industrial classes, a man with a modicum of diligence, initiative, and thrift might make his way in a tolerable fashion without special advantages in the way of prescriptive right or accumulated means. The principle of equal opportunity was, no doubt, met only in a very rough and dubious fashion; but so favorable became the conditions in this respect that men came to persuade themselves in the course of the eighteenth century that a substantially equitable allotment of opportunities would result from the abrogation of all prerogatives other than the ownership of goods.

But so precarious and transient was this approximation to a technologically feasible system of equal opportunity that, while the liberal movement which converged upon this great economic reform was still gathering head, the technological situation was already outgrowing the possibility of such a scheme of reform. After the Industrial Revolution came on, it was no longer true, even in the roughly approximate way in which it might have been true some time earlier, that equality before the law, barring property rights, would mean equal opportunity. In the leading, aggressive industries which were beginning to set the pace for all that economic system that centred about the market, the unit of industrial equipment, as required by the new technological era, was larger than one man could compass by his own efforts with the free use of the commonplace knowledge of ways and means. And the growth of business enterprise progressively made the position of the small, old-fashioned producer more precarious. But the speculative, theoreticians of that time still saw the phenomena of current economic life in the light of the handicraft traditions and of the preconceptions of natural rights associated with that system, and still looked to the ideal of "natural liberty" as the goal of economic development and the end of economic reform. They were ruled by the principles (habits of thought) which had arisen out of an earlier situation, so effectually as not to see that the rule of equal opportunity which they aimed to establish was already technologically obsolete[5] .

During the hundred years and more of this ascendency of the natural-rights theories in economic science, the growth of technological knowledge has unremittingly gone forward, and concomitantly the large-scale industry has grown great and progressively dominated the field. This large-scale, industrial regime is what the socialists, and some others, call "capitalism." "Capitalism," as so used, is not a neat and rigid technical term, but it is definite enough to be useful for many purposes. On its technological side the characteristic trait of this capitalism is that the current pursuit of industry requires a larger unit of material equipment than one individual can compass by his own labor, and larger than one person can make use of alone. So soon as the capitalist regime, in this some, comes in, it ceases to be true that the owner of the industrial equipment (of the controller of it) in any given case is or may be the producer of it, in any naive sense of "production."

He is under the necessity of acquiring its ownership or control by some other expedient than that of industrially productive work. The pursuit of industry requires an accumulation of wealth, and, barring force, fraud, and inheritance, the method of acquiring such an accumulation of wealth is necessarily some form of bargaining; that is to say, some form of business enterprise. Wealth is accumulated, within the industrial field, from the gains of business; that is to say, from the gains of advantageous bargaining[6] .Taking the situation by and large, looking to the body of business enterprise as a whole, the advantageous bargaining from which gains accrue and from which, therefore, accumulations of capital are derived, is necessarily, in the last analysis, a bargaining between those who own (or control) industrial wealth and those whose work turns this wealth to account in productive industry. This bargaining for hire - commonly a wage agreement - is conducted under the rule of free contract, and is concluded according to the play of demand and supply, as has been well set forth by many writers.

On this technological view of capital, as here spoken for, the relations between the two parties to the bargain, the, capitalist-employer and the working class, stand as follows. More or less rigorously, the technological situation enforces a certain scale and method in the various lines of indus-

---

[5] For a more extended discussion of this point see the Quarterly Journal of Economics, July, 1899, "The Preconceptions of Economic Science"; also the Theory of Business Enterprise, chap. iv. especially pp. 70-82.

[6] Marx holds that the "primitive accumulation" from which capitalism takes its rise is a matter of force and fraud (Capital, Book I., chap. xxiv.). Sombart holds the source to have been landed wealth (Moderne Kapitalismus, Book II., Part II., especially chap. xii.). Ehrenberg and other critics of Sombart incline to the view that the most important source was usury and the petty trade (Zeitalter der Fugger, chaps. i., ii.).

try[7] .The industry can, in effect, be carried on only by recourse to the technologically requisite scale and method, and this requires a material equipment of a certain (large) magnitude; while material equipment of this required magnitude is held exclusively by the capitalist-employer, and is de facto beyond the reach of the common man. A corresponding body of immaterial equipment - knowledge and practice of ways and means - is likewise requisite, under the rule of the same technological exigencies.

This immaterial equipment is in part drawn on in the making of the material equipment held by the capitalist-employers, in part in the use to be made of this material equipment in the further processes of industry. This body of immaterial equipment so drawn on in any line of industry is, relatively, still larger, being, on any exhaustive analysis, virtually the whole body of industrial experience accumulated by the community up to date. A free draft on this common stock of technological wisdom must be had both in the construction and in the subsequent use of the material equipment; although no one person can master, or himself employ, more than an inconsiderable fraction of the immaterial equipment so drawn on for the installation or operation of any given block of the material equipment.

The owner of the material equipment, the capitalist-employer, is, in the typical case, not possessed of any appreciable fraction of the immaterial equipment necessarily drawn on in the construction and subsequent use of the material equipment owned (controlled) by him. His knowledge and training, so far as it enters into the question, is a knowledge of business, not of industry[8] .The slight technological proficiency which he has or needs for his business ends is of a general character, wholly superficial and impracticable in point of workmanlike efficiency; nor is it turned to account in actual workmanship. He therefore "needs in his business" the service of persons who have a competent working mastery of this immaterial technological equipment, and it is with such persons that his bargains for hire are made. By and large, the measure of their serviceability for his ends is the measure of their technological competency. No workman not possessed of some fractional mastery of the technological requirements is employed, - imbeciles are useless in proportion to their imbecility; and even unskilled and "unintelligent" workmen, so called, are of relatively little use, altho they may be possessed of a proficiency in the commonplace industrial details such as would bulk large in absolute magnitude.

---

[7] The phrase "more or less" covers a certain margin of tolerance in respect of scale and method, which may be very appreciably wider in some lines of industry than in others, and which, cannot be more adequately defined or described here within such space as could reasonably be allowed. The requirement of scale and method is enforced by competition. The force and reach of this competitive adjustment can also not be dealt with here, but the familiar current acceptance of the fact will dispense with details.

[8] Cf. Theory of Business Enterprise, chap. III.

The "common laborer" is, in fact, a highly trained and widely proficient workman when contrasted with the conceivable human blank supposed to have drawn on the community for nothing but his physique. In the hands of these workmen - the industrial community, the bearers of the immaterial, technological equipment - the capital goods owned by the capitalist become a "means of production." Without them, or in the hands of men who do not know their use, the goods in question would be simply raw materials, somewhat deranged and impaired through having been given the form which now makes them "capital goods." The more proficient the workmen in their mastery of the technological expedients involved, and the greater the facility with which they are able to put these expedients into effect, the more productive will be the processes in which the workmen turn the employer's capital goods to account.

So, also, the more competent the work of "superintendence," the foreman like oversight and correlation of the work in respect of kind, speed, volume, the more will it count in the aggregate of productive efficiency. But this work of correlation is a function of the foreman's mastery of the technological situation at large and his facility in proportioning one process of industry to the requirements and effects of another. Without this due and sagacious correlation of the processes of industry, and their current adaptation to the demands of the industrial situation at large, the material equipment engaged would have but slight efficiency and would count for but little in tire way of capital goods. The efficiency of the control exercised by the master-workman, engineer, superintendent, or whatever term may be used to designate the technological expert who controls and correlates the productive processes, - this workmanlike efficiency determines how far the given material equipment is effectually to be rated as "capital goods.

"Through all this functioning of the workman and the foreman the capitalist's business ends are ever in the background, and the degree of success that attends his business endeavors depends, other things equal, on the efficiency with which these technologists carry on the processes of industry in which be has invested. His working arrangements with these workmen, the bearers of the immaterial equipment engaged, enables the capitalist to turn the processes for which his capital goods are adapted to account for his own profit, but at the cost of such a deduction from the aggregate product of these processes as the workmen may be able to demand in return for their work. The amount of this deduction is determined by the competitive bidding of other capitalists who may have use for the same lines of technological efficiency, in the manner set forth by writers on wages. With the conceivable consolidation of all material assets under one business management, so as to eliminate competitive bidding between employers, it is plain that the resulting business concern would command the undivided forces of the technological situation, with such deduction as is involved in the livelihood of the working population. This livelihood would in such a case be reduced to the most economical footing, as seen from the standpoint of the employer. And the employer (capitalist) would be the de facto owner of the community's aggregate knowledge of ways and means, except so far as this body of immaterial equipment serves also the housekeeping routine of the working population.

How nearly the current economic situation may approach to this finished state is a matter of opinion. There is also place for a broad question whether the conditions are more or less favorable to the working population under the existing business regime, involving competitive bidding between the several business concerns, than they would be in case a comprehensive business consolidation had eliminated competition and placed the ownership of the material assets on a footing of unqualified monopoly. Nothing but vague surmises can apparently be offered in answer to these questions. But as bearing on the question of monopoly and the use of the community's immaterial equipment it is to be kept in mind that the technological situation as it stands to-day does not admit of a complete monopolization of the community's technological expedients, even if a complete monopolization of the existing aggregate of material property were effected. There is still current a large body of industrial processes to which the large-scale methods do not apply and which do not presume such a large unit of material equipment or involve such rigorous correlation with the large-scale industry as to take them out of the range of discretionary use by persons not possessed of appreciable material wealth.

Typical of such lines of work, hitherto not amenable to monopolization, are the details of housekeeping routine alluded to above. It is, in fact, still possible for an appreciable fraction of the population to "pick up a living," more or less precarious, without recourse to the large-scale processes that are controlled by the owners of the material assets. This somewhat precarious margin of free recourse to the commonplace knowledge of ways and means appears to be what stands in the way of a neater adjustment of wages to the "minimum of subsistence" and the virtual ownership of the immaterial equipment by the owners of the material equipment. It follows from what has been said that all tangible[9] assets owe their productivity and their value to the immaterial industrial expedients which they embody or which their ownership enables their owner to engross. These immaterial industrial expedients are necessarily a product of the community, the immaterial residue of the community's experience, past and present, which has no existence apart from the community's life, and can be transmitted only in the keeping of the community at large. It may be objected by those who make much of the productivity of capital that tangible capital goods on hand are themselves of value and have a specific productive efficiency, if not apart from the industrial processes in which they serve, then at least as a prerequisite to these processes, and therefore a material condition-precedent standing in a causal relation to the industrial product.

---

[9] "Tangible assets" is here taken to signify serviceable capital goods considered as valuable possessions yielding income to their owner.

But these material goods are themselves a product of the past exercise of technological knowledge, and so back to the beginning. What there is involved in the material equipment, which is not of this immaterial, spiritual nature, and so what is not an immaterial residue of the community's experience, is the raw material out of which the industrial appliances are constructed, with the stress falling wholly on the "raw. "The point is illustrated by what happens to a mechanical contrivance which goes out of date because of a technological advance and is displaced by a new contrivance embodying a new process. Such a contrivance "goes to the junk-heap," as the phrase has it. The specific technological expedient which it embodies ceases to be effective in industry, in competition with "improved methods."

It ceases to bean immaterial asset. When it is in this way eliminated, the material repository of it ceases to have value as capital. It ceases to be a material asset. "The original and indestructible powers" of the material constituents of capital goods, to adapt Ricardo's phrase, do not make these constituents capital goods; nor, indeed, do these original and indestructible powers of themselves bring the objects in question into the category of economic goods at all. The raw materials - land, minerals, and the like - may, of course, be valuable property and may be counted among the assets of a business. But the value which they so have is a function of the anticipated use to which they may be put, and that is a function of the technological situation under which it is anticipated that they will be useful. All this may seem to undervalue or perhaps to overlook the physical facts of industry and the physical nature of commodities. There is, of course, no call to understate the importance of material goods or of manual labor. The goods about which this inquiry turns are the products of trained labor working on the available materials; but the labor has to be trained, in the large sense, in order to be labor, and the materials have to be available in order to be materials of industry. And both the trained efficiency of the labor and the availability of the material objects engaged are a function of the "state of the industrial arts."

Yet the state of the industrial arts is dependent on the traits of human nature, physical, intellectual, and spiritual, and on the character of the material environment. It is out of these elements that the human technology is made up; and this technology is efficient only as it meets with the suitable material conditions and is worked out, practically, in the material forces required. The brute forces of the human animal are an indispensable factor in industry, as are likewise the physical characteristics of the material objects with which industry deals. And it seems bootless to ask how much of the products of industry or of its productivity is to be imputed to these brute forces, human and non-human, as contrasted with the specifically human factors that make technological efficiency. Nor is it necessary to go into questions of that import here, since the inquiry here turns on the productive relation of capital to industry; that is to say, the relation of the material equipment and its ownership to men's dealings with the physical environment in which the race is placed.

The question of capital goods (including that of their ownership and therefore including the question of investment) is a question of how mankind as a species of intelligent animals deals with the brute force at its disposal. It is a question of how the human agent deals with his means of life, not of how the forces of the environment deal with man. Questions of the latter class belong under the head of ecology, a branch of the biological sciences dealing with the adaptive variability of plants and animals. Economic inquiry would belong under that category if the human response to the forces of the environment were instinctive and variational only, including nothing in the way of a technology. But in that case there would be no question of capital goods, or of capital, or of labor. Such questions do not arise in relation to the non-human animals.

In an inquiry into the productivity of labor some perplexity might be met with as to the share or the place of the brute forces of the human organism in the theory of production; but in relation to capital that question does not arise, except so far as these forces am involved in the production of the capital goods. As a parenthesis, more or less germane to the present inquiry into capital, it may be remarked that an analysis of the productive powers of labor would apparently take account of the brute energies of mankind (nervous and muscular energies) as material forces placed at the disposal of man by circumstances largely beyond human control, and in great part not theoretically dissimilar to the like nervous and muscular forces afforded by the domestic animals.

II. INVESTMENT, INTANGIBLE ASSETS, AND THE PECUNIARY MAGNATE.

What has been said in the earlier section of this paper[10] applies to "capital goods," so called, and it is intended to apply to these in their character of "productive goods" rather than in their character of "capital"; that is to say, what is had in mind is the industrial, or technological, efficiency and subservience of the material means of production rather than the pecuniary use and effect of invested wealth. The inquiry has dealt with the industrial equipment as "plant" rather than as "assets." In the course of this inquiry it has appeared that out of the profitable engrossing of the community's industrial efficiency through control of the material equipment there arises the practise of investment, which has further consequences that merit more detailed attention.

Investment is a pecuniary transaction, and its aim is pecuniary gain, - gain in terms of value and ownership. Invested wealth is capital, a pecuni-

---

[10] See this Journal for August 1908. By an oversight the sub-title of the earlier section was omitted. It should have read "The Productivity of Capital Goods."

ary magnitude, measured in terms of value and determined in respect of its magnitude by a valuation which proceeds on an appraisement of the gain expected from the ownership of this invested wealth. In modern business practise, capital is distinguished into two co-ordinate categories of assets, tangible and intangible. "Tangible assets" is here taken to designate pecuniarily serviceable capital goods, considered as a valuable possession yielding an income to their owner. Such goods, material items of wealth, are "assets" to the amount of their capitalizable value, which may be more or less closely related to their industrial serviceability as productive goods.

"Intangible assets" are immaterial items of wealth, immaterial facts owned, valued, and capitalized on an appraisement of the gain to be derived from their possession. These are also assets to the amount of their capitalizable value, which has commonly little, if any, relation to the industrial serviceability of these items of wealth considered as factors of production.

Before going into the matter of intangible assets, it is necessary to speak further of the consequences which investment - and hence capitalization - has for the use and serviceability of (material) capital goods. It has commonly been assumed by economists, without much scrutiny, that the gains which accrue from invested wealth are derived from and (roughly) measured by the productivity of the industrial process in which the items of wealth so invested are employed, productivity being counted in some terms of material serviceability to the community, conduciveness to the livelihood, comfort, or consumptive needs of the community. In the course of the present inquiry it has appeared that the gainfulness of such invested wealth (tangible assets) is due to a more or less extensive engrossing of the community's industrial efficiency.

The aggregate gains of the aggregate material capital accrue from the community's industrial activity, and bear some relation to the productive capacity of the industrial traffic so engrossed. But it will be noted that them is no warrant in the analysis of these phenomena as here set forth for alleging that the gains of investment bear a relation of equality or proportion to the material serviceability of the capital goods, as rated in terms of effectual usefulness to the community. Given capital goods, tangible assets, may owe their pecuniary serviceability to their owner, and so their value, to other things than their serviceability to the community; altho the gains of investment in the aggregate are drawn from the aggregate material productivity of the community's industry.

The ownership of the material equipment gives the owner not only the right of use over the community's immaterial equipment, but also the right of abuse and of neglect or inhibition. This power of inhibition may be made to afford an income, as well as the power to serve; and whatever will yield an income may be capitalized and become an item of wealth to its possessor. Under modern conditions of investment it happens not infrequently that it becomes pecuniarily expedient for the owner of the material equipment to curtail or retard the processes of industry, - "restraint of trade." The motive in all such cases of retardation is the pecuniary expediency of the measure for the owner (controller) of capital, - expediency in terms of income from investment, not expediency in terms of serviceability to the community at large or to any fraction of the community except the owner (manager).

Except for the exigencies of investment, i.e., exigencies of pecuniary gain to the investor, phenomena of this character would have no place in the industrial system. They invariably come of the endeavors of business men to secure a pecuniary gain or to avoid a pecuniary loss. More frequently, perhaps, manoeuvres of inhibition - advised idleness of plant - in industry aim to effect a saving or avoid a waste than to procure an increase of gain; but the saving to be effected and the waste to be avoided am always pecuniary saving to the owner and pecuniary waste in the matter of ownership, not a saving of goods to the community or a prevention of wasteful consumption or wasteful expenditure of effort and resources on the part of the community. Pecuniary - that is to say, differential - advantage to the capitalist-manager has, under the regime of investment, taken precedence of economic advantage to the community; or rather, the differential advantage of ownership is alone regarded in the conduct of industry under this system.

Business practises which inhibit industrial efficiency and curtail the industrial output are too well known to need particular enumeration. Nor is it necessary to cite evidence to show that such inhibition and curtailment am resorted to from motives of pecuniary expediency. But an illustrative example or two will make the theoretical point clearer, and perhaps more plainly bring out the wholly pecuniary grounds of such business procedure. The most comprehensive principle involved in this class of business management is that of raising prices, and so increasing the net gains of business, by limiting the supply, or "charging what the traffic will bear." Of a similar effect, for the point here in question, are the obstructive tactics designed to hinder the full efficiency of a business rival.

These phenomena lie along the line of division between tangible and intangible assets. Successful strategy of this kind may, by force of custom, legislation, or the "freezing-out" of rival concerns, pass into settled conditions of differential advantage for the given business concern, which so may be capitalized as an item of intangible assets and take their place in the business community as articles of invested wealth. But, aside from such capitalization of inefficiency, it is at least an equally consequential fact that the processes of productive industry are governed in detail by the exigencies of investment, and therefore by the quest of gain as counted in terms of price, which leads to the dependence of production on the course of prices. So that, under the regime of capital, the community is unable to turn its knowledge of ways and means to account for a livelihood except at such seasons and in so far as the course of prices affords a differential advantage to the owners of the material equipment.

The question of advantageous - which commonly means rising - prices for the owners (managers) of the capital goods is made to decide the question of livelihood for the rest of the community. The recurrence of hard times, unemployment, and the rest of that familiar range of phenomena, goes to show how effectual is the inhibition of industry exercised by the ownership of capital under the price system[11] .So also as regards the discretionary abuse of the community's industrial efficiency vested in the owner of the material equipment. Disserviceability may be capitalized as readily as serviceability, and the ownership of the capital goods affords a discretionary power of misdirecting the industrial processes and perverting[12] industrial efficiency, as well as of inhibiting or curtailing industrial processes and their output, while the outcome may still be profitable to the owner of the capital goods. There is a large volume of capital goods whose value lies in their turning the technological inheritance to the injury of mankind. Such are, e.g., naval and military establishments, together with the docks, arsenals, schools, and manufactories of arms, ammunition, and naval and military stores, that supplement and supply such establishments.

These armaments and the like are, of course, public and quasi-public enterprises, under the current regime, with somewhat disputable relations to the system of current business enterprise. But it is no far-fetched interpretation to say that they are, in great part, a material equipment for the maintenance of law and order, and so enable the owners of capital goods with immunity to inhibit or pervert the industrial processes when the exigencies of business profits make it expedient; that they are, further, a means - more or less ineffectual, it is true - for extending and protecting trade, and so serve the differential advantage of business men at the cost of the community; and that they are also in large part a material equipment set apart for the diversion of a livelihood from the community at large to the military, naval, diplomatic, and other official classes.

These establishments may in any case be taken as illustrating how items of material equipment may be devoted to and may be valued for the use of the technological expedients for the damage and discomfort of mankind, without sensible offset or abatement. Typical of a class of investments which derive profits from capital goods devoted to uses that are altogether dubious, with a large presumption of net detriment, are such establishments as race-tracks, saloons, gambling-houses, and houses of prostitution[13] .

---

[11] For the concretion between prices and prosperity, hard times, unemployment, etc, see The Theory of Business Enterprise, chap. vii (pp. 185-252, especially, 196-212).

[12] By "perversion" is here meant such disposition of the industrial forces as entails a net waste or detriment to the community's livelihood.

[13] Should the connection at this point with the main argument of the paper as set forth in the earlier section seem doubtful or obscure, it may be called to mind that these dubious enterprises in dissipation are cases of investment for a profit, and that the "capital goods" engaged are invested wealth yielding an income, but that they yield an income only on the fulfilment of two conditions (a) the possession and employment of these capital goods enables their holder to turn to account the common stock of technological proficiency, in those bearings in which it may be of

Some spokesmen of the "non-Christian tribes" might wish to include churches under the same category, but the consensus of opinion in modern communities inclines to look on churches as serviceable, on the whole; and it may be as well not to attempt to assign them a specific place in the scheme of serviceable and disserviceable use of invested wealth. There is, further, a large field of business, employing much capital goods and many technological processes, whose profits come from products in which serviceability and disserviceability are mingled with waste in the most varying proportion.

Such are the production of goods of fashion, disingenuous proprietary articles, sophisticated household supplies, newspapers and advertising enterprise. In the degree in which business of this class draws its profits from wasteful practises, spurious goods, illusions and delusions, skilled mendacity, and the like, the capital goods engaged must be said to owe their capitalizable value to a perverse use of the technological expedients employed. These wasteful or disserviceable uses of capital goods have been cited, not as implying that the technological proficiency embodied in these goods or brought into effect in their use, intrinsically has a disserviceable bearing, nor that investment in these things, and business enterprise in the management of them, need aim at disserviceability, but only to bring out certain minor points of theory, obvious but commonly overlooked: (a) technological proficiency is not of itself and intrinsically serviceable or disserviceable to mankind, - it is only a means of efficiency for good or ill; (b) the enterprising use of capital goods by their businesslike owner aims not at serviceability to the community, but only at serviceability to the owner; (c) under the price system - under the rule of pecuniary standards and management - circumstances make it advisable for the business man at times to mismanage the processes of industry, in the sense that it is expedient for his pecuniary gain to inhibit, curtail, or misdirect industry, and so turn the community's technological proficiency to the community's detriment.

These somewhat commonplace points of theory are of no great weight in themselves, but they are of consequence for any theory of business or of life under the rules of the price system, and they have an immediate bearing hem on the question of intangible assets. At the risk of some tedium it is necessary to the theory of intangible assets to pursue this analysis and piecing together of commonplaces somewhat farther. As has already been

---

use in his enterprise; and (b) as limited amount of wealth available for the purpose enables their holder to "engross" the usufruct of such a fraction of the common stock of technological proficiency, in the degree determined by this limitation of the amount available. In so far, these enterprises are like any other industrial enterprise, but beyond this they have the peculiarity that they do not, or need not, even ostensibly, turn the current knowledge and use of ways and means to "productive" account for the community at large, but simply take their stand on the (institutionally sacred) "accomplished fact" of invested wealth. They have less of the fog of apology about them than the common run of business enterprise.

remarked, "assets" is a pecuniary concept, not a technological one; a concept of business, not of industry. Assets are capital, and tangible assets are items of material equipment and the like, considered as available for capitalization. The tangibility of tangible assets is a matter of the materiality of the items of wealth of which they are made up, while they are assets to the amount of their value. Capital goods, which typically make up the category of tangible assets, are capital goods by virtue of their technological serviceability, but they are capital in the measure, not of their technological serviceability, but in the measure of the income which they may yield to their owner. The like is, of course, true of intangible assets, which are likewise capital, or assets, in the measure of their income-yielding capacity. Their intangibility is a matter of the immateriality of the item of wealth - objects of ownership - of which they are made up, but their character and magnitude as assets is a matter of the gainfulness to their owner of the processes which their ownership enables him to engross. The facts so engrossed, in the case of intangible assets, are not of a technological or industrial character; and herein lies the substantial disparity between tangible and intangible assets. Mankind has other dealings with the material means of life, besides those covered by the community's technological proficiency.

These other dealings have to do with the use, distribution, and consumption of the goods procured by the employment of the community's technological proficiency, and are carried out under working arrangements of an institutional character, - use and wont, law and custom. The principles and practise of the distribution of wealth vary with the changes in technology and with the other cultural changes that are going forward; but it is probably safe to assume that the principles of apportionment, - that is to say, the consensus of habitual opinion as to what is right and good in the distribution of the product, - these principles and the concomitant methods of carrying them out in practise have always been such as to give one person or group or class something of a settled preference above another. Something of this kind, something in the way of a conventionally arranged differential advantage in the apportionment of the common livelihood, is to be found in all cultures and communities that have been observed at all carefully; and it is perhaps needless to remark that in the higher cultures such economic preferences, privileges, prerogatives, differential advantages and disadvantages, are numerous and varied, and that they make up an intricate fabric of economic institutions. Indeed, peculiarities of class difference in some such respect are among the most striking and decisive features that distinguish one cultural era from another. In all phases of material civilization these preferential advantages are sought and valued.

Classes or groups which are in a position to make good a claim to such differential advantages commonly come, in due course, to put forward such claims; as, e.g., the priesthood, the princely and ruling class, the men as contrasted with the women, the adults as against minors, the able-bodied as against the infirm. Principles (habits of thought) countenancing some form of class or personal preference in the distribution of income are to be found incorporated in the moral code of all known civilizations and embodied in some form of institution. Such items of immaterial wealth are of a differential character, in that the advantage of those who secure the preference is the disadvantage of those who do not; and it may be mentioned in passing, that such a differential advantage inuring to any one class or person commonly carries a more than equal disadvantage to some other class or person or to the community at large5[14] .When property rights fall into definite shape and the price system comes in, and more particularly when the practise of investment arises and business enterprise comes into vogue, such differential advantages take on something of the character of intangible assets. They come to have a pecuniary value and rating, whether they are transferable or not; and if they are transferable, if they can be sold and delivered, they become assets in a fairly clear and full sense of that term. Such immaterial wealth, preferential benefits of the nature of intangible assets, may be a matter of usage simply, as the vogue of a given public house, or of a given tradesman, or of a given brand of consumable goods; or may be a matter of arrogation, as the King's Customs in early times, or the once notorious Sound Dues, or the closing of public highways by large land-owners; or of contractual concession, as the freedom of a city or a gild, or a franchise in the Hanseatic League or in the Associated Press; or of government concession, whether on the basis of a bargain or otherwise, as the many trade monopolies of early modern times, or a corporation charter, or a railway franchise, or letters of marque, or letters patent; or of statutory creation, as trade protection by import, export, or excise duties or navigation laws; or of conventionalized superstitious punctilio, as the creation of a demand for wax by the devoutly obligatory consumption of consecrated tapers, or the similar devout consumption of and demand for fish during Lent.

Under the regime of investment and business enterprise these and the like differential benefits may turn to the business advantage of a given class, group, or concern, and in such an event the resulting differential business advantage in the pursuit of gain becomes an asset, capitalized on the basis of its income-yielding capacity, and possibly vendible under the cover of a corporation security (as, e.g., common stock), or even under the usual form of private sale (as, e.g., the appraised good-will of a business concern).But the regime of business enterprise has not only taken over various forms of institutional privileges and prerogatives out of the past: it also gives rise to new kinds of differential advantage and capitalizes them into intangible assets. These are all (or virtually all) of one kind, in that

---

[14] This statement may not seem clear without indicating in a more concrete manner some terms in which to measure the relative differential advantage and disadvantage which so emerge in such a case of prerogative or privilege. Where, as in the earlier non-pecuniary phases of culture, no price test is applicable, the statement in the text may be taken to mean that the differential disadvantage at the cost of which the differential benefit in question is gained is greater than the beneficiary would be willing to undergo in order to procure this benefit.

their common aim and common basis of value and capitalization is a preferentially advantageous sale. Naturally so, since the end of all business endeavor, in the last analysis, is an advantageous sale. The commonest and typical kind of such intangible assets is "good-will," so called, - a term which has come to cover a great variety of differential business advantages, but which in the original business usage of it meant the customary resort of a clientele to the concern so possessed of the good-will. It seems originally to have implied a kindly sentiment of trust and esteem on the part of a customer, but as the term is now used it has lost this sentimental content.

In the broad and loose sense in which it is now currently employed it is extended to cover such special advantages as inure to a monopoly or a combination of business concerns through its power to limit or engross the supply of a given line of goods or services. So long as such a special advantage is not specifically protected by special legislation or by a due legal instrument, - as in the case of a franchise or a patent right, - it is likely to be spoken of loosely as "good-will. "The results of the analysis may be summed up to show the degree of coincidence and the distinctions between the two categories of assets: (a) the value (that is to say, the amount) of given assets, whether tangible or intangible, is the capitalized (or capitalizable) value of the given articles of wealth, rated on the basis of their income-yielding capacity to their owner; (b) in the case of tangible assets there is a presumption that the objects of wealth involved have some (at least potential) serviceability at large, since they serve a materially productive work, and there is therefore a presumption, more or less well founded, that their value represents, tho it by no means measures, an item of serviceability at large; (c) in the ease of intangible assets there is no presumption that the objects of wealth involved have any serviceability at large, since they serve no materially productive work, but only a differential advantage to the owner in the distribution of the industrial product6 .[15](d)

---

[15] A doubt has been offered as to the applicability of this characterization to such intangible assets as a patent right and other items of the same class. The doubt seems to arise from a misapprehension of the analysis and of its intention. It should be remarked that there is no intention to condemn or disapprove any of the items here spoken of as intangible assets. The patent right may be justifiable or it may not - there is no call to discuss that question here. Other intangible assets are in the same case in this respect. Further, as to the character of a patent right considered as an asset. The invention or innovation covered by the patent right is a contribution to the common stock of technological proficiency. It may be (immediately) serviceable to the community at large, or it may not; - e.g., a cash register, a bank-check punch, a street-car fare register, a burglar-proof safe and the like are of no immediate service to the community at large, but serve only a pecuniary use to their users. But, whether the innovation is useful or not, the patent right, as an asset, has no (immediate) usefulness at large, since its essence is the restriction of the usufruct of the innovation to the patentee. Immediately and directly the patent right must be considered a detriment to the community at large, since its purport is to prevent the community from making use of the patented innovation, whatever may be its ulterior beneficial effects or its ethical justification.

given tangible assets may be disserviceable to the community, - a given material equipment may owe its value as capital to a disserviceable use, tho in the aggregate or on an average the body of tangible assets are (presumptively) serviceable; (e) given intangible assets may be indifferent in respect of serviceability at large, tho in the aggregate, or on an average, intangible assets are (presumably) disserviceable to the community.

On this showing it would appear that the substantial difference between tangible and intangible assets lies in the different character of the immaterial facts which are turned to pecuniary account in the one ease and in the other. The former, in effect, capitalize such fraction of the technological proficiency of the community as the ownership of the capital goods involved enables the owner to engross. The latter capitalize such habits of life, of a non-technological character, - settled by usage, convention, arrogation, legislative action, or what not, - as will effect a differential advantage to the concern to which the assets in question appertain. The former owe their existence and magnitude to the usufruct of technological expedients involved in the industrial process proper; while the latter are in like manner due to the usufruct of what may be called the interstitial correlations and adjustments both within the industrial system and between industry proper and the market, in so far as these relations are of a pecuniary rather than a technological character. Much the same distinction may be put in other words, so as to bring the expression nearer the current popular apprehension of the matter, by saying that tangible assets, commonly so called, capitalize the processes of production, while intangible assets, so called, capitalize certain expedients and processes of acquisition, not productive of wealth, but affecting only its distribution.

Formulated in either way, the distinction seems not to be an altogether hard-and-fast one, as will immediately appear if it is called to mind that intangible assets may be converted into tangible assets, and conversely, as the exigencies of business may decide. Yet, while the two categories of assets stand in such close relation to one another as this state of things presumes, it is still evident from the same state of things that they are not to be confounded with one another. Taking "good-will" as typical of the category of "intangible assets," as being the most widely prevalent and at the same time the farthest removed in its characteristics from the range of "tangible assets," some slight further discussion of it may serve to bring out the difference between the two categories of assets and at the same time to enforce their essential congruity as assets as well as the substantial connection between them. In the earlier days of the concept, in the period of growth to which it owes its name, when good-will was coming into recognition as a factor affecting assets, it was apparently looked on habitually as an adventitious differential advantage accruing spontaneously to the business concern to which it appertained; an immaterial by-product of the concern's conduct of business, - commonly presumed to be an adventitious blessing incident to an upright and humane course of business life. Poor Richard would express this sense of the matter in the saying that "honesty is the best policy."

But presently, no doubt, some thought would be taken of the acquirement of good-wilt and some effort would be expended by the wise business man in that behalf. Goods would be given a more elegant finish for the sake of a readier sale, beyond what would conduce to their brute serviceability simply; smooth-spoken and obsequious salesmen and solicitors, gifted with a tactful effrontery, have come to be preferred to others, who, without these merits, may be possessed of all the diligence, dexterity, and muscular force required in their trade; something is expended on convincing, not to say vain-glorious, show-windows that shall promise something more than one would like to commit one's self to in words; itinerant agents, and the like, are employed at some expense to secure a clientele; much thought and substance is spent on advertising of many kinds. This last-named item may be taken as typical of the present stage of growth in the production or generation of good-will, and therefore in the creation of intangible assets. Advertising has come to be an important branch of business enterprise by itself, and it employs a large and varied array of material appliances and processes (tangible assets). Investment is made in certain material items (productive goods), such as printed matter, signboards, and the like, with a view to creating a certain body of good-will.

The precise magnitude of the product may not be foreseen, but, if sagaciously made, such investment rarely fails of the effect aimed at - unless a business rival with even greater sagacity should out-manoeuvre and offset these endeavors with a superior array of appliances (productive goods) and workmen for the generation of good-will. The product aimed at, commonly with effect, is good-will, - an intangible asset, - which may be considered to have been generated by converting certain tangible assets into this intangible; or it may be considered as an industrial product, the output of certain industrial processes in which the given items of material equipment are employed and give effect to the requisite technological proficiency.

Whichever view be taken of the causal relation between the material equipment and processes employed, on the one hand, and the output of good-will, on the other hand, the result is substantially the same for the purpose in hand. The ulterior end of the advertising is, it may be said, the sale of an increased quantity of the advertised articles, at an increased net gain; which would mean an increased value of the material items offered for sale; which, in turn, is the same as saying an increase of tangible assets. It may be assumed without debate that the end of business endeavor is a gain in final terms of tangible values. But this ulterior end is, in the ease of advertising enterprise, to be gained only by the intermediate step of a production of an immaterial item of good-will, an intangible asset. So the case in illustration shows not only the conversion of tangible assets (material capital goods, such as printed matter) into intangible wealth, or, if that formula be preferred, the production of immaterial wealth by the productive use of material wealth, but also, conversely, in the second step of the process, it shows the conversion of intangible assets into tangible wealth (enhanced value of vendible goods), or, if the expression seems preferable, the production of tangible assets by the use of intangible wealth.

This creation of tangible wealth out of intangible assets is seen perhaps at its neatest in the enhancement of land values by the endeavors of interested parties. Real estate is, of course, a tangible asset of the most authentic tangibility, and it is an asset to the amount of its value, which is determined, say, by the figures at which the real estate in question is currently bought and sold. This is the current value of the real estate, and therefore its current actual magnitude as a tangible asset. The value of the real estate might also be computed by capitalizing its rental value; but, where the current market value does not coincide with the capitalized rental value, the former must, according to business conceptions, be accepted as the actual value. In many parts of this country, perhaps in most, but particularly in the Western States and in the neighborhood of flourishing towns, these two methods of rating the pecuniary magnitude of real estate will habitually not coincide.

Due allowance, often very considerable, being made, the capitalized rental value of the land may be taken as measuring its current serviceability as an item of material equipment; while the amount by which the market value of the land exceeds its capitalized rental value may be taken as the product, the tangible residue, of an intangible asset of the nature of good-will, turned to account, or "productively employed," in behalf of this parcel of land[16] .Some of the lands of California may be taken as a very good, tho perhaps not an extreme, example of such a creation of real estate by spiritual instrumentalities. It is probably well within the mark to say that some of these lands owe not more than one-half their current market value to their current serviceability as an instrument of production or use. The excess may be attributable to illusions touching the chances of future sale, to anticipation of a prospective enhanced usefulness, and the like; but all these are immaterial factors, of the nature of good will. Like other assets, these lands are capitalized on the basis of the anticipated income from them, part of which income is anticipated from profitable sales to persons who, it is hoped, will be persuaded to take a very sanguine view of the land situation, while part of it may be due to over-sanguine anticipations of usefulness generated by the advertising matter and the efforts of the land agents directed to what is called "developing the country."

To any one preoccupied with the conceit that "capital" means "capital goods" such a conversion of intangible into tangible goods, or such a gen-

---

[16] Neither as a physical magnitude ("land") nor as a pecuniary magnitude ("real estate") is the capitalized land in question an item of "good-will"; but its value as real estate, i.e., its magnitude as an asset - is in part a product of the "good-will" (illusions and the like) worked up in its behalf and turned to account, by the land agent. The real estate is a tangible asset, an item of material wealth, while the "good-will" to which in part it owes its magnitude as an item of wealth is an intangible asset, an item of immaterial wealth.

eration of intangible assets by the productive use of tangible assets, might be something of a puzzle. If "assets" were a physical concept, covering a range of physical things, instead of a pecuniary concept, such conversion of tangible into intangible assets, and conversely, would be a case of transubstantiation. But there is nothing miraculous in the matter. "Assets" are a pecuniary magnitude, and belong among the facts of investment. Except in relation to investment the items of wealth involved are not assets. In other words, assets are a matter of capitalization, which is a special case of valuation; and the question of tangibility or intangibility as regards a given parcel of assets is a question what article or class of articles the valuation shall attach to or be imputed to. If, e.g., the fact to which value is imputed in the valuation is the habitual demand for a given article of merchandise, or the habitual resort of a given group of customers to a particular shop or merchant, or a monopolistic control or limitation of price and supply, then the resulting item of assets will be "intangible," since the object to which the capitalized value in question is imputed is an immaterial object. If the fact which is by imputation made the bearer of the capitalized value is a material object, as, e.g., the merchantable goods of which the supply is arbitrarily limited or the price arbitrarily fixed, or if it is the material means of supplying such goods, then the capitalized value in question is a case of tangible assets. The value involved is, like all value, a matter of imputation, and as assets it is a matter of capitalization; but capitalization is an appraisement of a pecuniary "income-stream" in terms of the vendible objects to the ownership of which the income is assumed to inure. To what object the capitalized value of the "income-stream" shall be imputed is a question of what object of ownership secures to the owner an effectual claim on this "income-stream"; that is to say, it is a question of what object of ownership the strategic advantage is assumed to attach to, which is a question of the play of business exigencies in the given case.

The "income-stream" in question is a pecuniary income stream, and is in the last resort traceable to transactions of sale. Within the confines of business - and therefore within the scope of capital, investments, assets, and the like business concepts - transactions of purchase and sale are the final terms of any analysis. But beyond these confines, comprehending and conditioning the business system, lie the material facts of the community's work and livelihood. In the final transaction of sale the merchantable goods are valued by the consumer, not as assets, but as livelihood[17] and in the last analysis and long run it is to some such transaction that all business imputations of value and capitalistic appraisement of assets must have regard and by which they must finally be checked. Dissociated from the facts of work and livelihood, therefore, assets cease to be

---

[17] "Livelihood" is, of course, here taken in a loose sense, not as denoting the means of subsistence simply or even the means of physical comfort, but as signifying that the purchases in question are made with a view to the consumptive use of the goods rather than with a view to their use for a profit.

assets; but this does not preclude their relation to these facts of work and livelihood being at times somewhat remote and loose.

Without recourse, immediately or remotely, to certain material facts of industrial process and equipment, assets would not yield earnings; that is to say, wholly disjoined from these material facts, they would in effect not be assets. This is true for both tangible and intangible assets, altho the relation of the assets to the material facts of industry is not the same in the two cases. The case of tangible assets needs no argument. Intangible assets, such as patent right or monopolistic control, are likewise of no effect except in effectual contact with industrial facts. The patent right becomes effective for the purpose only in the material working of the innovation covered by it; and monopolistic control is a source of gain only in so far as it effectually modifies or divides the supply of goods. In the light of these considerations it seems feasible to indicate both the congruence and the distinction between the two categories of assets a little more narrowly than was done above. Both are assets, - that is to say, both are values determined by a capitalization of anticipated income-yielding capacity; both depend for their income-yielding capacity on the preferential use of certain immaterial factors; both depend for their efficiency on the use of certain material objects; both may increase or decrease, as assets, apart from any increase or decrease of the material objects involved. The tangible assets capitalize the preferential use of technological, industrial expedients, - expedients of production, dealing with the facts of brute nature under the laws of physical cause and effect, - this preferential use being secured by the ownership of material articles employed in the processes in which these expedients are put into effect.

The intangible assets capitalize the preferential use of certain facts of human nature - habits, propensities, beliefs, aspirations, necessities - to be dealt with under the psychological laws of human motivation; this preferential use being secured by custom, as in the case of old-fashioned good-will, by legal assignment, as in patent or copyright, by ownership of the instruments of production, as in the case of industrial monopolies[18] .

Intangible assets are capital as well as tangible assets; that is to say, they are items of capitalized wealth. Both categories of assets, therefore, represent expected "income-streams" which are of such definite character as to admit of their being rated in set terms per cent per time unit; although the expected income need not therefore be anticipated to come in an even flow or to be distributed in any equable manner over a period of time. The income-streams to be so rated and capitalized are associated in such a manner with some external fact (impersonal to their claimant), whether material or immaterial, as to permit their being traced or attributed to an

---

[18] The instruments of production so monopolized are, of course, tangible assets, but the ownership of such means of production in amount sufficient to enable the owner to monopolize or control the market, whether for purchase (as of materials or labor) or for sale (as of marketable goods or services), gives rise to a differential business advantage which is to be classed as intangible assets.

income-yielding capacity on the part of this external fact, to which their valuation as a whole may be imputed and which may then be capitalized as an item of wealth yielding this income-stream. Income-streams which do not meet these requirements do not give rise to assets, and so do not swell the volume of capitalized wealth. There are income-streams which do not meet the necessary specifications of capitalizable wealth; and in modern business traffic, particularly, there are large and secure sources of income that are in this way not capitalizable and yet yield a legitimate business income. Such are, indeed, to be rated among the most consequential factors in the current business situation.

Under the guidance of traditions carried over from a more primitive business situation, it has been usual to speak of income-streams derived in such a manner as "wages of superintendence," or "undertaker's wages," or "entrepreneur's profits," or, latterly, as "profits" simply and specifically. Such phenomena of this class as are of consequence in business are commonly accounted for, theoretically, under this head; and the effort so to account for them is to be taken as, at least, a laudable endeavor to avoid an undue multiplication of technical terms and categories[19] .Yet the most striking phenomena of this class, and the most consequential for modern business and industry, both in respect of their magnitude and in respect of the pecuniary dominion and discretion which they represent, cannot well be accounted undertaker's gains, in the ordinary sense of that term.

The great gains of the great industrial financiers or of the great "interests," e.g., do not answer the description of undertaker's gains, in that they do not accrue to the captain of industry on the basis of his "managerial ability" alone, apart from his wealth or out of relation to his wealth; and yet it is not safe to say that such gains (which are over and above ordinary returns on his investments) accrue on the ground of the requisite amount of wealth alone, apart from the exercise of a large business discretion on the part of the owner of such wealth or on the part of his agent to whom discretion has been delegated. Administrative, or strategic, discretion and activity must necessarily be present in the case: otherwise, the income in question would rightly be rated as income from capital simply.

The captain of industry, the pecuniary magnate, is normally in receipt of income in excess of the ordinary rate per cent on investment; but apart from his large holdings he is not in a position to get those large gains. Dissociated from his large holdings, he is not a large captain of industry; but it is not the size of his holdings alone that determines what the gains of the pecuniary magnate in modern industry shall be. Gains of the kind and magnitude that currently come to this class of business men come only on condition that the owner (or his agent) shall exercise a similarly large discretion and control in the affairs of the business community; but the mag-

---

[19] One writer even goes so far in the endeavor to bring the facts within the scope of the staple concepts of theory at this point as to rate the persons concerned in such a case as "capital," after having satisfied himself that much income-streams are traceable to a personal source - See Fisher, Nature of Capital and Income, chap. v.

nitude of the gains, as well as of the discretion and control exercised, is somewhat definitely conditioned by the magnitude of the wealth which gives effect to this discretion.

The disposition of pecuniary forces in such matters may be well seen in the work and remuneration of any coalition of "interests," such as the modern business community has become familiar with. The "interests" in such a case are of a personal character, - they are "interested parties," - and the sagacity, experience, and animus of these various interested parties counts in the outcome, both as regards the aggregate gains of the coalition and as regards the distribution of these gains among the several parties in interest; but the weight of any given "interest " in a coalition or "system" is more nearly proportioned to the wealth controlled by the given "interest," and to the strategic position of such wealth, than to any personal talents or proficiency of the "interested party." The talents and proficiency involved are not the main facts. Indeed, the movements of such a "system," and of the several component "interests," are largely a matter of artless routine, in which the greatest ingenuity and initiative engaged in the premises are commonly exercised by the legal counsel working for a fee.

A dispassionate student of the current business traffic, who is not over-awed by round numbers, will be more impressed by the ease and simplicity of the manoeuvres that lead to large pecuniary results in the higher business finance than by any evidence of pre-eminent sagacity and initiative among the pecuniary magnates. One need only call to mind the simple and obvious way in which the promoters of the Steel Corporation were magnificently checkmated by the financiers of the Carnegie "interest," when that great and reluctant corporation was floated, or the pettyfogging tactics of Standard Oil in its later career. In extenuation of their visible lack of initiative and insight it may not be ungraceful to call to mind that many of the discretionary heads of the great "interests" are men of advanced years, and that in the nature of the case the pecuniary magnates of the present generation must commonly be men of a somewhat advanced age; and it is only during the present generation that the existing situation has arisen, with its characteristic opportunities and demands.

To take their present foremost rank in the new business finance which is here under inquiry, they have had to accumulate the great wealth on which alone their discretionary control of business affairs rests, and their best vigor has been spent in this work of preparation; so that they have commonly attained the requisite strategic position only after they had outlived their "years of discretion. "But there is no intention here to depreciate the work of the pecuniary magnates or the spokesmen of the great "interests." The matter has been referred to only as it bears on this category of capitalistic income which accrues on other ground than the "earning-capacity" of the assets involved, and which still cannot be imputed to the "earning-capacity" of these business men apart from these assets. The case is evidently not one of "wages of superintendence" or "undertaker's profits"; but it is as evidently not an ease of the earning-capacity of the assets.

The proof of the latter point is quite as easy as of the former. If the gains of the "system" or of its constituent "interests" and magnates were imputable to the earning-capacity of the assets involved, - in any accepted sense of "earnings," - then it would immediately follow that those assets would be recapitalized on the basis of these extraordinary earnings, and that the income derived in this class of traffic should reappear as interest or dividends on the capital so increased to correspond with the increased earnings. But such recapitalization takes place only to a relatively very limited extent, and he question then bears on the income which is not so accounted for in the recapitalization.

The gains of this class of traffic are, of course, themselves capitalized, - for the most part they accrue in the capitalized form, as issues of securities and the like; but the sources of this income are not capitalized as such. The (large) accumulated wealth, or assets, which gives weight to the movements of the "interests" and magnates in question, and which affords the ground for the discretionary control of business affairs exercised by them, are, for the most part at least, invested in ordinary business ventures, in the form of corporation securities and the like, and are there earning dividends or interest at current rates; and these assets are valued in the market (and thereby capitalized) on the basis of their current earnings in the various enterprises in which they are so invested. But their being so invested in profitable business enterprises does not in the least hinder their usefulness in the hands of the magnates as a basis or means of carrying on the large and highly profitable transactions of the higher industrial finance. To impute these gains to those assets as "earnings," therefore, would be to count the assets twice as capital, or rather to count them over and over.

An additional perplexity in endeavoring to handle gains of this class theoretically as earnings, in the ordinary sense, arises from the fact that they stand in no definable time relation to their underlying assets. They have no definable "time-shape," as Mr. Fisher might put it[20] .Such gains am timeless, in the sense that the time relation does not count in any substantial manner or in any sensible degree in their determination[21] .

In a more painstaking statement of this point of theory it would be necessary to note that these gains are "timeless," in the sense indicated, in so far as the enterprise from which they accrue is dissociated from the technological circumstances and processes of industry, and only in so far. Technological (industrial) procedure, being of the nature of physical causation, is subject to the time relation under which causal sequence runs. This is the basis of such discussions of capital and interest as those of Bohm-Bawerk, and of Fisher. But business traffic, as distinguished from

---

[20] Cf. Fisher, Rate of Interest, chap. vi.

[21] This conclusion is reached, e.g., by Mr. G. P. Watkins (The Growth of Large Fortunes, chap. iii, sec. 10), although, through a curious etymological misapprehension he rejects the term "timeless" as not available.

the processes of industry, being not immediately concerned with the technological process, is also not immediately or uniformly subject to the time relation involved in the causal sequence of the technological process. Business traffic is subject to the time relation because and in so far as it depends upon and follows up the processes of production.

The commonplace or old-fashioned business enterprise, the competitive system of investment in industrial business simply, commonly rests pretty directly on the due sequence of the industrial processes in which the investments of such enterprise are placed. Such enterprise, as conceived by the current theories of capital, does business at first hand in the industrial efficiency of the community, which is conditioned by the time relation of the causal sequence, and which is, indeed, in great measure a function of the time consumed in the technological processes. Therefore, the gains, as well as the transactions, of such enterprise are also commonly somewhat closely conditioned by the like time relation, and they typically emerge under the form of a per cent. per time unit; that is to say, as a function of the lapse of time.

Yet the business transactions themselves are not a matter of the lapse of time. Time is not of the essence of the case. The magnitude of a pecuniary transaction is not a function of the time consumed in concluding it, nor are the gains which accrue from the transaction. In business enterprise on the higher plane, which is here under inquiry, the relation of the transactions, and of their gains, to the consecution of the technological processes remotely underlying them is distant, loose, and uncertain, so that the time element here does not obtrude itself: rather, it somewhat obviously falls into abeyance, marking the degree of its remoteness. Yet this phase of business enterprise, like any other, of course takes place in time; and, it is also to be remarked, the volume of the traffic and the gains derived from it are, no doubt, somewhat closely conditioned in the long run by the time relation which dominates that technological (industrial) efficiency on which this enterprise, too, ultimately and indirectly rests and from which in the last resort its gains are finally drawn, however remotely and indirectly.

An analysis of these phenomena on lines similar to those which have been followed in the discussion of assets above is not without difficulty, nor can it fairly be expected to yield any but tentative and provisional results. The matter has received so little attention from economic theoreticians that even significant mistakes in this connection are of very rare occurrence[22] .The cause of this scant attention to these matters lies, no doubt, in the relative novelty of the facts in question. The facts may be roughly drawn together under the caption "Traffic in Vendible Capital"; although that term serves rather as a comprehensive designation of the

---

[22] Even Mr. Watkins (as cited above), e.g., is led by a superficial generalization to class these gains as "speculative," and so to excuse himself from a closer acquaintance with their character and with the bearings of tho class of business enterprise out of which they arise.

class of business enterprise from which these gains accrue than as an adequate characterization of the play of forces involved[23] .Traffic in vendible capital has not been unknown in the past, but it is only recently that it has come into the foreground as the most important line of business enterprise. Such it now is, in that it is in this traffic that the ultimate initiative and discretion in business are now to be found. It is at the same time the most gainful of business enterprise, not only in absolute terms, but relatively to the magnitude of the assets involved as well.

One reason for this superior gainfulness is the fact that the assets involved in this traffic are at the same time engaged as assets to their full extent in ordinary business, so that the peculiar gains of this traffic, are of the nature of a bonus above the earnings of the invested wealth. "It is like finding money." As was said above, the method, or the ways and means, characteristic of this superior business enterprise is a traffic in vendible capital. The wealth gained in this field is commonly in the capitalized form, and constitutes in each transaction or "deal," a deduction or abstraction from the capitalized wealth of the business commonly in favor of the magnates or "interests" to whom the gains accrue. Its proximate aim is a transfer of capitalized wealth from other capitalists to those who so gain. This transfer or abstraction of capitalized wealth from the former owners is commonly effected by all augmentation of the nominal capital, based on a (transient) advantage inuring to the particular concerns whose capitalization is so augmented[24] .

Any such increase of the community's aggregate capitalization, without a corresponding increase of the material wealth on which the capitalization is based, involves, of course, in effect a redistribution of the aggregate capitalized wealth; and in this redistribution the great financiers are in a position to gain. The gains in question, it will be seen, come out of the business community, out of invested wealth, and only remotely and indirectly out of the community at large from which the business community draws its income. These gains, therefore, we a tax on commonplace business enterprise, in much the same manner and with much the like effect as the gains of commonplace business (ordinary profits and interest) are a tax on industry[25] .

In a manner analogous to the old-fashioned capitalist-employer's engrossing of the industrial community's technological efficiency does the modern pecuniary magnate engross the business community's capitalistic

---

[23] Cf. Theory of Business Enterprise, chap v., pp. 119-130; chap. vi, pp. 162-174.

[24] Cf. Theory of Business Enterprise, footnote on pp. 169-170.

[25] As should be evident from the run of the argument in the earlier portions of this paper, the use of the words "tax," "deduction," "abstraction," in this connection, is not to be taken as implying approval or disapproval of the phenomena, so characterized. The words are used for want of better terms to indicate the source of business gains, and objectively to characterize the relation of give-and-take between industry and ordinary capitalistic business, on the one hand, and between ordinary business and this business enterprise on the higher plane, on the other hand.

efficiency. This capitalistic efficiency lies in the capitalist-employer's ability - by force of the ownership of the material equipment - to induce the industrial community, through suitable bargaining, to turn over to the owner of the material equipment the excess of the product above the industrial community's livelihood. The fortunes of the capitalist-employer are closely dependent on the run of the market, - the conjunctures of advantageous purchase and sale; and it is his constant endeavor to create or gain for himself some peculiar degree of advantage in the market, in the way of monopoly, good-will, legalized privilege, and the like, - something in the way of intangible assets. But the pecuniary magnate, in the measure in which he truly answers to the concept, is superior to the market on which the capitalist-employer depends, and can make or mar its conjunctures of advantageous purchase and sale of goods; that is to say, he is in a position to make or mar any peculiar advantage possessed by the given capitalist-employer who comes in his way. He does this by force of his large holdings of capital at large, the weight of which he can shift from one point of investment to another as the relative efficiency - earning-capacity - of one and another line of investment may make it expedient; and at each move of this kind, in so far as it is effective for his ends, he cuts into and assimilates a fraction of the invested wealth involved, in that he cuts into and sequesters a fraction of the capital's earning-capacity in the given line.

That is to say, in the measure in which he is a pecuniary magnate, and not simply a capitalist-employer, he engrosses the capitalistic efficiency of invested wealth; he turns to his own account the capitalist-employer's effectual engrossing of the community's industrial efficiency. He engrosses the community's pecuniary initiative and proficiency. In the measure, therefore, in which this relatively new-found serviceability of extraordinarily large wealth is effective for its peculiar business function, the old-fashioned capitalist-employer loses his discretionary initiative and becomes a mediator, an instrumentality of extraction and transmission, a collector and conveyer of revenue from the community at large to the pecuniary magnate, who, in the ideal case, should leave him only such an allowance out of the gross earnings collected and transmitted as will induce him to continue in business. To the community at large, whose industrial efficiency is already virtually engrossed by the capitalist-employer's ownership and control of the material equipment, this later step in the evolution of the economic situation should apparently not be a matter of substantial consequence or a matter for sentimental disturbance.

On the face of it, it should appear to have little more than a speculative interest for those classes of the community who do not derive an income from investments; particularly not for the working classes, who own nothing to speak of and whose only dependence is their technological efficiency, which has virtually ceased to be their own. But such is not the current state of sentiment. This inchoate new phase of capitalism, this business enterprise on the higher plane, is in fact viewed with the most lively apprehension. In a maze of consternation and solicitude the boldest, wisest, most public-spirited, most illustrious gentlemen of our time are spending their manhood in an endeavor to make the hen continue sitting on the nest after the chickens are out of the shell. The modern community is imbued with business principles - of the old dispensation. By precept and example, men have learned that the business interests (of the authentic superannuated scale and kind) are the palladium of our civilization, as Mr. Dooley would say; and it is felt that any disturbance of the existing pecuniary dominion of the capitalist-employer - as contrasted with the pecuniary magnate - would involve the well-being of the community in one common agony of desolation.

The merits of this perturbation, or of the remedies proposed for saving the pecuniary life of the old-fashioned capitalist-employer, of course do not concern the present inquiry; but the matter has been referred to here as evidence that the pecuniary magnate's work, and the dominion which his extraordinarily large wealth gives him, are, in effect, substantially a new phase of the economic development, and that these phenomena are distastefully unfamiliar and are felt to be consequential enough to threaten the received institutional structure. That is to say, it is felt to be a new phase of business enterprise, - distasteful to those who stand to lose by it.The basis of this business enterprise on the higher plane is capital-at-large, as distinguished from capital invested in a given line of industrial enterprise, and it becomes effective when wealth has accumulated in holdings sufficiently large to give the holder (or combination of holders, the "system") a controlling weight in any group or ramification of business interests into which he may throw his weight by judicious investment (or by underwriting and the like).

The pecuniary magnate must be able effectually to engross the pecuniary initiative and the business opportunities on which such a section or ramification of the business community depends for its ordinary gains. How large a proportion of the business community's capital is needed for such an effectual engrossing of its capitalistic efficiency, in any given bearing, is a question that cannot be answered in anything like absolute terms, or even in relative terms of a satisfactorily definite kind. It is, of course, evident that a relatively large disposable body of capital is needed for such a purpose; and it is also evident, from the current facts of business, that the body of capital so disposed of need not amount to a majority, or anything near a majority, of the investments involved, - at least not at the present relatively inchoate phase of this larger business enterprise. The larger the holdings of the magnate, the more effectual and expeditious will be his work of absorbing the holdings of the smaller capitalist-employer, and the more precipitately will the latter yield his assets to the new claimant.

Evidently, this work of the pecuniary magnate, bears a great resemblance to the creation of intangible assets under the ordinary competitive system. This is, no doubt, the point of its nearest relation to the current capitalistic enterprise. But, as has already been indicated above, it cannot be said that the magnate's peculiar work is the creation of intangible, or other assets, although there is commonly some recapitalization involved in his manoeuvres, and although his gains commonly come as assets, i.e., in the capitalized form. Nor can it, as has also been indicated above, be said that the wealth which serves him as the means of his peculiar enterprise stands in the relation of assets to this enterprise or to the gains in question, since this wealth already stands in an exhaustive relation as assets to some corporate enterprise in ordinary business and to the corresponding items of interest and dividends.

It may, of course, be contended that the present state of things on this higher plane of enterprise is transient and transitional only, and that in the settled condition which may conceivably supervene the magnate's relation to business at large will be capitalized in some form of intangible assets, after the manner in which the monopoly advantage of an ordinary "trust" is now capitalized. But this is at the best only a surmise, guided by inapplicable generalizations drawn from a past situation in which this higher enterprise has not engrossed the pecuniary initiative and played the ruling part.

Chapter 4

Bohm-Bawerk's Definition
Of Capital And The Source Of Wages

In his exposition of the term "capital" Professor Bohm-Bawerk briefly touches on the wages-fund doctrine, so far as to reject summarily the proposition that the means of subsistence of productive laborers is drawn from the capital of the community, although, from the point of view of the employer, these "real wages" are to be regarded as drawn from his private capital. With the distinction which the discussion establishes between social capital and private capital, this position is, of course, in itself perfectly consistent. The position is, indeed, contained in the definition of capital previously arrived at (pp. 42, 43, and 21).

The ground of the position taken is the unquestioned or, at all events, unquestionable truth that the laborer is a member of society, and his consumption of products is, in a broad view, a fact of the same kind, and of like theoretical significance with consumption on the part of any other member of society. The satisfaction of wants, whether it be the wants of the laborer or of any other, is the end, not the means, of productive activity. While the exposition at this point undeniably sheds a strong light on the question, it can hardly be said to have finally disposed of all ground for difference of opinion, still less to have explained away the wages-fund controversy, or that point of the controversy which concerns the question of the source of wages. And that controversy has been of such extent and earnestness as to raise the presumption that something is to be said for both sides of the dispute, and to leave little hope of its being finally put at rest by any other method than that of explaining away the ground of difference. For reaching this end, I believe Professor Bohm-Bawerk's exposition of capital has given us the means.

It is to be remarked, by the way, however, that there is a lacuna in the exposition at this point which seems, at least, not of first-rate theoretical consequence, and is, perhaps, the result of oversight of a not very important point, but which might afford a foothold for carping criticism. It will be best to speak of it at the outset, and put it out of the way before going on. This difficulty arises from the inclusion, as a subhead under Social Capital of "stocks of goods for consumption which are still in the hands of producers or dealers" (p. 70); that is to say, goods which have not yet passed that final stage of preparation for consumption which consists in their transfer, through the mechanism of exchange, into the ownership of the ultimate consumer. Now, this classification may afford ground for persons unduly given to nice distinctions to take exception to Professor Bohm-Bawerk's position on the question of the source of wages that, (1) inasmuch as the payment of wages, actually for the most part, and in theory normally, is a transfer to the laborer not of the particular goods he wants, but of an item of value by means of which he may obtain the particular goods through this final productive step of exchange, therefore the payment of wages simply gives the recipient a claim on goods which have not yet passed the final stage of production, and so are as yet a part of the general capital by the terms of the definition, and which will pass that stage only in consequence of this claim; (2) that, without regard to the mechanism by which the transaction is carried out, the claim on goods, which accrues to the laborer in the payment of wages, constitutes a drain on the stocks in the hands of producers or merchants, and tends to diminish such stocks, and this without regard to the point in time of the payment, relative to the production of the goods, which ultimately go to satisfy the laborer's wants.

The payment of the wages, as a matter to be considered in a theory of the methods of production, precedes the consumption, or the ownership on the part of the recipient, of the goods which the claim so transferred to him ultimately puts into his hands for consumption, and so is a claim that can be satisfied only by drawing on a class of goods included under the head of social capital. This criticism, it will be seen, touches a point of classification, and may perhaps be avoided without deranging the main structure of the theory now, as to the theory of the source of wages, in the light of Professor Bohm-Bawerk's definition of capital. It is not too much to say that the controversy has owed much of its bitterness and sterility to inadequate definition of the terms employed, especially to a lack of accuracy in the concept of capital. The *'Positive Theorie des Kapitals'* has given to the concept of capital, and of its relation to other elements of economic theory, a conciseness and adequacy of which earlier speculators were sorely in need. If the distinction which this discussion formulates between social and private capital had been apprehended earlier, with the same full and clear consciousness, the means would have been at hand by which the wages-fund controversy might have been put to rest.

But the completed definition of capital does not of itself dispose of the question. A further analysis in the same direction is necessary. It seems to me that economic theory is at this point in the presence of a distinction necessary to be made between "the laborer's share of consumable goods", or "earnings", on the one hand, and "wages", on the other, analogous to the distinction taken by Wagner - and perfected by Professor Bohm-Bawerk - between capital as a "purely economic category" and capital "in a juridico-historical sense." Wages, in this stricter definition, and private capital both are facts of usage, while the laborer's income, or earnings, and social capital both are facts intrinsic and fundamental to any theory of industrial society. Wages is a fact incident to the relation of employer and employed. It is, in the sense fixed by colloquial use, an economic category whose scope is entirely within the theory of production as carried on by the method based on that relation; and the term is not used in precisely the same sense when the discussion shifts to the standpoint of production simply as such, still less when the point of view is that of distribution or consumption. It is by an unconscious equivocation, in shifting the point of view, that wages is identified with earnings and spoken of as an element in the theory of distribution or consumption.

The laborer, from the point of view of consumption of products, is no longer "laborer": he is a member of society simply, and his share of the product of industry is the share of an individual member of society. As consumer, he is not "laborer", and his share of consumable goods is not "wages", in the strict technical sense of the term. Wages may coincide in range of comprehension with the labor's share of the product - with earnings - and may likewise coincide with the aggregate of his consumption; but wages is a category having a different significance for economic theory from that of earnings or of goods consumed. The item of value, which from the point of view of production as carried on by the method of private capital as wages is, from the point of view of the laborer, as being productively employed in his own interest, earnings.

From the point of view of consumption of goods produced, neither of these terms can be employed with entirely the same meaning as they have in the use just specified. If this distinction be allowed as theoretically legitimate, it appears that Professor Bohm-Bawerk's discussion does not upset the wages-fund doctrine in any of its essential texts. The one proposition, that the sustenance of men while productively employed is drawn from the product of past industry, is of course not impugned; the other, that wages are paid out of capital, is conceded in conceding that it will hold true when capital is understood to mean private capital; for it is only then that the term "wages", in the strict technical sense, can properly be employed. At the same time this discrimination of terms leaves the position of the opponents of the wages-fund doctrine, as to this particular point, perfectly tenable; for whenever "wages" is used in the sense of "earnings", as, I believe, is invariably the case in the usage of these writers, they are undoubtedly drawn from the product of industry, inasmuch as earnings are the product, to the laborer, of his labor.

All this may seem to be a web of excessively fine-spun technicalities, but in apology it is to be said that it is also directed exclusively to a point of pure theory. And the whole controversy about the source of wages has also been in the region of pure theory, having never directly involved questions of physical fact or of expediency.

Chapter 5

Gustav Schmoller's Economics

Professor Schmoller's *Grundriss*[1] is an event of the first importance in economic literature. It appears from later advices that the second and concluding volume of the work is hardly to be looked for at as early a date as the author's expressions in his preface had led us to anticipate. What lies before Professor Schmoller's readers, therefore, in this first volume of the Outlines is but one-half of the compendious statement which he here purposes making of his theoretical position and of his views and exemplification of the scope and method of economic science. It may accordingly seem adventurous to attempt a characterisation of his economic system on the basis of this avowedly incomplete statement.

And yet such an endeavor is not altogether gratuitous, nor need it in any great measure proceed on hypothetical grounds. The introduction comprised in the present volume sketches the author's aim in an outline sufficiently full to afford a convincing view of the "system" of science for which he speaks; and the two books by which the introduction is followed show Professor Schmoller's method of inquiry consistently carried out, as well as the reach and nature of the theoretical conclusions which he considers to lie within the competency of economic science. And with regard to an economist who is so much of an innovator, - not to say so much of an iconoclast, - and whose work touches the foundations of the science so intimately and profoundly, the interest of his critics and associates must, at least for the present, center chiefly about these questions as to the scope and nature assigned to the theory by his discussion, as to the range and character of the material of which he makes use, and as to the methods of inquiry which his sagacity and experience commend.

So, therefore, while the Outlines is yet incomplete, considered as a compendium of details of doctrine, the work in its unfinished state need not thereby be an inadequate expression of Professor Schmoller's relation to economic science. Herewith for the first time economic readers are put in possession of a fully advised deliverance on economic science at large as seen and cultivated by that modernised historical school of which Professor Schmoller is the authoritative exponent. Valuable and characteristic as his earlier discussions on the scope and method of the science are, they are but preliminary studies and tentative formulations as compared with this maturer work, which not only avows itself a definitive formulation, but has about it an air of finality perceptible at every turn.

But this comes near saying that it embodies the sole comprehensive working-out of the scientific aims of the historical school. Discussions

---

[1] Grundriss der allgemeinen Volkswirtschaftslehre. Erster Teil. Leipzig, 1900.

partially covering the field, monographs and sketches there are in great number, showing the manner of economic theory that was to be looked for as an outcome of the "historical diversion." Some of these, especially some of the later ones, are extremely valuable in the results they offer, as well as significant of the trend which the science is taking under the hands of the German students[2] .

But a comprehensive work, aiming to formulate a body of economic theory on the basis afforded by the "historical method," has not hitherto been seriously attempted. To the broad statement just made exception might perhaps be taken in favor of Schaeffle's half-forgotten work of the seventies, together possibly with several other less notable and less consistent endeavors of a similar kind, dating back to the early decades of the school. Probably none of the younger generation of economists would be tempted to cite Roscher's work as invalidating such a statement as the one made above. Although time has been allowed for the acceptance and authentication of these endeavors of the earlier historical economists in the direction of a system of economic theory, - that is to say, of an economic science, - they have failed of authentication at the hands of the students of the science; and there seems no reason to regard this failure as less than definitive.

During the last two decades the historical school has branched into two main directions of growth, somewhat divergent, so that broad general statements regarding the historical economists can be less confidently made to-day than perhaps at any earlier time. Now, as regards the more conservative branch, the historical economists of the stricter observance, - these modern continuers of what may be called the elder line of the historical school can scarcely be said to cultivate a science at all, their aim being not theoretical work. Assuredly, the work of this elder line, of which Professor Wagner is the unquestioned head, is by no means idle. It is work of a sufficiently important and valuable order, perhaps it is indispensable to the task which the science has in hand, but, broadly speaking, it need not be counted with in so far as it touches directly upon economic theory.

This elder line of German economics, in its numerous modern representatives, shows both insight and impartiality; but as regards economic theory their work bears the character of eclecticism rather than that of a constructive advance. Frequent and peremptory as their utterances commonly are on points of doctrine, it is only very rarely that these utterances embody theoretical views arrived at or verified by the economists who make them or by such methods of inquiry as are characteristic of these economists. Where these expressions of doctrine are not of the nature of maxims of expediency, they are, as is well known, commonly borrowed somewhat uncritically from classical sources. Of constructive scientific work - that is to say, of theory - this elder line of German economics is in-

---

[2] E.g., K. Bücher's Entstehung der Volkswirtschaft, and Arbeit und Rythmus; R. Hildebrand's Recht und Sitte; Knapp's Grundherrschaft und Rittergut; Ehrenberg's Zeitalter der Fugger; R. Mucke's various works.

nocent; nor does there seem to be any prospect of an eventual output of theory on the part of that branch of the historical school, unless they should unexpectedly take advice, and make the scope, and therefore the method, of their inquiry something more than historical in the sense in which that term is currently accepted. The historical economics of the conservative kind seems to be a barren field in the theoretical respect.

So that whatever characteristic articles of general theory the historical school may enrich the science with are to be looked for at the hands of those men who, like Professor Schmoller, have departed from the strict observance of the historical method. A peculiar interest, therefore, attaches to his work as the best accepted and most authoritative spokesman of that branch of historical economics which professes to cultivate theoretical inquiry. It serves to show in what manner and degree this more scientific wing of the historical school have out grown the original "historical" standpoint and range of conceptions, and how they have passed from a distrust of all economic theory to an eager quest of theoretical formulations that shall cover all phenomena of economic life to better purpose than the body of doctrine received from the classical writers and more in consonance with the canons of contemporary science at large.

That this should have been the outcome of the half-century of development through which the school has now passed might well seem unexpected, if not incredible, to any who saw the beginning of that divergence within the school, a generation ago, out of which this modernised, theoretical historical economics has arisen. Professor Schmoller entered the field early, in the sixties, as a protestant against the aims and ideals then in vogue in economics. His protest ran not only against the methods and results of the classical writers, but also against the views professed by the leaders of the historical school, both as regards the scope of the science and as regards the character of the laws or generalisations sought by the science. His early work, in so far as he was at variance with his colleagues, was chiefly critical; and there is no good evidence that he then had a clear conception of the character of that constructive work to which it has been his persistent aim to turn the science. Hence he came to figure in common repute as an iconoclast and an extreme exponent of the historical school, in that he was held practically to deny the feasibility of a scientific treatment of economic matters and to aim at confining economics to narrative, statistics, and description.

This iconoclastic or critical phase of his economic discussion is now past, and with it the uncertainty as to the trend and outcome of his scientific activity. To understand the significance of the diversion created by Professor Schmoller as regards the scope and method of economics, it is necessary, very briefly, to indicate the position occupied by that early generation of historical economists from which his teaching diverged, and more particularly those points of the older canon at which he has come to differ characteristically from the views previously in vogue. As regards the situation in which the historical school, as exemplified by its leaders, was then placed, it is, of course, something of a commonplace that by the end of its first twenty years of endeavor in the reform of economic science the school bad, in point of systematic results, scarcely got beyond preliminaries. And even these preliminaries were not in all respects obviously to the purpose.

A new and wider scope had been indicated for economic inquiry, as well as a new aim and method for theoretical discussion. But the new ideals of theoretical advance, as well as the ways and means indicated for their attainment, still had mainly a speculative interest. Nothing substantial had been done towards the realisation of the former or the *mise en oeuvre* of the latter. The historical economists can scarcely be said at that time to have put their hand to the new engines which they professed to house in their workshop. Apart from polemics and speculation concerning ideals, the serious interest and endeavors of the school had up to that time been in the field of history rather than in that of economics, except so far as the adepts of the new school continued in a fragmentary way to inculcate and, in some slight and uncertain degree, to elaborate the dogmas of the classical writers whom they sought to discredit.

The character of historical economics at the time when Professor Schmoller entered on his work of criticism and revision is fairly shown by Roscher's writings. Whatever may be thought to-day of Roscher's rank as all economist, in contrast with Knies and Hildebrand, it will scarcely be questioned that at the close of the first quarter-century of the life history of the historical school it was Roscher's conception of the scope and method of economics that found the widest acceptance and that best expressed the animus of that body of students who professed to cultivate economics by the historical method.

For the purpose in hand Roscher's views may, therefore, be taken as typical, all the more readily since for the very general purpose here intended there are no serious discrepancies between Roscher and his two illustrious contemporaries. The chief difference is that Roscher is more naive and more specific. He has also left a more considerable volume of results achieved by the professed use of his method. Roscher's professed method was what he calls the "historico-physiological" method. This lie contrasts with the "philosophical" or "idealistic" method. But his air of depreciation as regards "philosophical" methods in economics must not be taken to mean that Roscher's own economic speculations were devoid of all philosophical or metaphysical basis. It only means that his philosophical postulates were different from those of the economists whom he discredits, and that they were regarded by him as self-evident.

As must necessarily be the case with a writer who had neither a special aptitude for nor special training in philosophical inquiries, Roscher's metaphysical postulates are, of course, chiefly tacit. They are the common-sense, commonplace metaphysics afloat in educated German circles in the time of Roscher's youth, - during tile period when his growth and education gave him his outlook on life and knowledge and laid the basis of his intellectual habits; which means that these postulates belong to what Hoffding has called the "Romantic" school of thought, and are of a Hegelian complexion. Roscher being not a professed philosophical student, it is neither easy nor safe to particularise closely as regards his fundamental metaphysical tenets; but, as near as so specific an identification of his philosophical outlook is practicable, he must be classed with the Hegelian "Right." But since the Hegelian metaphysics had in Roscher's youth an unbroken vogue in reputable German circles, especially in those ultra-reputable circles within which lay the gentlemanly life and human contact of Roscher, the postulates afforded by the Hegelian metaphysics were accepted simply as a matter of course, and were not recognised as metaphysical at all.

And in this his metaphysical affiliation Roscher is fairly typical of the early historical school of economics. The Hegelian metaphysics, in so far as bears upon the matter in hand, is a metaphysics of a self-realising life process. This life process, which is the central and substantial fact of the universe, is of a spiritual nature, "spiritual," of course, being here not contrasted with "material." The life process is essentially active, self-determining, and unfolds by inner necessity, by necessity of its own substantially active nature. The course of culture, in this view, is an unfolding (exfoliation) of the human spirit; and the task which economic science has in hand is to determine the laws of this cultural exfoliation in its economic aspect. But the laws of the cultural development with which the social sciences, in the Hegelian view, have to do are at one with the laws of the processes of the universe at large; and, more immediately, they are at one with the laws of the life process at large.

For the universe at large is itself a self-unfolding life process, substantially of a spiritual character, of which the economic life process which occupies the interest of the economist is but a phase and an aspect. Now, the course of the processes of unfolding life in organic nature has been fairly well ascertained by the students of natural history and the like; and this, in the nature of the case, must afford a clew to the laws of cultural development, in its economic as well as in any other of its aspects or hearings, - the laws of life in the universe being all substantially spiritual and substantially at one. So we arrive at a physiological conception of culture after the analogy of the ascertained physiological processes seen in the biological domain. It is conceived to be physiological after the Hegelian manner of conceiving a physiological process, which is, however, not the same as the modern scientific conception of a physiological process[3] .

---

3 A physiological conception of society, or of the community, had been employed before, - e.g., by the Physiocrats, - and such a concept was reached also by English speculators - e.g., Herbert Spencer - during Roscher's lifetime; but these physiological conceptions of society are reached by a different line of approach from that which led up to the late Hegelian physiological or biological conception of human culture as a spiritual structure and process. The outcome is also a different one, both as regards the use made of the analogy and as regards the theoretical results reached by its aid. It may be remarked, by the way, that neo-Hegelianism, of the "Left," likewise gave rise to a theory of a self-determining cultural exfoliation; namely, the so-called "Materialistic Conception of History" of the Marxian socialists. This Marxian conception, too, had much of a physiological air; but Marx and his coadjutors had an advantage over Roscher and his following, in that they were to

Since this quasi-physiological process of cultural development is conceived to be an unfolding of the self-realising human spirit, whose life history it is, it is of the nature of the case that the cultural process should run through a certain sequence of phases - a certain life history prescribed by the nature of the active, unfolding spiritual substance.

The sequence is determined on the whole, as regards the general features of the development, by the nature of life on the human plane. The history of cultural growth and decline necessarily repeats itself, since it is substantially the same human spirit that seeks to realise itself in every comprehensive sequence of cultural development, and since this human spirit is the only factor in the case that has substantial force. In its generic features the history of past cultural cycles is, therefore, the history of the future. Hence the importance, not to say the sole efficacy for economic science, of an historical scrutiny of culture. A well-authenticated sequence of cultural phenomena in the history of the past is conceived to have much the same binding force for the sequence of cultural phenomena in the future as a "natural law," as the term has been understood in physics or physiology, is conceived to have as regards the course of phenomena in the life history of the human body; for the onward cultural course of the human spirit, actively unfolding by inner necessity, is an organic process, following logically from the nature of this self-realising spirit.

If the process is conceived to meet with obstacles or varying conditions, it adapts itself to the circumstances in any given case, and it then goes on along the line of its own logical bent until it eventuates in the consummation given by its own nature. The environment, in this view, if it is not to be conceived simply as a function of the spiritual force at work, is, at the most, of subsidiary and transient consequence only. Environmental conditions can at best give rise to minor perturbations; they do not initiate a cumulative sequence which can profoundly affect the outcome or the ulterior course of the cultural process. Hence the sole, or almost sole, importance of historical inquiry in determining the laws of cultural development, economic or other.

The working conception which this romantic-historical school had of economic life, therefore, is, in its way, a conception of development, or evolution; but it is not to be confused with Darwinism or Spencerianism. Inquiry into the cultural development under the guidance of such preconceptions as these has led to generalisations, more or less arbitrary, regarding uniformities of sequence in phenomena, while the causes which determine the course of events, and which make the uniformity or variation of the sequence, have received but scant attention. The "natural laws" found by this means are necessarily of the nature of empiricism, colored by the bias or ideals of the investigator.

---

a greater extent schooled in the Hegelian philosophy, instead of being uncritical receptacles of the Romantic commonplaces left by Hegelianism as a residue in popular thought. They were therefore more fully conscious of the bearing of their postulates and less naive in their assumptions of self-sufficiency.

The outcome is a body of aphoristic wisdom, perhaps beautiful and valuable after its kind, but quite fatuous when measured by the standards and aims of modern science. As is well known, no substantial theoretical gain was made along this romantic-historical line of inquiry and speculation, for the reason, apparently, that there are no cultural laws of the kind aimed at, beyond the imprecise generalities that are sufficiently familiar beforehand to all passably intelligent adults. It has seemed necessary to offer this much in characterisation of that "historical" aim and method which afforded a point of departure for Professor Schmoller's work of revision.

When he first raised his protest against the prevailing ideals and methods, as being ill-advised and not thorough-going, he does not seem himself to have been entirely free from this Romantic, or Hegelian, bias. There is evidence to the contrary in his early writings[4] .It cannot even be said that his later theoretical work does not show something of the same animus, as, e.g., when he assumes that there is a meliorative trend in the course of cultural events[5] .What has differentiated his work from that of the group of writers which has above been called the elder line of historical economics is the weakness or relative absence of this bias in his theoretical work.

Particularly, he has refused to bring his researches in the field of theory definitely to rest on ground given by the Hegelian, or Romantic, school of thought. He was from the first unwilling to accept classificatory statements of uniformity or of normality as an adequate answer to questions of scientific theory. He does not commonly deny the truth or the importance of the empirical generalisations aimed at by the early historical economists. Indeed, he makes much of them and has been notoriously urgent for a full survey of historical data and a painstaking digestion of materials with a view to a comprehensive work of empirical generalisation. As is well known, in his earlier work of criticism and methodological controversy he was led to contend that for at least one generation economists must be content to spend their energies on descriptive work of this kind; and he thereby earned the reputation of aiming to reduce economics to a descriptive knowledge of details and to confine its method to the Baconian ground of generalisation by simple enumeration. But this exhaustive historical scrutiny and description of detail has always, in Professor Schmoller's view, been preliminary to an eventual theory of economic life. The survey of details and the empirical generalisations reached by its help are useful for the scientific purpose only as they serve the end of an eventual formulation of the laws of causation that work out in the process of economic life. The ulterior question, to which all else is subsidiary, is a question of the causes at work rather than a question of the historical uniformities observable in the sequence of phenomena. The scrutiny of his-

---

[4] E.g., in his controversy with Treitschke. See Grundfragen der Socialpolitik und der Volkswirtschaftslehre, particularly pp. 24, 25.

[5] E.g., Grundriss, pp. 225, 409, 411.

torical details serves this end by defining the scope and character of the several factors causally at work in the growth of culture, and, what is of more immediate consequence, as they are at work in the shaping of the economic activities and the economic aims of men engaged in this unfolding cultural process as it lies before the investigator in the existing situation.

In the preliminary work, then, of defining and characterising the causes or factors of economic life, historical investigation plays a large, if not the largest, part; but it is by no means the sole line of inquiry to which recourse is had for this purpose. Nor, it may be added, is this the sole use of historical inquiry. To the like end a comparative study of the climatic, geographical, and geological features of the community's environment is drawn into the inquiry; and more particularly there is a careful study of ethnographic parallels and a scrutiny of the psychological foundations of culture and the psychological factors involved in cultural change. Hence it appears that Professor Schmoller's work differs from that of the elder line of historical economics in respect of the scope and character of the preliminaries of economic theory no less than in the ulterior aim which he assigns the science. It is only by giving a very broad meaning to the term that this latest development of the science can be called an "historical" economics. It is Darwinian rather than Hegelian, although with the earmarks of Hegelian affiliation visible now and again; and it is "historical" only in a sense similar to that in which a Darwinian account of the evolution of economic institutions might be caller historical. For the distinguishing characteristic of Professor Schmoller's work, that wherein it differs from the earlier work of the economists of his general class, is that it aims at a Darwinistic account of the origin, growth, persistence, and variation of institutions, in so far as these institutions have to do with the economic aspect of life either as cause or as effect. In much of what he has to say, he is at one with his contemporaries and predecessors within the historical school; and he shows at many points both the excellences and weaknesses due to his "historical" antecedents. But his striking and characteristic merits lie in the direction of a post-Darwinian, causal theory of the origin and growth of species in institutions. In this line of theoretical inquiry Professor Schmoller is not alone, nor does he, perhaps, go so far or with such singleness of purpose in this direction as some others do at given points; but the seniority belongs to him, land he is also in the lead as regards the comprehensiveness of his work.

But to return to the Grundriss, to which recourse must be had to substantiate the characterisation here offered. The entire work as projected comprises an Introduction and four Books, of which the introduction and the first two books are contained in the volume already published. The two books yet to be published, in a second volume, promise to be of a length corresponding to the first two. The present volume should accordingly contain approximately three-fifths of the whole, counted by bulk. The scheme of the work is as follows: An Introduction (pp. 1-124) treats of (1) the Concept of Economics, (2) the Psychical, Ethical (or Conventional, sittliche), and Legal Foundations of Economic Life and of Culture, and (3) the Literature and Method of the Science. This is followed by Book I. (pp. 125-228) on Land, Population, and the Industrial Arts, considered as collective phenomena and factors in economic life, and Book II. (pp. 229-457), on the Constitution of Economic Society, its chief organs and the causal factors to which they are due. Books III and IV are to deal with the Circulation of Goods and the Distribution of Income, and to give a genetic account of the Development of Economic Society.

The course outlined differs noticeably from what has been customary in treatises on economics. The point of departure is a comprehensive general survey of the factors which enter into the growth of culture, with special reference to their economic bearing. This survey runs chiefly on psychological and ethnographic ground, historical inquiry in the stricter sense being relatively scant and obviously of secondary consequence. It is followed up with a more detailed and searching discussion of the factors engaged in the economic process in any given situation. The factors, or "collective phenomena," in question are not the time-honored Land, Labor, and Capital, but rather population, material environment, and technological conditions. Here, too, the discussion has to do with ethnographic rather than with properly historical material. The question of population concerns not the numerical force of laborers, but rather the diversity of race characteristics and the bearing of race endowment upon the growth of economic institutions.

The discussion of the material environment, again, has relatively little to say of the fertility of the soil, and gives much attention to diversities of climate, geographical situation, and geological and biological conditions. And this first book closes with a survey of the growth of technological knowledge and the industrial arts. In all this the significant innovation lies not so much in the character of the details. They are for the most part commonplace enough as details of the sciences from which they are borrowed. They are shrewdly chosen and handled in such a way as to bring out their bearing upon the ulterior questions about which the economist's interest centers; but there is, as might be expected, little attempt to go back of the returns given by specialists in the several lines of research that are laid under contribution. But the significance of it all lies rather in the fact that material of this kind should have been drawn upon for a foundation for economic theory, and that it should have seemed necessary to Professor Schmoller to make this introductory survey so comprehensive and so painstaking as it is. Its meaning is that these features of human nature and these forces of nature and circumstances of environment are the agencies out of whose interaction the economic situation has arisen by a cumulative process of change, and that it is this cumulative process of development, and its complex and unstable outcome, that are to be the economist's subject-matter. The theoretical outcome for which such a foundation is prepared is necessarily of a genetic kind. It necessarily seeks to know and explain the structure and functions of economic society in terms of how and why they have come to be what they are, not, as so many economic writers have explained them, in terms of what they are good for and what they ought to be. It means, in other words, a deliberate attempt to substitute an inquiry into the efficient causes of economic life in the place of empirical generalisations, on the one hand, and speculations as to the eternal fitness of things, on the other hand. It follows from the nature of the case that an economics of this genetic character, working on grounds of the kind indicated, comprises nothing in the way of advice or admonition, no maxims of expediency, and no economic, political, or cultural creed. How nearly Professor Schmoller conforms to this canon of continence is another question. The above indicates the scope of such doctrines as are consistently derivable from the premises with which the work under review starts out, not the scope of its writer's speculations on economic matters.

The second book, by the help of prehistoric and ethnographic material as well as history, deals with the evolution of the methods of social organisation, - the growth of institutions in so far as this growth shapes or is shaped by the exigencies of economic life. The "organs," or social-economic institutions, whose life history is passed in review are: the family; the methods of settlement and domicile, in town and country; the political units of control and administration; differentiation of functions between industrial and other classes and groups; ownership, its growth and distribution; social classes and associations; business enterprise, industrial organisations and corporations. As regards the singleness of purpose with which Professor Schmoller has carried out the scheme of economic theory for which he has sketched the outlines and pointed the way, it is not possible to speak with the same confidence as of his preliminary work. It goes without saying that this further work of elaboration is excellent after its kind; and this excellence, which was to be looked for at Professor Schmoller's hands, may easily divert the reader's attention from the shortcomings of the work in respect of kind rather than of quality. Now, while a broad generalisation on this head may be hazardous and is to be taken with a large margin, still, with due allowance, the following generalization will probably stand, so far as regards this first volume. So long as the author is occupied with the life-history of institutions down to contemporary developments, so long his discussion proceeds by the dry light of the scientific interest, simply, as the term "scientific" is understood among the modern adepts of the natural sciences; but so soon as he comes to close quarters with the situation of to-day, and reaches the point where a dispassionate analysis and exposition of the causal complex at work in contemporary institutional changes should begin, so soon the scientific light breaks up into all the colors of the rainbow, and the author becomes an eager and eloquent counselor, and argues the question of what ought to be and what modern society must do to be saved.

The argument at this point loses the character of a genetic explanation of phenomena, and takes on the character of appeal and admonition, urged on grounds of expediency, of morality, of good taste, of hygiene, of political ends, and even of religion. All this, of course, is what we are used to in the common run of writers of the historical school; but those students whose interest centers in the science rather than in the ways and means of maintaining the received cultural forms of German society have long fancied they had ground to hope for something more to the purpose when Professor Schmoller came to put forth his great systematic work. Brilliant and no doubt valuable in its way and for its end, this digression into homiletics and reformatory advice means that the argument is running into the sands just at the stage where the science can least afford it. It is precisely at this point, where men of less years and breadth and weight would find it difficult to bold tenaciously to the course of cause and effect through the maze of jarring interests and sentiments that make up the contemporary situation, - it is precisely at this point that a genetic theory of economic life most needs the guidance of the firm, trained, dispassionate hand of the master.

And at this point his guidance all but fails us. What has just been said applies generally to Professor Schmoller's treatment of contemporary economic development, and it should be added that it applies at nearly all points with more or less of qualification. But the qualifications required are not large enough to belie the general characterisation just offered. It would be asking too large an indulgence to follow the point up in this place through all the discussions of the volume that fairly come tinder this criticism. The most that may be done is to point for illustration to the handling which two or three of the social-economic "organs" receive. So, for instance, Book II opens with an account of the family and its place and function in the structure of economic society. The discussion proceeds along the beaten paths of ethnographic research, with repeated and well-directed recourse to the psychological knowledge that Professor Schmoller always has well in hand.

Coming down into recent times, the discussion still proceeds to show how the large economic changes of late mediaeval and early modern times acted to break down the patriarchal regime of the earlier culture; but at the same time there comes into sight (pp. 245-249) a bias in favor of the recent as against the earlier form of the household. The author is no longer content to show the exigencies which set the earlier patriarchal household aside in favor of the modified patriarchal household of more recent times. He also offers reasons why the later, modified form is intrinsically the more desirable; reasons, it should perhaps be said, which may be well taken, but which are beside the point so far as regards a scientific explanation of the changes under discussion.

The closing paragraphs of the section (91) dwell with a kindly insistence on the many elements of strength and beauty possessed by the form of household organisation handed down from the past generation to the present. The facts herewith recited by the author are, no doubt, of weight, and must be duly taken account of by any economist who ventures on a genetic discussion of the present situation and the changing fortunes of the received household. But Professor Schmoller has failed even to point out in what manner these elements of strength and beauty have in the recent past or may in the present and immediate future causally affect the fortunes of the institution. The failure to turn the material in question to scientific account becomes almost culpable in Professor Schmoller, since there are few, if any, who are in so favorable a position to outline the argument which a theoretical account of the situation at this point must take. Plainly, as shown by Professor Schmoller's argument, economic exigencies are working an incessant cumulative change in the form of organisation of the modern household; but he has done little towards pointing out in what manner and with what effect these exigencies come into play.

Neither has he gone at all into the converse question, equally grave as a question of economic theory, of how the persistence, even though qualified, of the patriarchal family has modified and is modifying economic structure and function at other points and qualifying or accentuating the very exigencies themselves to which the changes wrought in the institution are to be traced. Plainly, too, the strength and beauty of the traditionally received form of the household - that is to say, the habits of life and of complacency which are bound up with this household - are elements of importance in the modern situation as affects the degree of persistence and the direction of change which this institution shows under modern circumstances. They are psychological facts, facts of habit and propensity and spiritual fitness, the efficiency of which as live forces making for survival or variation is in this connection probably second to that of no other factors that could be named.

We had, therefore, almost a right to expect that Professor Schmoller's profound and comprehensive erudition in the fields of psychology and cultural growth should turn these facts to better ends than a preachment concerning an intrinsically desirable consummation. Regarding the present visible disintegration of the family, and the closely related "woman question," Professor Schmoller's observations are of much the same texture. He notes the growing disinclination to the old-fashioned family life on the part of the working population, and shows that there are certain economic causes for this growth or deterioration of sentiment. What he has to offer is made up of the commonplaces of latter-day social-economic discussion, and is charged with a strong undertone of deprecation. What the trend of the causes at work to alter or fortify this body of sentiment may be, counts for very little in what he says on the present movement or on the immediate future of the institution. The best he has to offer on the "woman question" is an off-hand reference of the ground of sentiment on which it rests to a recrudescence of the eighteenth century spirit of *egalite*.

This notion of the equality of the sexes he refutes in graceful and affecting terms, and he pleads for the unbroken preservation of woman's sphere and man's primacy; as if the matter of superiority or inferiority between the sexes could conceivably be anything more than a conventional outcome of the habits of life imposed upon the community by the circumstances under which they live. How it has come to pass that under the economic exigencies of the past the physical and temperamental diversity between the sexes has been conventionally construed into a superiority of the man and an inferiority of the woman, - on this head he has no more to say or to suggest than on the correlate question of why this conventional interpretation of the facts has latterly not been holding its ancient ground. The discussion of the family and of the relation of the sexes, in modern culture, is marked throughout by unwillingness or inability to penetrate behind the barrier of conventional finality. The discussion of the family just cited occupies the opening chapter of Book II. For a further instance of Professor Schmoller's handling of a modern economic problem, reference may be had to the closing chapter of Book I., on the "Development of Technological Expedients and its Economic Significance," but more particularly the sections (84-86) on the modern machine industry (pp. 211-228). In this discussion, also, the point of interest is the attention given to the latter-day phenomena of machine industry, and the author's method and animus in dealing with them. There is (pp. 211-218) a condensed and competent presentation of the main characteristics of the modern "machine age," followed (pp. 218-228) by a critical discussion of its cultural value.

The customary eulogy, but with more than the customary discrimination, is given to the advantages of the regime of the machine in point of economy, creature comforts, and intellectual sweep; and it is pointed out how the regime of the machine has brought about a redistribution of wealth and of population and a reorganisation and redistribution of social and economic structures and functions. It is pointed out (p. 223) that the gravest social effect of the machine industry has been the creation of a large class of wage laborers. The material circumstances into which this class has been thrown, particularly in point of physical comfort, are dealt with in a sober and discriminating way; and it is shown (p. 224) that in the days of its fuller development the machine's regime has evolved a class of trained laborers who not only live in comfort, but are sound and strong in mind and body. But with the citation of these facts the pursuit of the chain of cause and effect in this modern machine situation comes to an end.

The remainder of the space given to the subject is occupied with extremely sane and well-advised criticism, moral and esthetic, and indications of what the proper ideals and ends of endeavor should be. Professor Schmoller misses the opportunity he here has of dealing with this material in a scientific spirit and with some valuable results for economic theory. He could, it is not too bold to assume, have sketched for us an effective method and line of research to be pursued, for instance, in following up the scientific question of what may be the cultural, spiritual effects of the machine's regime upon this large body of trained workmen, and what this body of trained workmen in its turn counts for as a factor in shaping the institutional growth of the present and the economic and cultural situation of tomorrow. Work of this kind, there is reason to believe, Professor Schmoller could have done with better effect, than any of his colleagues in the science; for he is, as already noticed above, possessed of the necessary qualifications in the way of psychological training, broad knowledge of the play of cause and effect in cultural growth, and an ability to take a scientific point of view. Instead of this he harks back again to the dreary homiletical waste of the traditional Historismus.

It seems as if a topic which he deals with as an objective matter so long as it lies outside the sphere of every-day humanitarian and social solicitude, becomes a matter to be passed upon by conventional standards of taste, dignity, morality, and the like, so soon as it comes within the sweep of latter-day German sentiment. This habit of treating a given problem from these various and shifting points of view at times gives a kaleido-scopic effect that is not without interest. So in the matter of the technically trained working population in the machine industry, to which reference has already been made, something of an odd confusion appears when expressions taken from diverse phases of the discussion are brought side by side. He speaks of this class at one point (p. 224) as "sound, strong, spir-itually and morally advancing," superior in all these virtues to the working classes of other times and places. At another point (pp. 250-253) be speaks of the same popular element, under the designation of "socialists," as per-verse, degenerate, and reactionary. This latter characterisation may be substantially correct, but it proceeds on grounds of taste and predilection, not on grounds of scientifically determinable cause and effect. And the two characterisations apply to the same elements of population; for the substantial core and tone-giving factor of the radical socialistic element in the German community is, notoriously, just this technically trained popu-lation of the industrial towns where the discipline of the machine industry has been at work with least mitigation.

The only other fairly isolable element of a radical socialistic complexion is found among the students of modern science. Now, further, in his spec-ulations on the relation of technological knowledge to the advance of cul-ture, Professor Schmoller points out (e.g., p. 226) that a high degree of cul-ture connotes, on the whole, a high degree of technological efficiency, and conversely. In this connection he makes use of the terms Halbkulturvolker and Ganzkulturvolker to designate different degrees of cultural maturity. It is curious to reflect, in the light of what he has to say on these several heads, that if the socialistically affected, technically trained population of the industrial towns, together with the radical-socialistic men of science, were abstracted from the German population, leaving substantially the peasantry, the slums, and the aristocracy great and small, the resulting German community would unquestionably have to be classed as a Halbkulturvolk in Professor Schmoller's scheme. Whereas the elements abstracted, if taken by themselves, would as unquestionably be classed among the Ganzkulturvolker. In conclusion, one may turn to the conclud-ing chapter (Book II., Chapter vii.) of the present volume for a final illus-tration of Professor Schmoller's method and animus in handling a modern economic problem.

All the more so as this chapter on business enterprise better sustains that scientific attitude which the introductory outline leads the reader to look for throughout. It shows how modern business enterprise is in the main an outgrowth of commercial activity, as also that it has retained the commercial spirit down to the present. The motive force of business en-terprise is the self-seeking quest of dividends; but Professor Schmoller shows, with more dispassionate insight than many economists, that this self-seeking motive is hemmed in and guided at all points in the course of its development by considerations and conventions that are not of a pri-marily self-seeking kind. He is not content to point to the beneficent working of a harmony of interests, but sketches the play of forces whereby a self-seeking business traffic has come to serve the interests of the community. Business enterprise has gradually emerged and come into its present central and dominant position in the community's industry as a concomitant of the growth of individual ownership and pecuniary discretion in modern life. It is therefore a phase of the modern cultural situation; and its survival and the direction of its further growth are therefore conditioned by the exigencies of the modern cultural situation. What this modern cultural situation is and what are the forces, essentially psychological, which shape the further growth of the situation, no one is better fitted to discuss than Professor Schmoller; and he has also given valuable indications (pp. 428-457) of what these factors are and how the inquiry into their working must be conducted. But even here, where a dispassionate tracing-out of the sequence of cause and effect should be easier to undertake, because less readily blurred with sentiment, than in the case, e.g., of the family, the work of tracing the developmental sequence tapers off into advice and admonition proceeding on the assumption that the stage now reached is, or at least should be, final.

The attention in the later pages diverges from the process of growth and its conditioning circumstances, to the desirability of maintaining the good results attained and to the ways and means of holding fast that which is good in the outcome already achieved. The question to which an answer is sought in discussing the present phase of the development is not a question as to what is taking place as respects the institution of business enterprise, but rather a question as to what form should be given to an optimistic policy of fostering business enterprise and turning it to account for the common good. At this point, as elsewhere, though perhaps in a less degree than elsewhere, the existing form of the institution is accepted as a finality. All this is disappointing in view of the fact that at no other point do modern economic institutions bear less of an air of finality than in the forms and conventions of business organisations and relations. As Professor Schmoller remarks (p. 455), the scope and character of business undertakings necessarily conform to the circumstances of the time, not to any logical scheme of development from small to great or from simple to complex.

So also, one might be tempted to say, the expediency and the chance of ultimate survival of business enterprise is itself an open question, to be answered by a scrutiny of the forces that make for its survival or alteration, not by advice as to the best method of sustaining and controlling it. What has here been said in criticism of Professor Schmoller's work, particularly as regards his departure from the path of scientific research in dealing with present-day phenomena, may, of course, have to be qualified, if not entirely set aside, when his work is completed with the promised genetic survey of modern institutions to be set forth in the concluding fourth book. Perhaps it may even be said that there is fair hope, on general grounds, of such a consummation; but the present volume does not afford ground for a confident expectation of this kind. It is perhaps needless, perhaps gratuitous, to add that the strictures offered indicate, after all, but relatively slight shortcomings in a work of the first magnitude.

Chapter 6

The Use of Loan Credit
in Modern Business

There is no intention here to offer a restatement of the general theory of credit, but merely to discuss certain features of the use of credit peculiarly relevant to the conduct of modern business. The subject of inquiry is the resort to credit as an expedient in the quest of profits. The larger, and in some relations perhaps the more important, aspects of credit are accordingly not touched on here, except so far as seems indispensable to the theory of that business traffic upon which the inquiry centers. The inquiry, therefore, turns about the business motives that lead to an extensive use of credit and about certain of the general consequences which credit extension has for the course of business affairs and for the working of the modern industrial system.

Such points of the theory of credit at large as unavoidably come into the discussion are passed in review in the most summary manner. Familiarity with the terms and concepts employed is presumed to the extent necessary to follow the discussion. The thesis is advisedly accepted, by men of affairs as well as by economists, that the use of credit is indispensable to a facile working of the modern industrial system. It may be added without hesitation that such use is also unavoidable under modern circumstances. The extensive use of credit follows necessarily from business competition. Credit serves two main uses in the regular course of such business as is occupied with the conduct of industry: (a) that of deferred payments in the purchase and sale of goods — book accounts, bills, checks, and the like belong chiefly under this head; and (b) loans or debts — notes, stock shares, interest-bearing securities, deposits, call loans, etc., belong chiefly here. These two categories of credit extension are by no means clearly distinct. Forms of credit which commonly serve the one purpose may be turned to the other use; but the two uses of credit are, after all, broadly distinguishable.

For many purposes of economic theory such a distinction might not be serviceable, or even practicable; it is here made merely for present use. It is chiefly with credits of the latter class, or rather with credit in so far as it is turned to use for the latter purpose, that this inquiry is concerned. The most obvious service of loan credit, to which attention is frequently directed, in this connection is that by its use the discretionary control of industrial property is transferred from owners who do not want to manage it to other business-men who wish to assume the management. Seen from the standpoint of the industrial process at large such a transfer may commonly be construed, without violence, as a transfer of management to more competent hands. To the extent to which this is the case there results a presumptive gain in industrial efficiency at large; the consequent advantage to the community is patent, as are also the advantages which result to the borrower or the organizer of any enterprise to which such advances of capital are invited. But it is to be noted that the business-man does not put his purposes in these terms in seeking an extension of credit, nor need such an extension serve simply this end of shifting the management of the material equipment of industry to more competent or more willing hands. If that were the extent of the functioning of loan credit in industry it would be wholly gratuitous, as well as presumptuous, to offer a discussion of the subject in this place, since that function of credit has been well and largely discussed by many competent economists[1] .This may be the most important function of loan credit, but for the purpose in hand its functioning beyond or aside from this, its main service, is of more immediate interest. That it has substantial consequences of a different kind becomes particularly evident in a period of acute liquidation.

At such a time the inconveniences, not to say the disastrous effects, of a large extension of loan credit attract general attention. These disadvantageous consequences, in the way of panic, insolvency, etc., are commonly said to come of an "undue," "abnormal," "excessive," or "illegitimate" extension of credit during that period of speculative advance which commonly precedes the liquidation. But there is no hard and fast line to be drawn between "due" and " undue," or "normal" and "abnormal," extensions of loan credit[2] as regards either the motives of the borrowers, the methods by which the transactions are carried through, the kind of collateral, or the uses to which the borrowed funds are turned. There may be a somewhat consistent difference on one or more of these points between items which are well within the limits of legitimacy, on the one hand, and of illegitimacy, on the other hand, but the two categories shade off into one another by insensible gradations.

Not only that, but with respect to a very appreciable proportion of the items the question as to whether they are an "excessive" extension of credit can be answered only in the light of subsequent facts. If, at a period of liquidation, a given item of loan credit ends its life-history in insolvency, then it was excessive or illegitimate; if not, then it was not. The question of excessiveness, therefore, may, and in the case of an appreciable proportion of loan-credit items it probably does, depend on circumstances of an essentially fortuitous character and which could, therefore, not be foreseen. The "excessive" or undue extension follows as a continuation of the conservative or moderate resort to credit, as a simple progressive change in magnitude, without its being possible to specify a point in the progression beyond which there comes a change in kind. The ulterior test of undueness is insolvency, which is not the result of a given arithmetical proportion of indebtedness to assets, simply, but is an eventuality conditioned by other circumstances as well. Circumstances may change in such

---

[1] Cf., e. g. Knies, Geld, chap, iii; Credit, chap, ix; J. S. Mill, Political Economy, Book III, chap. xi

[2] Cf. Laughlin, "Credit", Decennial Publications, Vol. IV, pp. 22-4.

a way that a credit extension which was normal or legitimate at its inception will in the course of time become undue or abnormal; as, e. g., if there supervenes a shrinkage in the value of the collateral[3].

In detail, a given item of credit extension, resting on a given block of collateral, may conceivably be moderate one week, excessive the next week, and moderate again the next week after, owing simply to a fluctuation in the market value of the collateral, without the creditor or debtor having done anything to upset the balance; as will happen, e, gr., in the case of a call loan secured by stocks or similar collateral whose quotations fluctuate. Looked at from this post factum standpoint, from which alone the question of an aggregate excessiveness can be confidently judged, the extension of credit is accounted "undue," "excessive," or "abnormal" in so far as the debtors are unable to repay loans falling due, and to pay interest on securities outstanding, without cutting into their paid-up capital or reducing their earnings much below a "reasonable" rate[4].

The disastrous consequences of an undue extension of credit primarily affect business — the immediate consequence is a liquidation between business-men; secondarily, of course, the liquidation carries a serious disturbance to the industrial process proper. The incentives which determine the business-man's recourse to credit are of the same kind whether the resulting extension proves "excessive" or not. The question therefore becomes: What are the business incentives in the case, and why do these incentives carry the extension of credit to a length which the sequel proves to be undue or illegitimate? It is this question which is here sought to be answered. Suppose due credit arrangements have already been made — in the way of investments in stocks, interest-bearing securities, and the like — such as to place the management of the industrial equipment in competent hands. This supposition is not a violent one, since a condition roughly approximating to this prevails in any quiescent period of industry, when there is no appreciable depression.

Under these "normal" conditions, the capital invested in any given industrial venture is turned over within a certain approximately definite length of time. The length of time occupied by the turnover may vary from one establishment to another, but in any given case the length of the turnover is one of the important factors that determine the chances of gain for the business concern in question. Indeed, if the general conditions of the trade and of the market are given, the two factors which determine the status and value of a given sound concern, as seen from the business-man's standpoint, are the magnitude of the turnover and the length of time it occupies. The business-man's object is to get the largest aggregate gain from his business. It is manifestly for his interest, as far as may be, to

---

[3] Ibid., p. 24.

[4] The question of "undueness" relates to a (varying) proportion between the credit extension and the capitalized value of the collateral, for the time being; it therefore relates to the presumptive earnings of the property represented by the collateral. - See pp. 11, 12, 16, n. 21, below.

shorten the process out of which his earnings are drawn[5] or, in other words, to shorten the period in which he turns over his capital. If the turnover consumes less than the time ordinarily allowed in the line of industry in which he is engaged, he gains more than the current rate of profits in that line of business, other things equal; whereas he loses if the turnover takes more than the normal time. This fact is forcibly expressed in the maxim:

"Small profits and quick returns." There are two chief means of shortening the interval of the turnover, currently resorted to in industrial business. The first is the adoption of more efficient, time-saving industrial processes. Improvements of technique having this in view are gaining in importance in the later developments of business, since a closer attention is now given to the time element in investments, and great advances have been made in this direction[6].A second expedient for accelerating the rate of turnover is the competitive pushing of sales, through larger and more persistent advertising, and the like. It is needless to say that this means of accelerating business also receives due attention at the hands of modern business-men. But the magnitude of the turnover, "the volume of business," is of no less consequence than its rapidity. It is, of course, a trite commonplace that the earnings of any industrial business are a joint function of the rate of turnover and the volume of business[7].The businessman may reach his end of increased earnings by either the one or the other expedient, and he commonly has recourse to both if he can. His means of increasing the magnitude of the turnover is a resort to credit and a close husbanding of his assets.

He is under a constant incentive to increase his liabilities and to discount his bills receivable. Indebtedness in this way comes to serve much the same purpose, as regards the rate of earnings, as does a time-saving improvement in the processes of industry[8]. The effect of the use of credit on the part of a businessman so placed is much the same as if his capital had been turned over a greater number of times in the year. It is accordingly to his interest to extend his credit as far as may be and as far as the state of the market will admit.

---

[5] This, of course, has nothing to say to Bohm-Bawerk's theory of the enhancement of production through lengthening the processes of industry. His theory of the "round-about method" applies to the technical, material efficiency of the mechanical process; whereas the point in question here is the interval occupied in the turning over of a given business capital. Bohm-Bawerk's position may be questionable, however, on other grounds.

[6] Cf. e. g. Werner Sombart, "Der Stil des modernen Wirthschaftslebens," Archiv für soz. Gesetzg. u. Statistik, Vol. XVII, pp. 1-20, especially pp. 4-15. Reprinted as chap. iv, Vol. II, of Der moderne Kapitalismus (Leipzig, 1902).

[7] Cf., e. g. Marshall, Principles of Economics (3d ed.), Book VI, chap, vii, secs. 3 and 4.

[8] Cf. Laughlin, "Credit," p. 8.

[9]But on funds obtained on credit the debtor has to pay interest, which, being deducted from the gross earnings of the business, leaves, as net gain due to his use of credit, only the amount by which the increment of gross earnings exceeds the interest charge. This sets a somewhat elastic limit to the advantageous use of loan credit in business. In ordinary times, however, and under capable management, the current rate of business earnings exceeds the rate of interest by an appreciable amount; and in times of ordinary prosperity, therefore, it is commonly advantageous to employ credit in the way indicated. Still more so in brisk times, when opportunities for earnings are many and promise to increase. To turn the proposition about, so as to show the run of business motives in the case: whenever the capable business manager sees an appreciable difference between the cost of a given credit extension and the gross increase of gains to be got by its use, he will seek to extend his credit.

But under the regime of competitive business whatever is generally advantageous becomes a necessity to all competitors. Those who take advantage of the opportunities afforded by credit are in a position to undersell any others who are similarly placed in all but this respect. Broadly speaking, recourse to credit becomes the general practice, the regular course of competitive business management, and competition goes on on the basis of such a use of credit, as an auxiliary to the capital in hand. So that the competitive earning capacity of business enterprises comes to rest on the basis, not of paid-up capital alone, but of capital plus such borrowed funds as this capital will support. The competitive rate of earnings is brought to correspond with this basis of operation; the consequence being that under such competitive employment of credit the aggregate earnings of an enterprise resting on a given bona fide capital will be but slightly larger than it might have been if such a general recourse to credit to swell the volume of business did not prevail.

But since such use of credit prevails, a further consequence is that any concern involved in the open business competition, which does not or cannot take recourse to credit to swell its volume of business, will be unable to earn a "reasonable" rate of profits. So that the general practice drives all competitors to the use of the same expedient; but since the advantage to be derived from this expedient is a relative advantage only, the

---

9 The turnover will count for more in gross earnings at current rates if instead of his own capital alone the business-man also engages whatever funds he can borrow by using his capital as collateral. The turnover counted on capital (value of the industrial equipment) plus credit, at current rates, will be greater than that counted on the capital alone used without credit extension. The turnover may be expressed as the product of the mass of values employed multiplied by the velocity. Hence, if credit be taken as an indeterminate fraction of the capital used as collateral, we may say that Turnover = $1/\text{time}$ (capital + capital/n); i. e., $T = 1/t$ (c+ c/n) = (c+c/n)/t; or t = (c+c/n)/T The algebraic statement serves to bring out the equivalence between an acceleration of the rate of turnover and an increase of the volume of business capital.

universality of the practice results in but a slight, if any, increase of the aggregate earnings of the business community.

Borrowed funds afford any given business-man a differential advantage as against other competitors; but it is, in the main, a differential advantage only. The competitive use of such borrowed funds in extending business operations may, incidentally, throw the management of some portion of the industrial process into more competent or less competent hands. So far as this happens, the credit operations in question and the use of the borrowed funds may increase or diminish the output of industry at large, and so may affect the aggregate earnings of the business community. But, apart from such individual shifting of the management of industry to more competent (or less competent) hands, this competitive use of borrowed funds is without aggregate effect. The current or reasonable rate of profits is, roughly, the rate of profits at which business-men are content to employ the actual capital which they have in hand[10] .

A general resort to credit extension as an auxiliary to the capital in hand results, on the whole, in a competitive lowering of the rate of profits, computed on capital plus credit, to such a point as would not be attractive to a business-man who must confine himself to the employment of capital without credit extension. On an average, it may be said, under the circumstances of this credit extension the aggregate earnings of the aggregate capital with credit extension are but slightly greater than the aggregate earnings of the same capital without credit extension would be in the absence of a competitive use of credit extension. But under modem conditions business cannot profitably be done by any one of the competitors without the customary resort to credit. Without the customary resort to credit a "reasonable" return could not be obtained on the investment.

All this applies to Such extension of credit as exceeds what may serve the purpose of distributing the management of the industrial, material apparatus to competent hands; or, in other words, it applies to such resort to credit as aims at a competitive extension of business on the part of competent managers. Probably at no point in the progressive competitive extension of credit is there no effect had in the way of shifting the management of industry to more competent hands; and at no point, therefore, can it confidently be said that a further extension of credit has no effect in the way of enhancing the efficiency of industry.

But, after all is said, it remains true that the extension of credit under modern conditions has the two distinguishable effects here spoken for; and this is the point of the argument. To the extent to which the competitive recourse to credit is of the character here indicated — to the extent to which it is a competitive bidding for funds between competent managers — it may be said that, taken in the aggregate, the funds so added to business capital represent no material capital or "productive goods." They are business capital only; they swell the volume of business, as counted in

---

[10] See Marshall, as above.

terms of price, etc., but they do not directly swell the volume of industry, since they do not add to the aggregate material apparatus of industry, or alter the character of the processes employed, or enhance the degree of efficiency with which industry is managed.

The "buoyancy" which a speculative inflation of values gives to industrial business may indirectly increase the material output of industry by enhancing the intensity with which the industrial process is carried on under the added stimulus; but apart from this psychological effect, the expansion of business capital through credit extension has no aggregate industrial effect. This secondary effect of credit inflation may be very considerable, and is always present in brisk times. It is commonly obvious enough to be accounted the chief characteristic of a period of "prosperity." For a theory of industry this indirect effect of credit inflation would be its main characteristic, but for a theory of business it occupies the place of a corollary only. To the view set forth above the objection may present itself that all funds borrowed represent property owned by someone (the lender or his creditors) and transferred, in usufruct, by the loan transaction to the borrower; and that these funds can, therefore, be converted to productive uses, like any other funds, by drawing into the industrial process, directly or indirectly, the material items of wealth whose fluent form these funds are.

The objection fails at two points: (a) while the loans may be covered by property held by the lender, they are not fully covered by property which is not already otherwise engaged; and even if such were the case, it would (b) not follow that the use of these funds would increase the technical (material) outfit of industry. As to the first point (a): Loans made by the financial houses in the way of deposits or other advances on collateral are only to a fractional extent covered by liquid assets[11] and anything but liquid assets is evidently beside the point of the present question. An inconsiderable fraction of these loans is represented by liquid assets. The greater part of the advances made by banking houses, for instance, rest on the lender's probable ability to pay eventually, on demand or at maturity, any claims that may in the course of business be presented against the lender on account of the advances made by him. It is a business truism that no banking house could at a moment meet all its outstanding obligations[12].

A necessary source of banking profits is the large excess of the volume of business over reserves. As to (b): Another great part of the basis of such loans is made up of invested funds and collateral held by the lender. These at the same time are much of the basis on which rests the lender's probable ability to pay claims presented. But these investments, in industry or real estate, in interest-bearing securities and collateral of whatever de-

---

[11] Property convertible into cash at will.

[12] The legally obligatory reserve for national banks in this country, for instance, is 25 per cent of combined note circulation and deposits in central reserve banks, 15 per cent in others. – Revised Statutes, 5191.

scription, represent future income of the lender's debtors (as, e. gr., government and municipal securities), or property which is already either engaged in the industrial process or tied up in forms of wealth (as, e. gr., real estate) which do not lend themselves to industrial uses. Loans obtained on property which has no present industrial use, which cannot in its present form or under existing circumstances be employed in the processes of industry (as, e. g., speculative real estate), or loans on property which is already engaged in the industrial process (as, e. g., stocks, industrial plant, goods on hand, real estate in use),[13] represent, for the purpose in hand, nothing more substantial than a fictitious duplication of material items that cannot be drawn into the industrial process. Therefore such loans cannot, at least not directly, swell the aggregate industrial apparatus or enhance the aggregate productivity of industry; for the items which here serve as collateral are already previously in use in industry to the extent to which they can be used.

Property of these kinds — what is already in use in industry and what is not of use for industrial purposes — may be "coined into means of payment" and so made to serve as additional pecuniary (business) capital, but such property is mechanically incapable of serving as additional material (industrial) capital. To a very considerable extent the funds involved in these loans, therefore, have only a pecuniary (business) existence, not a material (industrial) one; and, so far as that is true, they represent, in the aggregate, only fictitious industrial equipment. Even such inconsiderable portion of them, however, as represents metallic reserves also adds nothing to the effective material apparatus of industry; since money as such, whether metallic or promissory, is of no direct industrial effect; as is evident from the well-known fact that the absolute quantity of the precious metals in use is a matter of no consequence to the conduct of either business or industry, so long as the quantity neither increases nor decreases by an appreciable amount. *Nummus nummum parere non potest.* So that all advances made by banking houses or by other creditors in a like case; whether the advances are made on mortgage, collateral or personal notes, in the form of deposits, note issues, or what not; whether they are taken to represent the items of property covered by the collateral, the cash reserves of the banks, or the general solvency of the creditor or debtor — all these "advances" go to increase the "capital" of which business-men have the disposal; but for the material purposes of industry taken in the aggregate they are purely fictitious items[14].

---

[13] This takes account of advances made by other lenders than the regular banking houses who exclude mortgages on real estate from their collateral; such, e. g., as the long-time advances (investments in securities) made by savings banks, insurance companies, minor private and mortgage banks, private lenders, etc.

[14] This truism is frequently overlooked in theoretical discussions; hence, as the present argument requires its due recognition, it is here stated in this explicit way.

Cash loans (such as savings-bank deposits[15] and the like) belong in the same category. All these advances afford the borrower a differential advantage in bidding against other business-men for the control and use of industrial processes and materials; they afford him a differential advantage in the distribution of the material means of industry; but they constitute no aggregate addition to the material means of industry at large. Funds of whatever character are a pecuniary fact, not an industrial one; they serve the distribution of the control of industry only, not its mechanically productive work.

Loan credit in excess of what may serve to transfer the management of industrial materials from the owner to a more competent user — that is to say, in so far as it is not, in effect, of the nature of a lease of industrial plant — serves on the whole not to increase the quantity of the material means of industry nor, directly, to enhance the effectiveness of their use; but, taken in the aggregate, it serves only to widen the discrepancy between business capital and industrial equipment. So long as times are brisk this discrepancy ordinarily goes on widening through a progressive extension of credit. Funds obtained on credit are applied to extend the business; competing business-men bid up the material items of industrial equipment by the use of funds so obtained; the value of the material items employed in industry advances; the aggregate of values employed in a given undertaking increases, with or without a physical increase of the industrial material engaged; but since an advance of credit rests on the collateral as expressed in terms of value, an enhanced value of the property affords a basis for a further extension of credit, and so on. Now, the base line of business transactions is the money value (market or exchange value, price) of the items involved, not their material efficiency. The value of the money unit is by conventional usage held to be invariable, and the lenders perforce proceed on this assumption, so long as they proceed at all[16].

Consequently any increase of the aggregate money values involved in the industrial business enterprises concerned will afford a basis for an extension of loans, indistinguishable from any other basis of capitalized value, even if the increase of capitalized values is due to credit advances previously made on the full cash value of the property hypothecated. The extension of loans on collateral, such as stock and similar values involved in industrial business, has therefore in the nature of things a cumulative character. This cumulative extension goes on, if otherwise undisturbed, so

---

[15] The cash loans made by depositors to savings banks in the form of deposits

[16] Few perhaps would in set terms maintain an argument that the value of money does not vary, but still fewer would, in a credit transaction, proceed on a supposition at variance with that position. As the economists are accustomed to say, money is the standard of deferred payments. It is also, in the unreflecting apprehension of those who have practically to deal with wealth phenomena, felt to be the standard and inflexible measure of wealth. The fact that this conventional usage is embodied in law acts greatly to fortify the naive acceptance of money and price as the definitive terms of wealth.

long as no adverse price phenomenon obtrudes itself with sufficient force to convict this cumulative enhancement of capitalized values of imbecility.

The extension of credit proceeds on the putative stability of the money value of the capitalized industrial material, whose money value is cumulatively augmented by this extension itself. But the money value of the collateral is at the same time the capitalized value of the property computed on the basis of its presumptive earning capacity. These two methods of rating the value of collateral must approximately coincide, if the capitalization is to afford a stable basis for credit; and when an obvious discrepancy arises between the outcome given by the two ratings, then a re-rating will be had in which the rating on the basis of earning capacity must be accepted as definitive, since earnings are the ground fact about which all business transactions turn and to which all business enterprise converges. A manifest discrepancy presently arises in this way between the aggregate nominal capital (capital plus loans) engaged in business, on the one hand, and the actual rate of earning capacity of this business capital, on the other hand; and when this discrepancy has become patent a period of liquidation begins.

To give an easier view of the part played by loan credit in this discrepancy between the business capital and the earning capacity of industrial concerns, it will be in place to indicate more summarily what are the factors at play. The earnings of the business community, taken as a whole, are derived from the marketable output of goods and services turned out by the industrial process — disregarding such earnings as accrue to one concern merely at the cost of another. The effective industrial capital, from the use of which this output, and therefore these earnings, arise, is the aggregate of capitalized material items actually engaged in industry. The business capital, on the other hand, is made up of this capitalized industrial material, plus good-will, plus whatever funds are obtained on credit by using this capitalized industrial material as collateral, plus funds obtained on other, non-industrial, property used as collateral.

Through the competitive use of funds obtained on credit, as spoken of above, the nominal value of the capitalized industrial material is cumulatively augmented so as to make it approximately equal to its original capitalization plus whatever funds are obtained on credit of all kinds. On this basis of an expanded collateral a further extension of credit takes place, and the funds so obtained are incorporated in the business capital and turned to the like competitive use, and so on. Capital and earnings are counted in terms of the money unit. Counted in these terms, the earnings (industrial output) are also increased by the process of inflation through credit, since the competitive use of funds spoken of acts to bid up prices of whatever products are used in industry, and of whatever speculative property is presumed to have some eventual industrial use. But the nominal magnitude (value) of the earnings is not increased in as strong a ratio as that of the business capital; since the demand whereby the values of the output are regulated is not altogether a business demand (for productive goods), but is in great part, and, indeed, in the last resort mainly, reducible to a consumptive demand for finished goods[17].

Looking at credit extension and its use for purposes of capital as a whole, the outcome which presents itself most strikingly at a period of liquidation is the redistribution of the ownership of industrial property. The funds obtained on credit are in great measure invested competitively in the same aggregate of material items that is already employed in industry apart from any use of loan credit, with the result that the same range of items of wealth are rated at a larger number of money units. In these items of wealth — which, apart from the use of credit, are owned by their nominal owners -the creditors, by virtue of the credit extension, come to own an undivided interest proportioned to the advances which they have made. The aggregate of these items of property comes hereby to be potentially owned by the creditors in approximately the proportion which the loans bear to the collateral plus the loans. The outcome of credit extension, in this respect, is a situation in which the creditors have become potential owners of such a fraction of the industrial equipment as would be represented by the formula (loans/(capitalization (= collateral + loans))[18].

---

[17] The market value of the output does not, in fact, keep pace with the inflation of business capital during a period of speculative advance. In order that it should do so, and afford nominal earning proportionate to the inflated capital, it would be necessary that incomes should increase proportionately to the inflation of capital; but, even if this happened, the expenses of production would thereby be so increased (through the advance of wages and the like) as to offset the entire inflation of values for all consumptive goods and leave only the advance in the values of productive goods as a net margin from which to draw an increase of earnings. The discrepancy under discussion, however, is not due entirely to the presence of credit, and a fully detailed analysis of the causes out of which it arises can, therefore, not properly be presented in this place.

18 So long as the rating of the capitalized property remains undisturbed, the formula which expresses the creditors' claim maintains the form given above. It then signifies nothing more than that the creditors hold a claim on such a proportion of the aggregate capitalized property involved as their advances boar to the aggregate capitalization. But so soon as a re-rating of the capitalized property enters the problem the formula becomes (loans/(capitalization + delta capitalization)) or (loans/(capitalization — delta capitalization)) according as the re-rating of capitalization is in the direction of enhancement or depreciation: (1/(cap + delta cap)) or (1/(cap – delta cap)). During brisk times, when capitalization advances, the claim represented by a given loan covers a decreasing proportion of the aggregate capitalized property involved (1/(cap + delta cap)); the denominator increases and the quotient consequently decreases. Whereas, in a period of liquidation the ratio of the creditors' claim to the aggregate capitalization increases by force of the lowered rating of the capitalized property (1/(cap- delta cap)); the quotient increases because the denominator decreases. The numerator remains constant.

In a period of liquidation this potential ownership on the part of the creditors takes effect to the extent to which the liquidation is carried through[19].

The precise measure and proportion in which the industrial property of the business community passes into the hands of the creditors in a period of liquidation can of course not be specified; it depends on the degree of shrinkage in values, as well as on the degree of thoroughness with which the liquidation is carried out, and perhaps on other still less ascertainable causes, among which is the degree of closeness of organization of the business community. It is, however, through the shrinkage of market values of the output and the industrial plant that the transfer of ownership to the creditor class takes place. In case no shrinkage of values took place, no such general transfer of ownership to the creditors as a class would become evident.

In point of fact, the shrinkage commonly supervenes, in the course of modern business, when a general liquidation comes; although it is readily conceivable that the period of acute liquidation and its attendant shrinkage of values need not supervene. Such would probably be the case in the absence of competitive investment in industrial material on a large scale. Secondary effects, such as perturbations of the rate of interest, insolvency, forced sales, and the like, need scarcely be taken up here, although it may be well to keep in mind that these secondary effects are commonly very considerable and far-reaching, and that they may in specific instances very materially affect the outcome. The theoretical result of this summary sketch of loan credit in modem business, so far, seems to be: (a) an extension of loan credit beyond that involved in the transference of productive goods from their owners to more competent users is unavoidable under the regime of competitive business; (b) such a use of credit does not add to the aggregate of industrially productive equipment nor increase its material output of product, and therefore it does not add materially to the aggregate gross earnings obtained by the body of business-men engaged in industry, as counted in terms of material wealth or of permanent values[20] (c) it diminishes the aggregate net profits obtained by the business-men engaged in industry as counted in such terms, in that it requires them to pay interest, to creditors outside the industrial process proper, on funds which, taken as an aggregate, represent no productive goods and have no aggregate productive effect; (d) there results an overrating of the aggregate capital engaged in industry, compared with the value of the industrial equipment at the starting-point, by approximately the amount of the aggregate deposits and loans on collateral; (e) the overrating swells the business capital, thereby raises the valuation of collateral, and gives rise to a further extension of credit, with further results of a like nature; (f) com-

---

[19] All those who, at a period of liquidation, are holders of fluent funds or of claims to fixed sums of money are, for the present purpose, in the position of creditors.

[20] This disregards the indirect effects of a speculative advance in the way of heightened intensity of application and fuller employment of the industrial plant.

monly beginning at some point where the extension of credit is exceptionally large in proportion to the material substratum of productive goods, or where the discrepancy between nominal capital and earning capacity is exceptionally wide, the overrating is presently recognized by the creditor and a settlement ensues; (g) on the consequent withdrawal of credit a forced re-rating of the aggregate capital follows, bringing the nominal aggregate into approximate accord with the facts of earning capacity; (h) the shrinkage which takes place in reducing the aggregate rating of business capital from the basis of capital goods plus loans to the basis of capital goods alone, takes place at the expense of debtors and nominal owners of industrial equipment, in so far as they are solvent; (i) in the period of liquidation the gain represented by the credit inflation goes to the creditors and claimants of funds outside the industrial process proper, except that whatever is canceled in bad debts is written off; (j) apart from secondary effects, such as heightened efficiency of industry due to inflated values, changes of the rate of interest, insolvency, etc., the main final outcome is a redistribution of the ownership of property whereby the creditor class, including holders and claimants of funds, is benefited.

This characterization is intended to apply only to what may be called an "undue" extension of credit, and has nothing to say as to the substantial benefits derived by the business community from what may, by contrast, be called a "due" extension of credit. Neither does it imply deprecation of the use of "undue" credit in business. The view here spoken for plainly involves the position that there is always present, in ordinary times, some appreciable amount of loan credit of this "undue" or "abnormal" character. In brisk times the proportion of such undue credit is large and commonly increases progressively. But the extension of credit need not take on the cumulative character which it bears during a period of speculative advance, or "rising prosperity," unless some effective disturbance of prices and of the market outlook comes in to heighten the incentives that lead business-men to compete for loans. In other words, there seems to be some ill-defined point of equilibrium between prices, earning capacity of capital, interest, and loan credit; and when this equilibrium is seriously disturbed a cumulative extension of credits of an "undue" character is likely to follow. An effective disturbance of the equilibrium, such as is designated by the phrase "brisk times" or "good times," is commonly initiated by an advance in the prices or in the volume of demand for some one or more of the products that are extensively used in industry. It may also, though less commonly, arise from changes in the rate of interest. When this happens it is usually, if not invariably, accompanied by a somewhat general advance in prices. Indeed, in its primary incidence, such a movement may be said to run its course as a sequence of price phenomena turning about the earning capacity of business enterprises.

Since the modern industrial situation began to take form there have been two principal forms of credit transactions current in the usage of the business community for the purpose of investment — the old-fashioned loan, the usage of which has come down from an earlier day, and the stock share whereby funds are invested in a joint stock company or corporation.

The latter is a credit instrument, so far as touches the management of the property represented, in that (in earlier usage at least) it effects a transfer of a given body of property from the hands of an owner who resigns discretion in its control to a board of directors who assume the management of ii In addition to these two methods of credit relation there has, during the modern industrial period, come into extensive use for business purposes a third class of expedients, *viz.*, debentures of one form and another — bonds of various tenor, preferred stock, preference shares, etc., ranging, in point of technical character and degree of liability involved, from something approaching the nature of a bill of sale to something not readily distinguishable in effect from a personal note. The typical (latest and most highly specialized) instrument of this class is the preferred stock. This is in form a deed of ownership, and in effect an evidence of debt. It is typical of a somewhat comprehensive class of securities in use in the business community, in the respect that it ignores the distinction between capital and credit.

In this respect, indeed, preferred stock, more adequately perhaps than any other instrument, reflects the nature of the "capital concept" current among up-to-date business-men who are engaged in the larger industrial affairs. The part which debenture credit, nominal and virtual, plays in the financing of modem industrial corporations is very considerable, and the proportion which it bears in the capitalization of these corporations apparently grows larger as time passes and shrewder methods of business gain ground. In the field of the "industrials" proper, debenture credit has not until lately been employed with full effect. It seems to be from the corporation finance of American railway companies that business-men have learned the full use of an exhaustive debenture credit as an expedient for expanding business capital. It is not an expedient newly discovered, but its free use even in railway finance is relatively late.

Wherever it prevails in an unmitigated form, as with some railway companies and latterly in many other industrial enterprises, it throws the capitalization of the business concerns affected by it into a peculiar, characteristically modern, position in relation to credit. When carried out thoroughly it places virtually the entire capital, comprising the whole of the material equipment, on a credit basis. Stock being issued by the use of such funds as may be needed to pay for printing, a road will be built, or an industrial plant established, by the use of funds drawn from the sale of bonds; preferred stock or similar debentures will then be issued, commonly of various denominations, to the full amount that the property will bear, and not infrequently somewhat in excess of what the property will bear. When the latter case occurs, the market quotations of the securities will, of course, roughly adjust the current effective capitalization to the run of the facts, whatever the nominal capitalization may be. The common stock in such a case represents "goodwill," and in the later development usually nothing but "good- will." The material equipment is covered by credit instruments — debentures. Not infrequently the debentures cover appreciably more than the value of the material equipment, together with such property as useful patent rights or trade secrets; in such a case the good-will is also, to some extent, covered by debentures, and so serves as virtual collateral for a credit extension which is incorporated in the business capital of the company. In the ideal case, where a corporation is financed with due perspicacity, there will be but an inappreciable proportion of the market value of the company's good-will left uncovered by debentures. In the case of a railway company, for instance, no more should be left uncovered by debentures than the value of the "franchise," and probably in most cases not that much actually is uncovered.

Whether capitalized good-will (including "franchise" if necessary) is to be rated as a credit extension is a nice question that can apparently be decided only on a legal technicality. In any case so much seems clear — that good- will is the nucleus of capitalization in modem corporation finance. In a well-financed, flourishing corporation good- will, indeed, constitutes the total assets after liabilities have been met, but the total remaining assets may not nearly equal the total market value of the company's good-will; that is to say, the material equipment (plant, etc.) of a shrewdly managed concern is hypothecated at least once, commonly more than once, and its immaterial properties (good-will), together with its evidences of indebtedness, may also to some extent be drawn into the hypothecation[21] .

---

[21] Any student who harks back to archaic methods of business organization for a norm of what capitalization should be will object that what is said above applies only in a case of gross overcapitalisation or stock-watering. But the objection proceeds on obsolete premises. It supposes that the stock of a corporation must represent material wealth, in fact as well as in law. Such is not the case in fact, whatever may be held to be binding in law. The question of "stock-watering," "overcapitalization," and the like is scarcely pertinent in the case of a large industrial corporation, financed as the modern situation demands. Under modern circumstances the stock can scarcely fail to be all "water," unless in a small concern or under incompetent management. Nothing but "water" — under the name of good-will — belongs in the common stock; whereas the preferred stock, which represents material equipment, is a debenture. "Overcapitalization," on the other hand, if it means anything under modern business conditions, must mean overcapitalization as compared with earning capacity, for there is nothing else pertinent to compare with; and earning capacity fluctuates, while the basis (interest rates) on which the earning capacity is to be capitalized also fluctuates independently. In effect, the adjustment of capitalization to earning capacity is taken care of by the market quotations of stock and other securities; and no other method of adjustment is of any avail, because capitalization is a question of value, and market quotations are the last resort in questions of value. The value of any stock listed on the exchange, or otherwise subject to purchase and sale, fluctuates from time to time; which comes to the same thing as saying that the effectual capitalization of the concern, represented by the securities quoted, fluctuates from time to time. It fluctuates more or less, sometimes very slowly, but always at least so much as to compensate the long-period fluctuations of discount rates in the money market; which means that the purchase price of a given fractional interest in the corporation as a going concern fluctuates so as to equate it with the capitalized value of its putative earning capacity, computed at current rates of discount and allowing for risks.

What has just been said of the part borne by good-will and debentures in the capitalization of corporations should be taken in connection with what was said above (p. 9) as to the securities offered as collateral in procuring credit extension. The greater part of the securities used as collateral, and so coined into means of payment, are evidences of debt, at the first remove or farther from the physical basis, instruments of credit recording a previous credit extension.

In the earlier period of growth of this debenture financiering in industry, as, e.g., in the railroad financiering of the third quarter of the nineteenth century, the process of expansion by means of debenture credit, in any given case, worked out gradually over a more or less extended period of time. But as the possibilities of this expedient have grown familiar to the business community the time consumed in perfecting the structure of debentures in each case has been reduced; until it is now not unusual to perfect the whole organization, with its load of debentures, at the inception of a corporate enterprise. In such a case, when a corporation starts with a fully organized capital and debt, the owners of the concern are also its creditors — they are, at the start, the holders of both common and preferred stock, and probably also of the bonds of the company — so adding another increment of confusion to the relation between modern capital and credit, as seen from the old-fashioned position as to what capitalization and its basis should be.

This syncopated process of expanding capital by the help of credit financiering, however, is seen at its best in the latter-day reorganizations and coalitions of industrial corporations; and as this class of transactions also illustrate another interesting and characteristically modem feature of credit financiering, the whole matter may best be set out in the way of a sketch of what takes place in a case of coalition of industrial corporations on a large scale, such as recent industrial history has made familiar. The avowed end of these latter-day business coalitions is economy of production and sale and an amicable regulation of intercorporate relations. So far as bears on the functioning of credit in the attendant business transactions, the presence or absence of these purposes, of course, does not affect the course of events or the outcome. These avowed incentives do not touch the credit operations involved. On the other hand, the need of large credit in consummating the deal, as well as the presumptive gains to be drawn from the credit relations involved, offer inducements of their own. Inducements of this kind seem to have been quite effective in bringing on some of the recent operations of this class.

Credit operations come into these transactions mainly at two points: in the "financing" of the deal, and in the augmentation of debentures; and at both these points there is a chance of gain — on the one hand to the promoter (organizer) and the credit house which finances the operation, and on the other hand to the stockholders. The gain which accrues to the two former is the more unequivocal, and this seems in some cases to be the dominant incentive to effect the reorganization. The whole operation of reorganization may, therefore, best be taken up from the point of view of the promoter, who is the prime mover in the matter. A reorganization of industrial concerns on a large scale, such as are not uncommon at the present time, involves a campaign of business strategy, engaging, it is said, abilities and responsibilities of a very high order. Such a campaign of business strategy, as carried out by the modem captains of industry, runs, in the main, on credit relations, in the way of financial backing, options, purchases, leases, and the issuance and transfer of stock and debentures. In order to carry through these large "deals," in the first place, a very substantial basis of credit is required, either in the hands of the promoter (organizer) himself or in the hands of a credit house which "finances" the organization for him.

The strategic use of credit here involved is, in effect, very different from the use of loan credit in investments. In transactions of this class the time element, the credit period, is an inconspicuous factor at the most; it plays a very subordinate and uncertain part. The volume of credit at the disposal of a given strategist is altogether the decisive point, as contrasted with the lapse of time over which the incident credit extension may run. The usefulness of the credit extension is not measured in terms of time, nor are the gains which accrue to the creditor in the case proportioned to the length of time involved. This follows from the peculiar nature of the work which these great captains of industry have in hand, and more remotely, therefore, from the peculiar character of the earnings which induce them to undertake the work. Their work, though it is of the gravest consequence to industry, is not industrial business, in that it is not occupied with anything like the conduct of a continuous industrial process. Nor is it of the same class as commercial business, or even banking business, in that there is no investment in a continued sequence of transactions.

It differs also from stock and produce speculation, as that is currently conceived," in that it does not depend on the lapse of time to bring a change of circumstances; although it has many points of similarity with stock speculation. In its details this work resembles commercial business, in that it has to do with bargaining; but so does all business, and this peculiar work of the trust promoter differs from mercantile business in the absence of continuity. Perhaps its nearest business analogue is the work of the real-estate agent.

The volume of credit involved is commonly very great; whereas the credit period, the lapse of time, is a negligible factor. Indeed, if an appreciable credit period intervenes, it is a fortuitous circumstance. The time element in these credit operations is in abeyance, or, at the best, it is an indeterminate magnitude. Hence the formula shown above (p. 6, n. 9) is practically not applicable to business of this class. So far as bears upon the credit operations involved in these transactions of the large finance, the question about which interest turns is almost exclusively the volume of the turnover; its velocity is a negligible quantity. Such strategic use of credit is not confined to the business of making or marring industrial coalitions. It is habitually to be met with in connection with stock (and produce) speculation, and ramifications of the like use of credit run through the dealings of the business community at large in many directions; but it rarely attains the magnitude in the service of stock speculation which it reaches in the campaign incident to a trust-making deal.

The form of credit extension employed in these transactions with indeterminate time also varies. The older and more familiar form is that of the call loan, together with the stock-exchange transactions for which call loans are largely used. Here the time element is present, especially in form; but the credit period is somewhat indeterminate, as is also the gain that accrues to the creditor from the transaction; although the creditor's gain here continues to be counted at a (variable) rate per cent, per time-unit.

The strategic use of credit in the affairs of the large business finance has much in common with the call loan. Indeed, the call loan in set form is often resorted to as a valuable auxiliary expedient, although the larger arrangements for financing such a campaign of business strategy are not usually put in the form of a call loan. The arrangement between the promoter and the financial agent is commonly based on a less specific stipulation as to collateral, and the payment for credit obtained takes even less, if any, account of the length of the credit period. In financing a campaign of coalition the credit house that acts as financial agent assumes, in effect, an even less determinate credit responsibility.

Here, too, the gains accruing to the creditor are no longer, even nominally, counted per cent, per time-unit, but rather in the form of a bonus based mainly on the volume of the turnover, with some variable degree of regard to other circumstances. Answering to the essentially timeless character of the gains accruing to the financial agent, the earnings of the promoter engaged in transactions of this class are also not of the nature of profits per cent, per time-unit, but rather a bonus which commonly falls immediately into the shape of a share in the capitalization of the newly organized concern. Much of this increment of capital, or capitalization, that goes to the promoter is scarcely distinguishable from an increase of the liabilities of the new corporation (e.g., preferred stock); and the remainder (e.g., common stock) has also some of the characteristics of a credit instrument. It is worth noting that the cost of reorganization, including the bonus of the promoter and the financial agent, is, in the common run of cases, added to the capitalization; that is to say, as near as this class of transactions may be spoken of in terms borrowed from the old-fashioned business terminology, what answers to the "interest" due the creditor on the credit extension involved is incorporated in the "capital " of the debtor, without circumlocution or faltering.

The line between credit and capital, or between debt and property, in the values handled throughout these strategic operations of coalition, remains somewhat uncertain. Indeed, the old-fashioned concepts of "debt" and "property," or "liabilities" and "assets," are not fairly applicable to the facts of the case — except, of course, in the way of a technical legal distinction. The old-fashioned law and legal presumptions and the new-fashioned facts and usages are parting company, at this point as at some others in the affairs of modem business .When such a large transaction in the reorganization of industrial concerns has been completed, the values left in the hands of the former owners of the concerns merged in the new coalition are only to a fractional and uncertain extent of the nature of material goods. They are in large part debentures, and much of the remainder is of a doubtful character. A large proportion of the nominal collective capital resulting in such cases is made up of the capitalized good-will of the concerns merged. This good-will is chiefly a capitalization of the differential advantages possessed by the several concerns as competitors in business, and has for the most part no use for other than competitive business ends. It is for the most part of no aggregate industrial effect.

But the differential advantages possessed by business concerns as competitors disappear when the competitors are merged, in the degree in which they cease to compete with rival bidders for the same range of business. As an element in the capitalization of the new corporation, therefore, this defunct good-will has a value analogous to the present value of the competitive merits of last year's fashions in bonnets. To this aggregate good-will of the consolidated concerns (which in the nature of things can make only an imaginary aggregate) is added something in the way of an increment of good-will belonging to the new corporation as such; and the whole is then represented, approximately, by the common stock issued. The nominal capital of the concerns merged (in good part based on capitalized good-will) is aggregated, after an appraisement which commonly equalizes the proportion of each by increasing the nominal shares of all.

This aggregate is covered with common and preferred stock, chiefly preferred, which is a class of debentures issued under the form of capital. The stock, common and preferred, goes to the owners of the concerns merged, and to the promoter and the financial agent, as already indicated above. In case bonds are issued, these likewise go to the former owners, in so far as they do not replace outstanding liabilities of the concerns merged. "Capital" in modern business usage means "capitalized presumable earning capacity," and in this capitalization is comprised the usufruct of whatever credit extension the given business concern's industrial equipment and good-will will support.

By consequence the effectual capitalization (shown by the market quotations) as contrasted with the nominal capital (shown by the par value of the stock of all descriptions) fluctuates with the fluctuations of the prevalent presumption as to the solvency and earning capacity of the concern and the good faith of its governing board. When the modem captain of industry reorganizes and consolidates a given range of industrial business concerns, therefore, and gives them a collective form and name as an up-to-date corporation, the completed operation presents, in syncopated form and within a negligible lapse of time, all that intricate process of cumulative augmentation of business capital through the use of credit which otherwise may come gradually in the course of business competition. At the same time it involves a redistribution of the ownership of the property engaged in industry, such as otherwise occurs at a period of liquidation. The result is, of course, not the same at all points, but the equivalence between the two methods of expanding business capital and distributing the gains is close in some respects. The resemblances and the differences between the two processes, so far as relates to credit, are worth noticing. The trust-maker is in some respects a substitute for a commercial crisis.

When credit extension is used competitively in the old-fashioned way for increasing the business of competing concerns, as spoken of above (pp. 6-8, 12-14), the expansion of business capital through credit operations occupies a period of some duration, commonly running over an interval recognized as a period of speculative advance or "rising prosperity." The expansion of capitalized values then takes place more or less gradually through a competitive enhancement of the prices of industrial equipment and the like. The creditors then commonly come in for their resulting share in the industrial equipment only at the period of liquidation, with its attendant shrinkage of values. In the timeless credit transactions involved in the modem reorganizations of industrial business, on the other hand, the creditors' claim takes effect without an appreciable lapse of time, a liquidation, or a shrinkage of values.

The whole process of credit extension, augmentation of business capital, and distribution of proceeds is reduced to a very simple form. The credit extension is effected in two main forms: (a) the "financing" undertaken by the credit house in conjunction with the promoter, and (b) the issuance of debentures. The bonus of the financing house and promoter, as well as the debentures, are all included in the recapitalization, together with an increment of good-will and any other incidental items of expense or presumptive gain. The resulting collective capitalization (assets and liabilities) is then distributed to the several parties concerned in the transaction. The outcome, so far as touches the present argument, being that when the operation is completed the ownership of the recapitalized industrial equipment, with whatever other property is involved, appears distributed between the former owners, the promoter, and the credit house which financed the operation. But, by virtue of the debentures distributed, the former owners, together with the other parties named, appear in the role of creditors of the new corporation as well as owners of it; they commonly come out of the transaction with large holdings of preferred stock or similar debentures at the same time that they hold the common stock.

The preferred stock, of course, is presently disposed of by the large holders to outside parties. The material equipment is then practically the same as it was before; the business capital has been augmented to comprise such proportion of the good-will of the several concerns incorporated as had not previously been capitalized and hypothecated, together with the good-will imputed to the new corporation and the debentures which these items of wealth will float. The effective capitalization resulting is, of course, indicated by the market quotations of the securities issued rather than by their face value. The value of the corporation's business capital so indicated need suffer no permanent shrinkage; it will suffer none if the monopoly advantage (good-will) of the new corporation is sufficient to keep its earning capacity up to the rate on which the capitalization is based. It appears, then, that in the affairs of latter-day business, as shown by modern corporation finance, capital and credit extension are not always distinguishable in fact, nor does there appear to be a decisive business reason why they should be distinguished.

"Capital" means "capitalized putative earning capacity," expressed in terms of value, and this capitalization comprises the use of all feasible credit extension. The business capital of a modern corporation is a magnitude that fluctuates from day to day; and in the fluctuations of its debentures the magnitude of its credit extension also fluctuates from day to day with the course of the market. The precise pecuniary magnitude of the business community's invested wealth, as well as the aggregate amount of the community's indebtedness, depends from hour to hour on the quotations of the stock exchange; and it rarely happens that it remains nearly the same in the aggregate from one week's end to the next. Both capital and credit, therefore, vary from hour to hour and, within narrow limits, from place to place. The magnitude and fluctuations of business capital — "capital" in the sense in which that term is used in business affairs — of course stands in no hard and fast relation to the material magnitude of the industrial equipment; nor do variations in the magnitude of the business capital reflect variations in the magnitude or the efficiency of the industrial equipment in any but the loosest and most indecisive manner.

So also, and for the same reason, the magnitude and the variations of the aggregate credit afloat at a given time bear, at the most, but a remote, indirect, and shifty relation to the aggregate of material wealth and the changes to which it is subject. All this applies with peculiar cogency wherever and in so far as industry and business are carried on by modern expedients and in due contact with the modem market.

Chapter 7
Credit and Prices

At its last meeting (1904) the American Economic Association gave up one session to a discussion of the relation between credit and prices. The point of the discussion was, in substance, the question: Does the use of credit raise general prices? This was the only strictly theoretical topic taken up at the meeting. It is perhaps needless to say that the question was not finally disposed of, even in the apprehension of those who took part in its discussion. There was apparent a general reluctance to admit that credit is a price-making factor of considerable importance, at the same time that there seemed to prevail an apprehensive hesitancy about saying so in so many words.

This is true only with exceptions, however. On the whole, there may be said to have been a rough consensus to the effect that credit does not have much to do with prices in ordinary times and in the general run of business, however opinions may differ as to its effect on prices in exceptional circumstances. It should be added that the discussion at the meeting was directed mainly, or almost wholly, to those forms of credit instruments which serve as currency or as a substitute for currency. It is, of course, not intended here to offer an off-hand solution of this large question of credit and prices, but certain phases of the use of credit in modern business, neglected in the arguments of the association's experts, may well be taken up. What is of immediate interest to modern theory is, of course, the current use of credit in business, and the relation of this business credit to the current price-level rather than the occasional resort of credit under relatively primitive circumstances. Credit is an expedient of business, and as such it is unquestionably a factor of great importance.

The price-level is similarly a fact upon which the business community's hopes and fears center. If one looks to the field of business, sun ply, and neglects to go behind the immediate facts of business traffic to those of die industrial process and the output of consumable goods, certain commonplace facts bearing on credit stand out in relief - obvious facts which have commonly been overlooked, perhaps because they are too obvious to be seen except with the naked eye. These are such facts as the following: The issuance of a large government loan advances the general rate of discount and depresses the price of investment securities; Business men resort to credit for the sake of gain, the gain being counted in money values; The securities covering the capitalization of a modern corporation commonly have a larger aggregate market value than the underlying tangible assets have before the incorporation Banking is profitable, also in terms of money values; Prosperous times are attended with a large extension of credit as well as an advance in general prices Crises and depression bring a shrinkage of credit and a decline of general prices.

From these and other phenomena of the same commonplace character the rough generalization may be drawn that an advance of prices commonly accompanies a pronounced expansion of credit. It is not plain from these facts which of the two correlated phenomena is cause and which is effect, but the great generality with which they are found in company indicates that they stand in a causal relation to one another, possibly as being the effects of the same causes.

There is nothing in these general facts to preclude the view that they are mutually related as cause and effect. That a pronounced advance in prices results in an increased extension of credit seems plain from what happens during a period of prosperity, or speculative advance. The circumstantial evidence runs to that effect, at the same time that such a result is to be expected from the nature of die case. Notoriously, a period of advancing prosperity is a period of relatively high prices, at least in some of the important branches of industry, and usually it is also a period of advancing prices. Extensions of credit, of course, run in terms of money, and are based on the money value (price) of the property submitted as collateral. If this market value of the collateral advances, then the amount of the credit which it will support will likewise increase. The market value of the collateral may increase immediately, as an incident of the advance of general prices; or it may increase through the increased earning capacity of the business property submitted as collateral, this increased earning capacity being in part due to the increased price at which the output of the business can be disposed of, in part, perhaps to the increased volume of output which the market will carry off. In the latter case, the increased demand for the output is, at least in part, a consequence of the high course of general prices. In the case of crisis or pronounced depression all this chain of consequences is reversed.

Such seems to be the rough and general run of correlation between credit and prices as conditioned by the circumstances of prosperity or depression. A closer analysis would show variations of detail under this general rule, and would afford material for detailed study. The general statement which these facts seem to warrant is that in this connection an advance or decline of general prices brings an expansion or retrenchment of credit. Further attention to the same range of facts seems to warrant the further generalization that an expansion of credit in periods of prosperity, at the same time, causes an advance of general prices; while a general retrenchment of credit, such as occurs in time of crises or acute depression, acts to lower general prices. This point has been noted by nearly all writers on crises and inflation, and no argument need be spent in enforcing it. The manner in which it works has also been analyzed repeatedly.

Movements of general credit and general prices have apparently a mutual accelerating effect upon one another, both in case of advance and in case of decline, giving rise to the well-known cumulative process of expansion or of contraction that marks a period of prosperity or of crisis or depression. In practice this cumulative movement of credit and prices is more or less disguised and disturbed by certain (secondary) phenomena, such as the issuance of large loans, particularly government loans; extensive incorporation of new companies and consolidation of old ones, with the attendant recapitalization of the various items of wealth involved in these operations; the promotion or - in the case of depression or crisis - the collapse of extra-hazardous, speculative business enterprises, etc. These "disturbing causes" would have to be taken up separately. It will probably be admitted that the cumulative movement of credit and prices spoken of has substantially the character assigned it above.

Among the phenomena that usually accompany a period of marked prosperity, and closely related to the expansion of credit during such a period, is a large volume of new capitalization in the form of new incorporations or expansions and coalitions of corporations already in existence. The issuance of corporation securities is a credit transaction, in the sense in which economists have been accustomed to use the word. Indeed, the sale of such securities involves the typical form of credit, as contemplated by the older economists, in that its immediate effect is to transfer the use of the property which it covers from the owner to the debtor, who is presumed to be a more competent it user than the owner. All this applies perhaps more patently to the sale of preferred stock and bonds than to that of common stock, but for the present purpose there seems to be no very substantial difference between these different descriptions of securities.

It is currently believed, probably on sufficient grounds that the corporations can make more profitable use of the property than the buyers of the securities, particularly a more profitable use than the buyers could make of it without spending additional time and attention in the management of the property. It is this presumed differential advantage in favor of the corporations that makes incorporation practicable on any appreciable scale. Except for the presumed advantage in gainfulness, it is safe to say, the organization of joint-stock companies would not have become a general practice. This presumed greater earning capacity of the corporations, above the earning capacity of the properties in severalty, may be due to economies of production, superior management, economies of sale, or what not. For the present argument it is only necessary to note that the corporations are presumed to have a greater earning capacity than their underlying properties, and that this presumption shows itself in the market value of the corporations' securities.

This market value of the securities is commonly larger in the aggregate than the aggregate value of the underlying properties. That is to say, the credit transaction which results in the organization of a corporation and an attendant issue of marketable securities commonly increases the aggregate price of the property involved. It is not unusual, latterly, to incorporate a business concern at a nominal capitalization of about 200 per cent of the current market value of the underlying properties; the resulting securities will sell below par; but in the case of an ordinarily sound and sagacious incorporation the total capitalization will still have a market value of something more than 100 per cent of the value of the underlying properties. In this ease, then, a credit transaction raises the price of the property immediately involved. Whether and how it affects the prices of other items of wealth is a question not easily answered. If the advantages of incorporation are in all cases differential advantages only, then the presumption would be that the prices of other property engaged in similar lines of business should be depressed in consequence of the incorporation. It does not seem probable that the depression in the prices of similar property outside of the given corporation, if such a depression results at all, is sufficient to balance the increase in the price of the assets of the corporation. In case the given incorporation results in a monopoly, a more or less extensive enhancement of prices may be expected to follow in its marketable output of goods or services, apparently without any necessary countervailing effect upon the prices of other goods. Price changes of this latter class, however, will probably be regarded as the effects of monopoly rather than of the credit transactions which initiate the monopoly.

They need therefore not be discussed here. They could properly be discussed here only in so far as credit relations are to be accounted a necessary basis of any efficient monopoly. Under existing conditions this is probably the case, but the relation between the credit relations which enable monopolies to be organized and to operate and the resulting effect on prices is, after all, so remote that an analysis of its consequences would take the present argument out of its way. Again, the issuance of a very considerable loan, such as a war loan of the larger sort, is known to lower the general market value (prices) of securities with a fixed interest or dividend charge. At such a juncture, because of the large demand for credit, general interest advances, and the general level of capitalization correspondingly declines that is to say, the market value of incorporated business declines, while the "price of money" advances. The prices of such lines of goods as are to be bought with the borrowed funds are likely to advance, and this may induce an advance in such capital as is concerned with the supply of these goods, but all that is an indirect consequence of the credit transaction rather than an immediate effect of it[1] .

The phenomena spoken of so far are of the class which the older economists would call "disturbances," rather than developments in the normal course of business. What happens in the case of such disturbances need not be taken as evidence of the effect of credit upon prices in the regular course of business in ordinary times, where no such perturbations occur, or apart from all perturbations of this kind. In the regular course of business there is, no doubt, a larger aggregate volume of credit, proportionately either to the stock of specie or to the aggregate amount of tangible wealth owned in the community, in use at present and in this country than

---

[1] This phenomenon of an equilibration between the rate of discount and the market value of securities is one of the most characteristic and indicative features of the modern business situation. An exhaustive study of it may be expected to result in a revision of the received views of credit, capital, interest, and prices, and of the interdependence of these several phenomena; but it is out of the question to pursue an inquiry of that magnitude here. It seems evident, however, that a fuller inquiry along that line should confirm the view here spoken for, that general credit and prices are intimately bound together in a relation of mutual cause and effect.

here formerly or now anywhere else. Will general prices range higher or lower because of such a more extended use of credit? Does the more extended and the increasing use of credit during the past thirty or forty years affect the general course of prices during the same period? This question has been argued by comparing the state of things at present with the corresponding facts of a generation ago, but without conclusive results.

No canvass of the statistical material bearing on the case can directly reach a solution of the question, because the variables included in the problem are too many and too unprecise. On the other hand, something in the way of tenable general conclusions may probably be arrived at through an examination of the aims which actuate borrowers and lenders, and of the method by which the work of credit extension is carried on, although such a line of inquiry can not be expected to yield anything like precise results.

As has just been noted, the credit transaction known as the floating of corporation securities results in an increased market value of the aggregate properties involved. This increased market value is more or less permanent, somewhat in proportion as the capitalization is more or less "conservative." At the same time, it is one of the reasons for the promoting of new corporations. The promoter's bonus, with other like charges and perquisites, comes out of the margin of increase in price. The incentive to credit extensions of this kind is a prospective gain in terms of price, and in this class of transactions the business man's hope of gain is at least not commonly disappointed, even if the permanent increase of the values which lie manipulates may not be as large as his anticipations.

In other credit transactions which differ from the floating of new companies in that they do not materialize in the form of corporation securities, but which are of the same kind in that the borrowed funds are made to serve the conduct of business, the end sought is of the same kind - a gain in terms of price. This gain may appear primarily as an increase in the market value of the property in which the borrowed funds are invested, as in the case of a real-estate speculation and the like; or it may appear only as a secondary effect, as an increase in the aggregate value of the output of an industry in which the funds are invested. The presumption would be that in this case also the hope of gain is not altogether disappointed.

But even if the business man's hopes of gain could be shown to be false in the average of cases of this class of loans, it would not follow that credit transactions of this class initiate no enhancement of prices. Loans of the kind just spoken of, procured with a view to investing the borrowed funds in a somewhat fixed form in business, have the direct effect of enhancing the market value of the general description of property in which they seek investment. The borrowers bid up the kind of property which they seek to buy. Whether there is a countervailing decline in the general prices of other property is doubtful and may be left on one side for the present, particularly as the argument of the next few pages approaches that question from another side.

In the ordinary conduct of business there is an extensive and increasing resort to credit in the way of loans, extended by banks in the form of deposits and by other credit institutions, such as trust companies, insurance companies, and the like, without their taking the form of deposits. In general, but more particularly where such a loan takes the form of a deposit, these extensions of credit would, by economists who hold that normal credit does not affect prices, be considered to be an expedient for facilitating an exchange of goods. The goods which serve as collateral for the loan, it is held, are by a more or less roundabout process of accounting exchanged for the goods paid for out of the deposits. This is in substance the theory which has felicitously been named "the refined system of barter." As bearing on the question of credit and prices, this doctrine declares that such loans do not affect prices, because the borrowed funds are nothing but the fluent form of the value of the underlying collateral. The loan and the collateral are held to offset one another as demand and supply, the loan adding no more to the demand side - the effective purchasing power seeking goods than the collateral adds to the supply side of the market situation - the effective offering of goods seeking sale.

Hence, it is held, no enhancement of price can arise from such loans, the increase of funds offered in purchase being no greater than the underlying increase of goods offered for sale. A singular query presents itself at this point. Not only is it true that the funds procured by loans of this kind, in a case of "normal" credit extension, are no larger than the value of the underlying collateral, but in the ordinary run of things the loan is not as large as the value of the collateral. No banker would be held blameless if he should extend his loans to the full ascertained value of the collateral. If the argument of the "refined system" is sound, will it not lead to the conclusion that credit extensions of this class lower general prices, since it should follow that the increase of the market demand due to the borrowed funds is overbalanced by the increase in the supply of goods represented by the collateral? The answer to the question comes into sight, if this argument is pursued a step farther.

The argument for "the refined system of barter" assumes that the collateral is of the nature of a bill of sale. It appears to break down immediately in so far as the collateral is not of this character, fit consists of property not sold or not designed presently to be sold; as, e. g., where the collateral is corporation securities or paper similar to corporation securities in the respect that it represents property which the borrower has not sold and is not trying to sell, but which is held as security during the term of the loan. The doctrine seems tenable only in so far as the collateral is of the nature of a bill of sale. A good share of current deposits and the greater part of other current loans are not of this character. The borrower's resort to credit in these cases is not an incident in the sale of the collateral. The presumption, indeed, is that he does riot wish to sell. But it is safe to say that he ordinarily wishes to buy, whether it be goods, securities, or what not. Here the balance which is sought to be established between goods sold and goods bought, in the doctrine of "the refined system of barter," is upset by the fact that property not sold and not designed to be sold is made a basis of credit extension.

The (discounted) value of this collateral enters the market as a factor in the demand for goods. If the determination of price is conceived in the customary way to be an outcome of the play of demand and supply, it appears that these considerations force the admission that general prices should advance as a result of these credit extensions. The general demand has been increased by "coining into means of payment" property which is not included in the general supply. It appears that, in so far as it is of this character as it is to a very large extent, credit should raise prices. The objection is ready, indeed it has in substance been made by those who speak for the view under discussion, that in the end the borrower must sell something or other in order to meet obligations falling due, and that in this way the balance is maintained and the transaction reduces itself to a virtual barter.

All of which may conceivably be true as applies to a given transaction, although it is not unusual for such a transaction to be followed immediately on the maturity of the loan by another like transaction which virtually continues the life of the original loan. But this line of defense overlooks the time element, which is of the essence of any credit transaction. During the credit period the balance between demand and supply is not maintained, supposing the argument of the "refined system" to be otherwise sound. And from this it follows that the balance between general demand and general supply (conceiving supply in terms of goods) fails, constantly and in the nature of things, by the whole amount of outstanding credit obligations, after deducting such loans as have been sunk in the purchase of industrial equipment or have otherwise been withdrawn from the active market as a means of payment - indeed, it may even be an open question whether this deduction should be made, or just what force should be assigned to this qualification.

Evidently this argument applies to the whole mass of outstanding credit, whatever the nature of the collateral. During their term the loans secured by ordinary commercial paper constitute an addition to the means of purchase as well as those loans that are secured by property not intended for sale[2].

Accordingly, such portion of the outstanding mass of credit as is available as a means of purchase must be taken to constitute an effective price-making demand and to have a force, as a price-making factor, equal to that of a like amount of hard cash used as currency. The rest of the credit outstanding at any given time, not available as a means of payment, is, perhaps, larger than this that may be called the mass of active credit, and if this "dormant" credit be deducted it appears that what is left as an active price-making factor is an indeterminate fraction of the whole. The secondary price-making effects of the loans sunk in investment are here disregarded; they seem, on the whole, to go in the direction of an enhancement of general prices, but they are complex and variable, and cannot be

---

[2] Cf. also pp. 37-39 below.

taken account of here except as a factor for which an indefinite allowance is to be made. It remains true that the mass of active credit, which senses as a current means of payment and so immediately affects prices, is a function of the whole mass of credit outstanding.

Now, when the mass of outstanding credit shrinks appreciably, as in a period of depression or crisis, the shrinkage ordinarily affects the credit available for current means of payment first or primarily. The consequence is a shrinkage of prices, both of goods in the open market, actively seeking a purchaser, and (secondarily) of the prices of the industrial equipment and similar items of property not intended for direct sale. Herewith the value of the collateral shrinks, forcing a reduction of outstanding loans, leading to a sale of collateral and so to an increased supply of things for sale, at the same time that the effective demand has been reduced by a shrinkage of the credit extensions used as a means of purchase.

In the doctrines of the classical economists, who at this point have not been superseded, the phenomena of credit are formulated in terms of their presumed social expediency. The actual motives and aims which animate those business men who seek credit, as well as those who carry on the traffic in credit - bankers, brokers, etc. - are disregarded, and in the stead of these business motives the presumed beneficial results of the traffic are imputed to these business men as the motives of their traffic.

Perhaps for this reason the question of the banker's gain and its relation to credit and prices is commonly not broached in the received doctrines of credit and prices. Without the prospective gain the banker would not do business. So the question suggests itself: Why is banking profitable? And what, if any, relation is there between prices and the profits of banking? Broadly speaking, banking is profitable chiefly because the banker lends more than he has or borrows. This is his chief, though not his only, source of gain.

His gains are derived from payments for two distinct kinds of service which he renders his customers. The two are currently not distinguished, the remuneration for both being indiscriminately spoken of as discount or interest, but for the present purpose a distinction seems desirable. (a) Banks discount commercial paper, and (b) banks and other concerns doing a credit business make loans on collateral which is not of the nature of a bill of sale.

(a) In discounting commercial paper the banker does not create credit or increase the volume of outstanding credit obligations. In substance he guarantees or authenticates the credit extension already created by the writing of the commercial paper which he discounts.

A bill of sale for future payment is a credit instrument, and the extension of credit involved in its use is effected in the sale for future payment which it covers. The volume of credit so covered by the bill of sale is by the banker's authentication converted into a form available for circulation. In substance, he insures and authenticates it, and for this service he is paid in the discount of the bill. The form of the transaction gives the appearance of no increased demand for goods, since the volume of credit, and so the volume of money values available for purchase, has not been increased by the banker's intervention, This gives color to the claim that in this transaction there is no addition to the available purchasing power, and therefore no effect on prices; but this color is due to oversight of the fact that the bill itself is an instrument which covers an extension of credit already effected. It is an open question whether the banker's intervention in such a case, as authenticator of an existing volume of credit, is to be conceived as increasing the effective demand for goods.

But a negative answer to this question is only an evasion. If the increase of available credit in such a case is not made by the banker, it is made by the makers of the bill. The net result is much the same.

(b) In making a loan on collateral which is not of the nature of a bill of sale, but represents property not intended to be sold, the banker, or any similar concern doing a credit business of this kind, creates a new volume of credit. The remuneration for this service also is called interest or discount.

Such a transaction creates credit, and so adds to the borrower's funds available for purchase, and therefore increases the effective demand for goods, and by so doing helps to enhance prices. In such a transaction the banker lends funds which he does not possess. He is enabled to lend more in the aggregate than the whole of the funds which seek emplacement in loans through his agency. Or, to phrase it differently, he coins into means of payment goods which do not change hands in the resulting transactions of purchase and sale. Hence borrowers are enabled to borrow more in the aggregate than all the funds which the ultimate lenders have to dispose of - more than the whole of the funds seeking investment as loans plus that collateral which represents property sold or seeking sale. The purchasing power placed at the disposal of debtors is larger because of the banker's mediation than it would be without it[3].

From this augmented purchasing power the banker deducts his remuneration as a discount. This discount is not withdrawn from the aggregate loan fund. It serves the same purpose as any other item of banker's assets, and enables him to lend more than the whole of it, or, if the wording be preferred, it enables him to make advances on collateral exceeding its own amount. The banker's debtors, of course, negotiate their loans with a view to using the funds as a means of payment. The funds have no other use, except further lending, as in the hands of borrowing bankers. Hence, other things equal, it should follow that bank credit acts to raise prices by as much as it increases the nominal purchasing power in the hands of the business community.

---

[3] It may be that a closer analysis would show that the banker's service to his customers is also in this case, as in case (a), that of guarantor or authenticator of their credit and that his remuneration in the discount obtained is of the nature of a payment for responsibility assumed. If this view be taken, the form of the argument changes, but its bearing on the question in hand is not materially changed.

When the funds so secured by unmarketed collateral have been spent in the purchase of goods, the goods so purchased may in their turn be hypothecated in the negotiation of a further loan; with the result that there is a further augmentation of the volume of credit, a further increase of the effective demand for goods, and a further effect on prices. The whole movement may therefore take on a cumulative character, as it does in a marked degree in a period of prosperity, or speculative advance. Something of this cumulative character there no doubt is in the credit situation at any given time during ordinary times. For some time past the mass of outstanding credit has been growing gradually larger, on the whole, and the effect of this movement should logically have been to advance general prices in a corresponding degree. The enhancement of general prices due to this cause has apparently been offset by cheapened production of goods, due to technological improvements. How far this countervailing effect of cheapened production has neutralized, or more than neutralized, the enhancement due to credit cannot be considered here. The volume of goods seeking a market has also greatly increased during the same period, and this should also have a countervailing effect. It should mask or offset the enhancement of prices due to an increased resort to credit, but this is also a matter that does not belong here So also the relation of credit, as a price-making factor, to the production of the precious metals is no doubt a matter of some consequence in this connection, but that, too, is question of detail that requires treatment by itself.

Chapter 8

The Overproduction Fallacy – I.

In the April number of this Journal Mr. Uriel H. Crocker publishes what purports to be a rehabilitation of the "overproduction" theory of industrial depression[71]. The paper deals specifically with Mill's discussion of the question, and it is particularly Mill's position that is claimed to have been refuted. It may, therefore, not seem ungracious to call to mind that, so long as we employ "demand" and "supply" in the meaning attached to those terms by Mill and commonly accepted by those who are of his way of thinking, the proposition that aggregate demand equals aggregate supply is a truism. General overproduction, as defined by Mill - "a supply of commodities in the aggregate, surpassing the demand" - is a contradiction in terms. Aggregate supply is aggregate demand, neither more nor less.

The above-quoted definition of overproduction occurs in the pages cited from Mill by Mr. Crocker, and can therefore hardly have escaped his notice. But, as it seems not to have furnished any obstacle to the development of Mr. Crocker's argument, the simple calling attention to its significance will hardly be accepted as subverting the position taken by him. Mr. Crocker's position is not a simple, crude denial of Mill's proposition in this general form; but I believe it can be shown that the line of argument by which that position is supported is no less futile than the naive overproduction theories that have been laid away by past economic discussion. To Mr. Crocker's mind, the question as to a possible general overproduction takes form as follows: Is it possible that there should exist at any time an overproduction of one or more products, unless there is at the same time a corresponding underproduction of some other product or products?

In other words, is it possible that one product should be selling for less than the ordinary profit over the cost of its reproduction, unless some other product is at the same time selling at more than the ordinary profit over the cost of its reproduction? (p. 356.)His answer to this question is the following proposition: If at any time there is a production of a commodity not based upon and strictly proportioned to the adequate demand for it, but, with the knowledge of the producer, in excess of that demand, then there may at such time be an overproduction of that commodity and no corresponding underproduction of any other commodity. In other words, there may be in such case a general overproduction. (p. 356.)The final conclusion is stated in this second proposition:

A production of a commodity not based upon and strictly proportioned to the adequate demand for the product, but, with the knowledge of the producer, in excess of that demand, may arise, and has, in some cases,

---

[71] "The 'Over-Production' Fallacy" by Uriel H. Crocker, Vol. VI, April, 1892.

actually arisen, when machinery for the production of the commodity has been created with a capacity of production in excess of the adequate demand for the product. (p. 358.)

The use of the term "adequate demand" is to be noted. "Adequate demand" is "the demand for a commodity at such a value as will afford the ordinary profit over the necessary cost of its reproduction." (p. 355.)The concept of an "adequate demand" rests on the concept of an "ordinary profit." Now, we can intelligibly speak of adequate demand and ordinary profit without questioning either of those terms, so long as the discussion is concerned with the production of a particular commodity, or with a part, only, of the aggregate of industry. But a closer scrutiny will show that both terms break down when we come to deal with production in the aggregate.

The "ordinary profit," which an adequate demand must cover, is not a satisfactorily definite concept. It may be taken to mean the rate of profit commonly obtainable at the point of time with which the discussion deals, or it may mean the rate of profit that ought to be commonly obtainable at the time, or it may mean the rate of profit commonly obtainable during a more or less indefinite period preceding the time in question. In its colloquial use it has both the latter meanings, mingled in varying proportions. Which of these, or any other possible meaning, Mr. Crocker attaches to the term he does not say. The line of argument pursued by him requires the first of these definitions, or some definition which is like the first above given in being based on the rate of profit actually obtained at the time in question, and, therefore, to a good extent, if not entirely, of the nature of an average of the profits actually obtained.

The ordinary rate of profit, in this sense, notoriously varies from time to time. The variations to which it is subject are due to particular variations in particular occupations. Being of the nature of an average, it varies with the fluctuations of the items that go to make up the average. If, in the manner supposed in Mr. Crocker's first proposition (p. 356), a given commodity comes to be produced at less than the ordinary profit previously obtained, the ordinary profit obtainable thereby suffers a reduction, and, compared with the new ordinary profit therewith established, other commodities are now produced at more than ordinary profit; that is to say, overproduction of one commodity involves, other circumstances remaining unchanged, an underproduction of all other commodities, in the sense attached to "overproduction" by Mr. Crocker. The case supposed by Mr. Crocker resolves itself into a variation in the ordinary rate of profit.

From the general point of view, it is clear that any variation in the rate of profit in any one or more branches of industry, or in the production of any particular commodity, produces a variation, in the same direction, in the ordinary profit obtainable at the time in question, and a consequent divergence of the rate of profit in other occupations, in the opposite direction, from the new "ordinary profit." If the rate of profit in occupation B were to fall, without any change in the absolute rate of profit in occupation A, the ordinary rate of profit obtainable in the aggregate of occupations would fall; and consequently the rate of profit in occupation A would thereby rise, relatively to the altered general rate. The demand which previously was an "adequate demand," and no more, for the product of occupation A, would now have become an over-demand, not, conceivably, because of any change affecting the demand for that product directly, but simply in consequence of a change in the "ordinary profit" with which the rate of profit in occupation A is to be compared.

That is to say, there would be an underproduction in occupation A in consequence of there being an overproduction in occupation B. It is accordingly necessary to say that any over-supply of one commodity implies, or rather involves, an under-supply, in the strict economic sense, of some or all other commodities. The first of Mr. Crocker's propositions therefore breaks down. It is to be remarked that the typical case cited by Mr. Crocker (p. 358) of a production "not based upon ... the adequate demand" also breaks down when it comes to the concrete application in the second of the two propositions. And the like would probably be true of any conceivable case. It is a case of an excess of production of a particular commodity, due to the creation of more fixed capital of a given kind than the adequate demand for the product would warrant, and resolves itself into a case of misdirected or "ill-sorted" production, such as Mill has specially provided for in his discussion. It is a case of relative overproduction of a special kind of fixed capital, and a consequent depreciation of that fixed capital, either permanent or temporary. The reason for the continued production of goods to be sold at what the producer conceives to be less than a fair return is, professedly, the fact that an undue proportion of the aggregate capital has been fixed for the production of the particular commodity in question.

The Overproduction Fallacy – II.

While the doctrine of a general over-supply of goods -in the sense in which it has been criticised in economic theory-is palpably absurd, it must be admitted that the cry of "overproduction" that goes up at every season of industrial depression has a very cogent though perhaps not a very articulate meaning to the men who raise the cry. What is the nature of the fact that is symbolised by the colloquial use of "overproduction," and how it is related to "depression" and "liquidation," has never been satisfactorily made out. But no doubt it stands for an economic fact that merits the attention of any one who is curious to understand the phenomena of hard times and commercial crises.

The passages which Mr. Crocker quotes from D. A. Wells's *Recent Economic Changes* - and, more distinctly, certain other passages of that book - indicate the difficulty rather than solve it. It should be said, by the way, that Mr. Wells claims no originality with respect to the theory, or rather statement, which he puts forth, though he gives it a conciseness which it hardly had before. General "overproduction," in Mr. Wells's use, means a general production in excess of the "demand at remunerative prices." And a remunerative price may be defined, for the present purpose, as a price that will afford the customary profit on the capital invested. If general prices become "unremunerative," the meaning of that fact, as expressed in terms of this definition, is that the general run of profits has fallen below what is accepted as the customary rate of profits, or below the "ordinary profit," in the sense of what the business community accepts as the proper or adequate rate of profits for the time being. "Overproduction," in the colloquial use of the word, as appealed to in explanation of depression in trade, is used to describe a situation where goods have been produced in excess of the demand at such prices as will afford the customary profit on the capital employed in their production.

The average profit obtainable at the time on the capital invested falls short of the standard accepted as the proper, customary profit. This need not mean that the rate of discount at the time falls short of what is conceived to be the proper, customary rate. The trouble lies not primarily with the rate of profit on new investments, as indicated by the rate of interest on money seeking investment, but with the rate of profit on property already invested and capitalised in the past. The point of complaint is as to the earning capacity of investments already made. There may be much that is unsatisfactory with respect to the making of new investments; but that class of difficulties is evidently an effect, never a cause, of the trouble that exists with respect to the earning capacity of capital already invested and "capitalised" in the past. The average rate of profit from past investments, indicated by the ratio of their earning capacity to their accepted capitalisation, falls short of the accepted customary profit, indicated by the customary rate of interest on money seeking investment.

The precise difficulty is that a divergence has taken place between the accepted nominal value of property, based on its past capitalisation, and its actual present value, indicated by its present earning capacity or the present cost of replacing it. The actual present value of the property, as capitalised on the basis of its present earning capacity or on the cost of replacing it, falls short of its nominal, accepted value; and, as profits continue to be computed on the basis of this accepted nominal value, the rate of profit actually obtainable falls short of what is accepted as the customary and proper rate. The profit, computed on this basis, may even entirely disappear. The "remunerative price," then, on which Mr. Wells bases his conception of "overproduction," turns out to be such a price as will afford the customary rate of profit to capital, as computed on the basis of its nominal value, or, in other words, on the basis of its accepted capitalisation.

Now, whenever the course of industrial development compels a readjustment of the basis of capitalisation (as happens whenever the cost of production has been appreciably lowered), the customary basis on which the remunerative price has been computed becomes obsolete. The price, therefore, also becomes obsolete; and a reluctant acceptance of a new order of things follows, in which the capitalisation and nominal value of property are readjusted on a revised scale of prices, which, in the new epoch, fixes the "remunerative price" that now affords the customary rate of profit on the revised capitalisation. The immediate economic fact for which "overproduction" stands is, therefore, a divergence between the nominal, accepted valuation and the actual present value of property engaged in production, in consequence of which the nominal earnings of capital (and in some cases the real earnings as measured in means of livelihood) are diminished. The characteristic fact in a case of general "overproduction" is that the basis on which "remunerative prices" and customary profit are computed has become obsolete. This divergence may be due to several different causes, but usually and mainly to two general ones - a speculative movement, and an increased efficiency of industry[72].

The action of the former of these needs no discussion here. A speculative movement may have pushed prices up unwarrantably. A fall of general prices, due to improved processes of production, may have depressed the actual present money value of property engaged in production below its nominal value. For the present purpose the immediate result is in either case much the same: the nominal, accepted valuation of the capital, on which its returns are computed, exceeds its actual value as indicated by its present earning capacity. The property, perhaps the general aggregate property of the community, has come to be rated at a capitalised value

---

[72] The progressive accumulation of capital, by directly lowering the rate of profits, acts in the same direction as the two causes here mentioned; and some would perhaps rank it abreast with these two as an efficient agency in producing the situation for which an explanation is sought.

above the cost at which it, or its equivalent for purposes of production, could now be replaced.

The hard times of the past decade are an example going to show how this result may be reached by a lowering of the cost of production; or, as some would perhaps prefer to express it, by an increase of the efficiency of industry .If the analysis were carried a step further, it would appear that the divergence between the accepted valuation and the true present value of property, here ascribed to a lowering of the cost of production, is not due to the lowering of cost of production generally, simply as such, so much as to a lowering of the cost of production of some or all staple commodities as compared with the cost of production of the precious metals. The whole matter is very largely a matter of price - of "values" in the commercial sense.

Such a divergence between the accepted valuation and the actual value of capital may seem an inadequate basis for an economic fact of such magnitude as a period of industrial depression. And yet an industrial depression means, mainly, a readjustment of values. It is primarily, to a very great extent, a psychological fact. Secondarily, it is largely a matter of the shifting of ownership rather than a destruction of wealth or a serious reduction of the aggregate productiveness of industry as measured in goods. The act of readjusting one's conception of one's own belongings to the scale of a reduced number of dollars, even though the dollar is worth enough more to make up for the nominal depreciation, is in itself a sufficiently painful one, and is submitted to only reluctantly and tardily. But this subjective element, this lesion of the feelings of the property owner, is by no means all that is involved in a decrease of the nominal earning capacity of capital. Whenever the nominal owner of the means of production is not also the real owner, as happens in the case of borrowed capital, he becomes answerable to the real owner - the lender - for any amount by which the actual present value of the property may fall short of the accepted valuation. A decline in the market value of property represented by the debt, therefore, means a real loss to the debtor, although, so far as it is due to increased efficiency of industry, it may be only a nominal loss to the man who has to do with his own capital only, and may be, and generally is, a source of distinct though unrecognized gain to the lender. The borrower assumes the risk of depreciation of the property represented by the debt.

In a case such as has been witnessed in this country during the past ten or twelve years, when there has been a pretty general decline in the cost of production of staple commodities - as compared with the standard of value - and a consequent decline in the nominal earning capacity of property engaged in production, of perhaps 30 percent, this factor is of the very gravest consequence. Especially is this true in the case of a community where so great a proportion of capital is represented by interest-bearing securities.

SOCIAL THEORY

Chapter 1
The Barbarian Status of Women

It seems altogether probable that in the primitive groups of mankind, when the race first took to a systematic use of tools and so emerged upon the properly human plane of life, there was but the very slightest beginning of a system of status, with little of invidious distinction between classes and little of a corresponding division of employments. In an earlier paper, published in this JOURNA[73] it has been argued that the early division of labor between classes comes in as the result of an increasing efficiency of labor, due to a growing effectiveness in the use of tools.

When, in the early cultural development, the use of tools and the technical command of material forces had reached a certain degree of effectiveness, the employments which occupy the primitive community would fall into two distinct groups - (a) the honorific employments, which involve a large element of prowess, and (b) the humiliating employments, which call for diligence and into which the sturdier virtues do not enter. An appreciable advance in the use of tools must precede this differentiation of employments, because (1) without effective tools (including weapons) men are not sufficiently formidable in conflict with the ferocious beasts to devote themselves so exclusively to the hunting of large game as to develop that occupation into a conventional mode of life reserved for a distinct class; (2) without tools of some efficiency, industry is not productive enough to support a dense population, and therefore the groups into which the population gathers will not come into such a habitual hostile contact with one another as would give rise to a life of warlike prowess; (3) until industrial methods and knowledge have made some advance, the work of getting a livelihood is too exacting to admit of the consistent exemption of any portion of the community from vulgar labor; (4) the inefficient primitive industry yields no such disposable surplus of accumulated goods as would be worth fighting for, or would tempt an intruder, and therefore there is little provocation to warlike prowess.

With the growth of industry comes the possibility of a predatory life; and if the groups of savages crowd one another in the struggle for subsistence, there is a provocation to hostilities, and a predatory habit of life ensues. There is a consequent growth of a predatory culture, which may for the present purpose be treated as the beginning of the barbarian culture. This predatory culture shows itself in a growth of suitable institutions. The group divides itself conventionally into a fighting and a peace-keeping class, with a corresponding division of labor. Fighting, together with other work that involves a serious element of exploit, becomes the employment

---

[73] "The Instinct of Workmanship and the Irksomeness of Labor," September 1898, pp. 187-201.

of the able-bodied men; the uneventful everyday work of the group falls to the women and the infirm. In such a community the standards of merit and propriety rest on an invidious distinction between those who are capable fighters and those who are not. Infirmity, that is to say incapacity for exploit, is looked down upon.

One of the early consequences of this deprecation of infirmity is a tabu on women and on women's employments. In the apprehension of the archaic, animistic barbarian, infirmity is infectious. The infection may work its mischievous effect both by sympathetic influence and by transfusion. Therefore it is well for the able-bodied man who is mindful of his virility to shun all undue contact and conversation with the weaker sex and to avoid all contamination with the employments that are characteristic of the sex. Even the habitual food of women should not be eaten by men, lest their force be thereby impaired. The injunction against womanly employments and foods and against intercourse with women applies with especial rigor during the season of preparation for any work of manly exploit, such as a great hunt or a warlike raid, or induction into some manly dignity or society or mystery.

Illustrations of this seasonal tabu abound in the early history of all peoples that have had a warlike or barbarian past. The women, their occupations, their food and clothing, their habitual place in the house or village, and in extreme cases even their speech, become ceremonially unclean to the men. This imputation of ceremonial uncleanness on the ground of their infirmity has lasted on in the later culture as a sense of the unworthiness or levitical inadequacy of women; so that even now we feel the impropriety of women taking rank with men, or representing the community in any relation that calls for dignity and ritual competency; as for instance, in priestly or diplomatic offices, or even in representative civil offices, and likewise, and for a like reason, in such offices of domestic and body servants as are of a seriously ceremonial character - footmen, butlers, etc.

The changes that take place in the everyday experiences of a group or horde when it passes from a peaceable to a predatory habit of life have their effect on the habits of thought prevalent in the group. As the hostile contact of one group with another becomes closer and more habitual, the predatory activity and the bellicose animus become more habitual to the members of the group. Fighting comes more and more to occupy men's everyday thoughts, and the other activities of the group fall into the background and become subsidiary to the fighting activity. In the popular apprehension the substantial core of such a group - that on which men's thoughts run when the community and the community's life is thought of - is the body of fighting men. The collective fighting capacity becomes the most serious question that occupies men's minds, and gives the point of view from which persons and conduct are rated.

The scheme of life of such a group is substantially a scheme of exploit. There is much of this point of view to be found even in the common-sense views held by modern populations. The inclination to identify the community with its fighting men comes into evidence today whenever warlike interests occupy the popular attention in an appreciable degree. The work of the predatory barbarian group is gradually specialized and differentiated under the dominance of this ideal of prowess, so as to give rise to a system of status in which the non fighters fall into a position of subservience to the fighters. The accepted scheme of life or consensus of opinions which guides the conduct of men in such a predatory group and decides what may properly be done, of course comprises a great variety of details; but it is, after all, a single scheme - a more or less organic whole so that the life carried on under its guidance in any case makes up a somewhat consistent and characteristic body of culture.

This is necessarily the case, because of the simple fact that the individuals between whom the consensus holds are individuals. The thinking of each one is the thinking of the same individual, on whatever head and in whatever direction his thinking may run. Whatever may be the immediate point or object of his thinking, the frame of mind which governs his aim and manner of reasoning in passing on any given point of conduct is, on the whole, the habitual frame of mind which experience and tradition have enforced upon him. Individuals whose sense of what is right and good departs widely from the accepted views suffer some repression, and in case of an extreme divergence they are eliminated from the effective life of the group through ostracism.

Where the fighting class is in the position of dominance and prescriptive legitimacy, the canons of conduct are shaped chiefly by the common sense of the body of fighting men. Whatever conduct and whatever code of proprieties has the authentication of this common sense is definitively right and good, for the time being, and the deliverances of this common sense are, in their turn, shaped by the habits of life of the able-bodied men. Habitual conflict acts, by selection and by habituation, to make these male members tolerant of any infliction of damage and suffering. Habituation to the sight and infliction of suffering, and to the emotions that go with fights and brawls, may even end in making the spectacle of misery a pleasing diversion to them. The result is in any case a more or less consistent attitude of plundering and coercion on the part of the fighting body, and this animus is incorporated into the scheme of life of the community. The discipline of predatory life makes for an attitude of mastery on the part of the able-bodied men in all their relations with the weaker members of the group, and especially in their relations with the women.

Men who are trained in predatory ways of life and modes of thinking come by habituation to apprehend this form of the relation between the sexes as good and beautiful. All the women in the group will share in the class repression and depreciation that belongs to them as women, but the status of women taken from hostile groups has an additional feature. Such a woman not only belongs to a subservient and low class, but she also stands in a special relation to her captor. She is a trophy of the raid, and therefore an evidence of exploit, and on this ground it is to her captor's interest to maintain a peculiarly obvious relation of mastery toward her. And since, in the early culture, it does not detract from her subservience to the life of the group, this peculiar relation of the captive to her captor will meet but slight, if any, objection from the other members of the group. At the same time, since his peculiar coercive relation to the woman serves to mark her as a trophy of his exploit, he will somewhat jealously resent any similar freedom taken by other men, or any attempt on their part to parade a similar coercive authority over her, and so usurp the laurels of his prowess, very much as a warrior would under like circumstances resent a usurpation or an abuse of the scalps or skulls which he had taken from the enemy.

After the habit of appropriating captured women has hardened into custom, and so given rise on the one hand to a form of marriage resting on coercion, and on the other hand to a concept of ownership,[74] a development of certain secondary features of the institution so inaugurated is to be looked for. In time this coercive ownership-marriage receives the sanction of the popular taste and morality. It comes to rest in men's habits of thought as the right form of marriage relation, and it comes at the same time to be gratifying to men's sense of beauty and of honor. The growing predilection for mastery and coercion, as a manly trait, together with the growing moral and aesthetic approbation of marriage on a basis of coercion and ownership, will affect the tastes of the men most immediately and most strongly; but since the men are the superior class, whose views determine the current views of the community, their common sense in the matter will shape the current canons of taste in its own image.

The tastes of the women also, in point of morality and of propriety alike, will presently be affected in the same way. Through the precept and example of those who make the vogue, and through selective repression of those who are unable to accept it, the institution of ownership-marriage makes its way into definitive acceptance as the only beautiful and virtuous form of the relation. As the conviction of its legitimacy grows stronger in each succeeding generation, it comes to be appreciated unreflectingly as a deliverance of common sense and enlightened reason that the good and beautiful attitude of the man toward the woman is an attitude of coercion. "None but the brave deserve the fair."

As the predatory habit of life gains a more unquestioned and undivided sway, other forms of the marriage relation fall under a polite odium. The masterless, unattached woman consequently loses caste. It becomes imperative for all men who would stand well in the eyes of their fellows to attach some woman or women to themselves by the honorable bonds of seizure. In order to a decent standing in the community a man is required to enter into this virtuous and honorific relation of ownership-marriage, and a publicly acknowledged marriage relation which has not the sanction of capture becomes unworthy of able-bodied men. But as the group increases in size, the difficulty of providing wives by capture becomes very great, and it becomes necessary to find a remedy that shall save the requirements of decency and at the same time permit the marriage of wom-

---

[74] For a more detailed discussion of this point see a paper on "The Beginnings of Ownership" in this JOURNAL for November, 1898.

en from within the group. To this end the status of women married from within the group is sought to be mended by a mimic or ceremonial capture. The ceremonial capture effects an assimilation of the free woman into the more acceptable class of women who are attached by bonds of coercion to some master, and so gives a ceremonial legitimacy and decency to the resulting marriage relation. The probable motive for adopting the free women into the honorable class of bond women in this way is not primarily a wish to improve their standing or their lot, but rather a wish to keep those good men in countenance who, for dearth of captives, are constrained to seek a substitute from among the home-bred women of the group.

The inclinations of men in high standing who are possessed of marriageable daughters would run in the same direction. It would not seem right that a woman of high birth should irretrievably be outclassed by any chance-comer from outside. According to this view, marriage by feigned capture within the tribe is a case of mimicry - "protective mimicry," to borrow a phrase from the naturalists. It is substantially a case of adoption. As is the case in all human relations where adoption is practiced, this adoption of the free women into the class of the unfree proceeds by as close an imitation as may be of the original fact for which it is a substitute. And as in other cases of adoption, the ceremonial performance is by no means looked upon as a fatuous make-believe. The barbarian has implicit faith in the efficiency of imitation and ceremonial execution as a means of compassing a desired end. The entire range of magic and religious rites is testimony to that effect.

He looks upon external objects and sequences naively, as organic and individual things, and as expressions of a propensity working toward an end. The unsophisticated common sense of the primitive barbarian apprehends sequences and events in terms of will-power or inclination. As seen in the light of this animistic preconception, any process is substantially teleological, and the propensity imputed to it will not be thwarted of its legitimate end after the course of events in which it expresses itself has once fallen into shape or got under way. It follows logically, as a matter of course, that if once the motions leading to a desired consummation have been rehearsed in the accredited form and sequence, the same substantial result will be attained as that produced by the process imitated. This is the ground of whatever efficiency is imputed to ceremonial observances on all planes of culture, and it is especially the chief element in formal adoption and initiation. Hence, probably, the practice of mock-seizure or mock-capture, and hence the formal profession of fealty and submission on the part of the woman in the marriage rites of peoples among whom the household with a male head prevails.

This form of the household is almost always associated with some survival or reminiscence of wife-capture. In all such cases, marriage is, by derivation, a ritual of initiation into servitude. In the words of the formula, even after it has been appreciably softened under the latter-day decay of the sense of status, it is the woman's place to love, honor, and obey. According to this view, the patriarchal household, or, in other words, the household with a male head, is an outgrowth of emulation between the members of a warlike community. It is, therefore, in point of derivation, a predatory institution. The ownership and control of women is a gratifying evidence of prowess and high standing. In logical consistency, therefore, the greater the number of women so held, the greater the distinction which their possession confers upon their master. Hence the prevalence of polygamy, which occurs almost universally at one stage of culture among peoples which have the male household. There may, of course, be other reasons for polygamy, but the ideal development of polygamy which is met with in the harems of very powerful patriarchal despots and chieftains can scarcely be explained on other grounds. But whether it works out in a system of polygamy or not, the male household is in any case a detail of a system of status under which the women are included in the class of un-free subjects.

The dominant feature in the institutional structure of these communities is that of status, and the groundwork of their economic life is a rigorous system of ownership. The institution is found at its best, or in its most effectual development, in the communities in which status and ownership prevail with the least mitigation; and with the decline of the sense of status and of the extreme pretensions of ownership, such as has been going on for some time past in the communities of the western culture, the institution of the patriarchal household has also suffered something of a disintegration. There has been some weakening and slackening of the bonds, and this deterioration is most visible in the communities which have departed farthest from the ancient system of status, and have gone farthest in reorganizing their economic life on the lines of industrial freedom. And the deference for an indissoluble tie of ownership-marriage, as well as the sense of its definitive virtuousness, has suffered the greatest decline among the classes immediately engaged in the modern industries.

So that there seems to be fair ground for saying that the habits of thought fostered by modern industrial life are, on the whole, not favorable to the maintenance of this institution or to that status of women which the institution in its best development implies. The days of its best development are in the past, and the discipline of modern life - if not supplemented by a prudent inculcation of conservative ideals - will scarcely afford the psychological basis for its rehabilitation. This form of marriage, or of ownership, by which the man becomes the head of the household, the owner of the woman, and the owner and discretionary consumer of the household's output of consumable goods, does not of necessity imply a patriarchal system of consanguinity.

The presence or absence of maternal relationship should, therefore, not be given definite weight in this connection. The male household, in some degree of elaboration, may well coexist with a counting of relationship in the female line, as, for instance, among many North American tribes. But where this is the case it seems probable that the ownership of women, together with the invidious distinctions of status from which the practice of such an ownership springs, has come into vogue at so late a stage of the cultural development that the maternal system of relationship had already been thoroughly incorporated into the tribe's scheme of life. The male household in such cases is ordinarily not developed in good form or entirely free from traces of a maternal household. The traces of a maternal household which are found in these cases commonly point to a form of marriage which disregards the man rather than places him under the surveillance of the woman. It may well be named the household of the unattached woman. This condition of things argues that the tribe or race in question has entered upon a predatory life only after a considerable period of peaceable industrial life, and after having achieved a considerable development of social structure under the regime of peace and industry, whereas the unqualified prevalence of the patriarchate, together with the male household, may be taken to indicate that the predatory phase was entered early, culturally speaking.

Where the patriarchal system is in force in fully developed form, including the paternal household, and hampered with no indubitable survivals of a maternal household or a maternal system of relationship, the presumption would be that the people in question has entered upon the predatory culture early, and has adopted the institutions of private property and class prerogative at an early stage of its economic development. On the other hand, where there are well-preserved traces of a maternal household, the presumption is that the predatory phase has been entered by the community in question at a relatively late point in its life history, even if the patriarchal system is, and long has been, the prevalent system of relationship. In the latter case the community, or the group of tribes, may, perhaps for geographical reasons, not have independently attained the predatory culture in accentuated form, but may at a relatively late date have contracted the agnatic system and the paternal household through contact with another, higher, or characteristically different, culture, which has included these institutions among its cultural furniture.

The required contact would take place most effectually by way of invasion and conquest by an alien race occupying the higher plane or divergent line of culture. Something of this kind is the probable explanation, for instance, of the equivocal character of the household and relationship system in the early Germanic culture, especially as it is seen in such outlying regions as Scandinavia. The evidence, in this latter case, as in some other communities lying farther south, is somewhat obscure, but it points to a long-continued coexistence of the two forms of the household; of which the maternal seems to have held its place most tenaciously among the subject or lower classes of the population, while the paternal was the honorable form of marriage in vogue among the superior class. In the earliest traceable situation of these tribes there appears to have been a relatively feeble, but growing, preponderance of the male household throughout the community.

This mixture of marriage institutions, as well as the correlative mixture or ambiguity of property institutions associated with it in the Germanic culture, seems most easily explicable as being due to the mingling of two distinct racial stocks, whose institutions differed in these respects. The race or tribe which had the maternal household and common property would probably have been the more numerous and the more peaceable at the time the mixing process began, and would fall into some degree of subjection to its more warlike consort race. No attempt is hereby made to account for the various forms of human marriage, or to show how the institution varies in detail from place to place and from time to time, but only to indicate what seems to have been the range of motives and of exigencies that have given rise to the paternal household, as it has been handed down from the barbarian past of the peoples of the western culture. To this end, nothing but the most general features of the life history of the institution have been touched upon, and even the evidence on which this much of generalization is based is, per force, omitted. The purpose of the argument is to point out that there is a close connection, particularly in point of psychological derivation, between individual ownership, the system of status, and the paternal household, as they appear in this culture. This view of the derivation of private property and of the male household, as already suggested, does not imply the prior existence of a maternal household of the kind in which the woman is the head and master of a household group and exercises a discretionary control over her husband or husbands and over the household effects.

Still less does it imply a prior state of promiscuity. What is implied by the hypothesis and by the scant evidence at hand is rather the form of the marriage relation above characterized as the household of the unattached woman. The characteristic feature of this marriage seems to have been an absence of coercion or control in the relation between the sexes. The union (probably monogamic and more or less enduring) seems to have been terminable at will by either party, under the constraint of some slight conventional limitations. The substantial difference introduced into the marriage relation on the adoption of ownership-marriage is the exercise of coercion by the man and the loss on the part of the woman of the power to terminate the relation at will. Evidence running in this direction, and in part hitherto unpublished, is to be found both in the modern and in the earlier culture of Germanic communities.

It is only in cases where circumstances have, in an exceptional degree, favored the development of ownership-marriage that we should expect to find the institution worked out to its logical consequences. Wherever the predatory phase of social life has not come in early and has not prevailed in unqualified form for a long time, or wherever a social group or race with this form of the household has received a strong admixture of another race not possessed of the institution, there the prevalent form of marriage should show something of a departure from this paternal type. And even where neither of these two conditions is present, this type of the marriage relation might be expected in the course of time to break down with the change of circumstances, since it is an institution that has grown up as a detail of a system of status, and, therefore, presumably fits into such a social system, but does not fit into a system of a different kind. It is at present visibly breaking down in modern civilized communities, apparently because it is at variance with the most ancient habits of thought of the race, as well as with the exigencies of a peaceful, industrial mode of life.

There may seem some ground for holding that the same reassertion of ancient habits of thought which is now apparently at work to disintegrate the institution of ownership-marriage may be expected also to work a disintegration of the correlative institution of private property; but that is perhaps a question of speculative curiosity rather than of urgent theoretical interest.

Chapter 2

The Economic Theory of Women's Dress

In human apparel the element of dress is readily distinguishable from that of clothing. The two functions - of dress and of clothing the person - are to a great extent subserved by the same material goods, although the extent to which the same material serves both purposes will appear very much slighter on second thought than it does at first glance. A differentiation of materials has long been going on, by virtue of which many things that are worn for the one purpose no longer serve, and are no longer expected to serve, the other. The differentiation is by no means complete. Much of human apparel is worn both for physical comfort and for dress; still more of it is worn ostensibly for both purposes.

But the differentiation is already very considerable and is visibly progressing. But, however united in the same object, however the two purposes may be served by the same material goods, the purpose of physical comfort and that of a reputable appearance are not to be confounded by the meanest understanding. The elements of clothing and of dress are distinct; not only that, but they even verge on incompatibility; the purpose of either is frequently best subserved by special means which are adapted to perform only a single line of duty. It is often true, here as elsewhere, that the most efficient tool is the most highly specialised tool.

Of these two elements of apparel dress came first in order of development, and it continues to hold the primacy to this day. The element of clothing, the quality of affording comfort, was from the beginning, and to a great extent it continues to be, in some sort an afterthought. The origin of dress is sought in the principle of adornment. This is a well-accepted fact of social evolution. But that principle furnished the point of departure for the evolution of dress rather than the norm of its development. It is true of dress, as of so much else of the apparatus of life, that its initial purpose has not remained its sole or dominant purpose throughout the course of its later growth. It may be stated broadly that adornment, in the naive aesthetic sense, is a factor of relatively slight importance in modern dress.

The line of progress during the initial stage of the evolution of apparel was from the simple concept of adornment of the person by supplementary accessions from without, to the complex concept of an adornment that should render the person pleasing, or of an enviable presence, and at the same time serve to indicate the possession of other virtues than that of a well-favored person only. In this latter direction lies what was to evolve into dress. By the time dress emerged from the primitive efforts of the savage to beautify himself with gaudy additions to his person, it was already an economic factor of some importance. The change from a purely aesthetic character (ornament) to a mixture of the aesthetic and economic took place before the progress had been achieved from pigments and trinkets to what is commonly understood by apparel. Ornament is not properly an economic category, although the trinkets which serve the purpose of ornament may also do duty as an economic factor, and in so far be assimilated to dress. What constitutes dress an economic fact, properly falling within the scope of economic theory, is its function as an index of the wealth of its wearer - or, to be more precise, of its owner, for the wearer and owner are not necessarily the same person. It will hold with respect to more than one half the values currently recognised as "dress," especially that portion with which this paper is immediately concerned - woman's dress - that the wearer and the owner are different persons. But while they need not be united in the same person, they must be organic members of the same economic unit; and the dress is the index of the wealth of the economic unit which the wearer represents.

Under the patriarchal organisation of society, where the social unit was the man (with his dependents), the dress of the women was an exponent of the wealth of the man whose chattels they were. In modern society, where the unit is the household, the woman's dress sets forth the wealth of the household to which she belongs. Still, even today, in spite of the nominal and somewhat celebrated demise of the patriarchal idea, there is that about the dress of women which suggests that the wearer is something in the nature of a chattel; indeed, the theory of woman's dress quite plainly involves the implication that the woman is a chattel. In this respect the dress of women differs from that of men. With this exception, which is not of first-rate importance, the essential principles of woman's dress are not different from those which govern the dress of men; but even apart from this added characteristic the element of dress is to be seen in a more unhampered development in the apparel of women.

A discussion of the theory of dress in general will gain in brevity and conciseness by keeping in view the concrete facts of the highest manifestation of the principles with which it has to deal, and this highest manifestation of dress is unquestionably seen in the apparel of the women of the most advanced modern communities.

The basis of the award of social rank and popular respect is the success, or more precisely the efficiency, of the social unit, as evidenced by its visible success. When efficiency eventuates in possessions, in pecuniary strength, as it eminently does in the social system of our time, the basis of the award of social consideration becomes the visible pecuniary strength of the social unit. The immediate and obvious index of pecuniary strength is the visible ability to spend, to consume unproductively; and men early learned to put in evidence their ability to spend by displaying costly goods that afford no return to their owner, either in comfort or in gain. Almost as early did a differentiation set in, whereby it became the function of woman, in a peculiar degree, to exhibit the pecuniary strength of her social unit by means of a conspicuously unproductive consumption of valuable goods.

Reputability is in the last analysis, and especially in the long run, pretty fairly coincident with the pecuniary strength of the social unit in question. Woman, primarily, originally because she was herself a pecuniary possession, has become in a peculiar way the exponent of the pecuniary strength of her social group; and with the progress of specialisation of functions in the social organism this duty tends to devolve more and more entirely upon the woman. The best, most advanced, most highly developed societies of our time have reached the point in their evolution where it has (ideally) become the great, peculiar, and almost the sole function of woman in the social system to put in evidence her economic unit's ability to pay. That is to say, woman's place (according to the ideal scheme of our social system) has come to be that of a means of conspicuously unproductive expenditure.

The admissible evidence of the woman's expensiveness has considerable range in respect of form and method, but in substance it is always the same. It may take the form of manners, breeding, and accomplishments that are, prima facie, impossible to acquire or maintain without such leisure as bespeaks a considerable and relatively long-continued possession of wealth. It may also express itself in a peculiar manner of life, on the same grounds and with much the same purpose. But the method in vogue always and everywhere, alone or in conjunction with other methods, is that of dress. "Dress," therefore, from the economic point of view, comes pretty near being synonymous with "display of wasteful expenditure."

The extra portion of butter, or other unguent, with which the wives of the magnates of the African interior anoint their persons, beyond what comfort requires, is a form of this kind of expenditure lying on the border between primitive personal embellishment and incipient dress. So also the brass-wire bracelets, anklets, etc., at times aggregating some thirty pounds in weight, worn by the same class of persons, as well as, to a less extent, by the male population of the same countries. So also the pelt of the arctic fur seal, which the women of civilised countries prefer to fabrics that are preferable to it in all respects but that of expense. So also the ostrich plumes and the many curious effigies of plants and animals that are dealt in by the milliners.

The list is inexhaustible, for there is scarcely an article of apparel of male or female, civilised or uncivilised, that does not partake largely of this element and very many may be said, in point of economic principle, to consist of virtually nothing else. It is not that the wearers or the buyers of these wasteful goods desire the waste. They desire to make manifest their ability to pay. What is sought is not the de facto waste, but the appearance of waste. Hence there is a constant effort on the part of the consumers of these goods to obtain them at as good a bargain as may be; and hence also a constant effort on the part of the producers of these goods to lower the cost of their production, and consequently to lower the price. But as fast as the price of the goods declines to such a figure that their consumption is no longer prima facie evidence of a considerable ability to pay, the particular goods in question fall out of favor, and consumption is diverted to something which more adequately manifests the wearer's ability to afford wasteful consumption.

This fact, that the object sought is not the waste but the display of waste, develops into a principle of pseudo-economy in the use of material; so that it has come to be recognised as a canon of good form that apparel should not show lavish expenditure simply. The material used must be chosen so as to give evidence of the wearer's (owner's) capacity for making it go as far in the way of display as may be; otherwise it would suggest incapacity on the part of the owner, and so partially defeat the main purpose of the display. But what is more to the point is that such a mere display of crude waste would also suggest that the means of display had been acquired so recently as not to have permitted that long-continued waste of time and effort required for mastering the most effective methods of display. It would argue recent acquisition of means; and we are still near enough to the tradition of pedigree and aristocracy of birth to make long-continued possession of means second in point of desirability only to the possession of large means. The greatness of the means possessed is manifested by the volume of display; the length of possession is, in some degree, evidenced by the manifestation of a thorough habituation to the methods of display. Evidence of a knowledge and habit of good form in dress (as in manners) is chiefly to be valued because it argues that much time has been spent in the acquisition of this accomplishment; and as the accomplishment is in no wise of direct economic value, it argues pecuniary ability to waste time and labor. Such accomplishment, therefore, when possessed in a high degree, is evidence of a life (or of more than one life) spent to no useful purpose; which, for purposes of respectability, goes as far as a very considerable unproductive consumption of goods.

The offensiveness of crude taste and vulgar display in matters of dress ii, in the last analysis, due to the fact that they argue the absence of ability to afford a reputable amount of waste of time and effort. Effective use of the means at hand may, further, be taken to argue efficiency in the person making the display; and the display of efficiency, so long as it does not manifestly result in pecuniary gain or increased personal comfort, is a great social desideratum. Hence it happens that, surprising as it may seem at first glance, a principle of pseudo-economy in the use of materials has come to hold a well-secured though pretty narrowly circumscribed place in the theory of dress, as that theory expresses itself in the facts of life. This principle, acting in concert with certain other requirements of dress, produces some curious and otherwise inexplicable results, which will be spoken of in their place.

The first principle of dress, therefore, is conspicuous expensiveness. As a corollary under this principle, but of such magnificent scope and consequence as to claim rank as a second fundamental principle, there is the evidence of expenditure afforded by a constant supersession of one wasteful garment or trinket by a new one. This principle inculcates the desirability, amounting to a necessity wherever circumstances allow, of wearing nothing that is out of date. In the most advanced communities of our time, and so far as concerns the highest manifestations of dress - e.g., in ball dress and the apparel worn on similar ceremonial occasions, when the canons of dress rule unhampered by extraneous considerations - this principle expresses itself in the maxim that no outer garment may be worn more than once.

This requirement of novelty is the underlying principle of the whole of the difficult and interesting domain of fashion. Fashion does not demand continual flux and change simply because that way of doing is foolish; flux and change and novelty are demanded by the central principle of all dress - conspicuous waste. This principle of novelty, acting in concert with the motive of pseudo-economy already spoken of, is answerable for that system of shams that figures so largely, openly and aboveboard, in the accepted code of dress. The motive of economy, or effective use of material, furnishes the point of departure, and, this being given, the requirement of novelty acts to develop a complex and extensive system of pretenses, ever varying and transient in point of detail, but each imperative during its allotted time-facings, edgings, and the many (pseudo) deceptive contrivances that will occur to any one that is at all familiar with the technique of dress. This pretense of deception is often developed into a pathetic, child-like make-believe. The realities which it simulates, or rather symbolises, could not be tolerated.

They would be in some cases too crudely expensive, in others inexpensive and more nearly adapted to minister to personal comfort than to visible expense; and either alternative is obnoxious to the canons of good form. But apart from the exhibition of pecuniary strength afforded by an aggressive wasteful expenditure, the same purpose may also be served by conspicuous abstention from useful effort. The woman is, by virtue of the specialisation of social functions, the exponent of the economic unit's pecuniary strength, and it consequently also devolves on her to exhibit the unit's capacity to endure this passive form of pecuniary damage. She can do this by putting in evidence the fact (often a fiction) that she leads a useless life. Dress is her chief means of doing so. The ideal of dress, on this head, is to demonstrate to all observers, and to compel observation of the fact, that the wearer is manifestly incapable of doing anything that is of any use.

The modern civilised woman's dress attempts this demonstration of habitual idleness, and succeeds measurably. Herein lies the secret of the persistence, in modern dress, of the skirt and of all the cumbrous and otherwise meaningless drapery which the skirt typifies. The skirt persists because it is cumbrous. It hampers the movements of the wearer and disables her, in great measure, for any useful occupation. So it serves as an advertisement (often disingenuous) that the wearer is backed by sufficient means to be able to afford the idleness, or impaired efficiency, which the skirt implies. The like is true of the high heel, and in less degree of several other features of modern dress. Herein is also to be sought the ground of the persistence (probably not the origin) of the one great mutilation practiced by civilised occidental womankind-the constricted waist, as well as of the analogous practice of the abortive foot among their Chinese sisters.

This modern mutilation of woman is perhaps not to be classed strictly under the category of dress; but it is scarcely possible to draw the line so as to exclude it from the theory, and it is so closely coincident with that category in point of principle that an outline of the theory would be incomplete without reference to it. A corollary of some significance follows from this general principle.

The fact that voluntarily accepted physical incapacity argues the possession of wealth practically establishes the futility of any attempted reform of woman's dress in the direction of convenience, comfort, or health. It is of the essence of dress that it should (appear to) hamper, incommode, and injure the wearer, for in so doing it proclaims the wearer's pecuniary ability to endure idleness and physical incapacity. It may be noted, by the way, that this requirement, that women must appear to be idle in order to be respectable, is an unfortunate circumstance for women who are compelled to provide their own livelihood. They have to supply not only the means of living, but also the means of advertising the fiction that they live without any gainful occupation; and they have to do all this while encumbered with garments specially designed to hamper their movements and decrease their industrial efficiency.

The cardinal principles of the theory of woman's dress, then, are these three:

1. Expensiveness: Considered with respect to its effectiveness as clothing, apparel must be uneconomical. It must afford evidence of the ability of the wearer's economic group to pay for things that are in themselves of no use to any one concerned-to pay without getting an equivalent in comfort or in gain. From this principle there is no exception.

2. Novelty: Woman's apparel must afford *prima facie* evidence of having been worn but for a relatively short time, as well as, with respect to many articles, evidence of inability to withstand any appreciable amount of wear. Exceptions from this rule are such things as are of sufficient permanence to become heirlooms, and of such surpassing expensiveness as normally to be possessed only by persons of superior (pecuniary) rank. The possession of an heirloom is to be commended because it argues the practice of waste through more than one generation.

3. Ineptitude: It must afford *prima facie* evidence of incapacitating the wearer for any gainful occupation; and it should also make it apparent that she is permanently unfit for any useful effort, even after the restraint of the apparel is removed. From this rule there is no exception. Besides these three, the principle of adornment, in the aesthetic sense, plays some part in dress. It has a certain degree of economic importance, and applies with a good deal of generality; but it is by no means imperatively present, and when it is present its application is closely circumscribed by the three principles already laid down. Indeed, the office of the principle of adornment in dress is that of handmaid to the principle of novelty, rather than that of an independent or co-ordinate factor.

There are, further, minor principles that may or may not be present, some of which are derivatives of the great central requisite of conspicuous waste; others are of alien origin, but all are none the less subject to the controlling presence of the three cardinal principles enumerated above. These three are essential and constitute the substantial norm of woman's dress, and no exigency m, permanently set them aside so long as the chance of rivalry between persons in respect of wealth remains. Given the possibility of a difference in wealth, and the sway of this norm of dress is inevitable. Some spasm of sense, or sentiment, or what not, may from time to time create a temporary and local diversion in woman's apparel; but the great norm of "conspicuous waste" cannot be set aside or appreciably qualified so long as this its economic ground remains.

To single out an example of the temporary effect of a given drift of sentiment, there has, within the past few years, come, and very nearly gone, a recrudescence of the element of physical comfort of the wearer, as one of the usual requirements of good form in dress. The meaning of this proposition, of course, is not what appears on its face; that seldom happens in matters of dress. It was the show of personal comfort that was lately imperative, and the show was often attained only at the sacrifice of the substance. This development, by the way, seems to have been due to a ramification of the sentimental athleticism (flesh-worship) that has been dominant of late; and now that the crest of this wave of sentiment has passed, this alien motive in dress is also receding.

The theory of which an outline has now been given is claimed to apply in full force only to modern woman's dress. It is obvious that, if the principles arrived at are to be applied as all-deciding criteria, "woman's dress" will include the apparel of a large class of persons who, in the crude biological sense, are men. This feature does not act to invalidate the theory. A classification for the purpose of economic theory must be made on economic grounds alone, and cannot permit considerations whose validity does not extend beyond the narrower domain of the natural sciences to mar its symmetry so far as to exclude this genial volunteer contingent from the ranks of womankind.

There is also a second, very analogous class of persons, whose apparel likewise, though to a less degree, conforms to the canons of woman's dress. This class is made up of the children of civilised society. The children, with some slight reservation of course, are, for the purpose of the theory, to be regarded as ancillary material serving to round out the great function of civilised womankind as the conspicuous consumers of goods. The child in the hands of civilised woman is an accessory organ of conspicuous consumption, much as any tool in the hands of a laborer is an accessory organ of productive efficiency.

Chapter 3

The Beginnings of Ownership

In the accepted economic theories the ground of ownership is commonly conceived to be the productive labor of the owner. This is taken, without
reflection or question, to be the legitimate basis of property; he who has
produced a useful thing should possess and enjoy it. On this head the socialists and the economists of the classical line - the two extremes of economic speculation - are substantially at one.

The point is not in controversy, or at least it has not been until recently;
it has been accepted as an axiomatic premise. With the socialists it has
served as the ground of their demand that the laborer should receive the
full product of his labor. To classical economists the axiom has, perhaps,
been as much trouble as it has been worth. It has given them no end of
bother to explain how the capitalist is the "producer" of the goods that
pass into his possession, and how it is true that the laborer gets what he
produces. Sporadic instances of ownership quite dissociated from creative
industry are recognized and taken account of as departures from the normal; they are due to disturbing causes. The main position is scarcely questioned, that in the normal case wealth is distributed in proportion to - and
in some cogent sense because of - the recipient's contribution to the
product.

Not only is the productive labor of the owner the definitive ground of his
ownership today, but the derivation of the institution of property is similarly traced to the productive labor of that putative savage hunter who
produced two deer or one beaver or twelve fish. The conjectural history of
the origin of property, so far as it has been written by the economists, has
been constructed out of conjecture proceeding on the preconceptions of
Natural Rights and a coercive Order of Nature. To anyone who approaches
the question of ownership with only an incidental interest in its solution
(as is true of the classical, pre-evolutionary economists), and fortified with
the preconceptions of natural rights, all this seems plain. It sufficiently
accounts for the institution, both in point of logical derivation and in
point of historical development. The "natural" owner is the person who
has "produced" an article, or who, by a constructively equivalent expenditure of productive force, has found and appropriated an object. It is conceived that such a person becomes the owner of the article by virtue of the
immediate logical inclusion of the idea of ownership under the idea of
creative industry.

This natural-rights theory of property makes the creative effort of an isolated, self-sufficing individual the basis of the ownership vested in him. In
so doing it overlooks the fact that there is no isolated, self-sufficing individual. All production is, in fact, a production in and by the help of the
community, and all wealth is such only in society. Within the human period of the race development, it is safe to say, no individual has fallen into

industrial isolation, so as to produce any one useful article by his own independent effort alone. Even where there is no mechanical co-operation, men are always guided by the experience of others. The only possible exceptions to this rule are those instances of lost or cast-off children nourished by wild beasts, of which half-authenticated accounts have gained currency from time to time. But the anomalous, half-hypothetical life of these waifs can scarcely have affected social development to the extent of originating the institution of ownership. Production takes place only in society - only through the co-operation of an industrial community. This industrial community may be large or small; its limits are commonly somewhat vaguely defined; but it always comprises a group large enough to contain and transmit the traditions, tools, technical knowledge, and usages without which there can be no industrial organization and no economic relation of individuals to one another or to their environment. The isolated individual is not a productive agent.

What he can do at best is to live from season to season, as the non-gregarious animals do. There can be no production without technical knowledge; hence no accumulation and no wealth to be owned, in severalty or otherwise. And there is no technical knowledge apart from an industrial community. Since there is no individual production and no individual productivity, the natural-rights preconception that ownership rests on the individually productive labor of the owner reduces itself to absurdity, even under the logic of its own assumptions. Some writers who have taken up the question from the ethnological side hold that the institution is to be traced to the customary use of weapons and ornaments by individuals. Others have found its origin in the social group's occupation of a given piece of land, which it held forcibly against intruders, and which it came in this way to "own." The latter hypothesis bases the collective ownership of land on a collective act of seizure, or tenure by prowess, so that it differs fundamentally from the view which bases ownership on productive labor.

The view that ownership is an outgrowth of the customary consumption of such things as weapons and ornaments by individuals is well supported by appearances and has also the qualified sanction of the natural-rights preconception. The usages of all known primitive tribes seem at first sight to bear out this view. In all communities the individual members exercise a more or less unrestrained right of use and abuse over their weapons, if they have any, as well as over many articles of ornament, clothing, and the toilet. In the eyes of the modern economist this usage would count as ownership. So that, if the question is construed to be simply a question of material fact, as to the earliest emergence of usages which would in the latter-day classification be brought under the head of ownership, then it would have to be said that ownership must have begun with the conversion of these articles to individual use. But the question will have to be answered in the contrary sense if we shift our ground to the point of view of the primitive men whose institutions are under review.

The point in question is the origin of the institution of ownership, as it first takes shape in the habits of thought of the early barbarian. The question concerns the derivation of the idea of ownership or property. What is of interest for the present purpose is not whether we, with our preconceptions, would look upon the relation of the primitive savage or barbarian to his slight personal effects as a relation of ownership, but whether that is his own apprehension of the matter. It is a question as to the light in which the savage himself habitually views these objects that pertain immediately to his person and are set apart for his habitual use. Like all questions of the derivation of institutions, it is essentially a question of folk-psychology, not of mechanical fact; and, when so conceived, it must be answered in the negative.

The unsophisticated man, whether savage or civilized, is prone to conceive phenomena in terms of personality; these being terms with which he has a first-hand acquaintance. This habit is more unbroken in the savage than in civilized men. All obvious manifestations of force are apprehended as expressions of conation - effort put forth for a purpose by some agency similar to the human will. The point of view of the archaic culture is that of forceful, pervading personality, whose unfolding life is the substantial fact held in view in every relation into which men or things enter. This point of view in large measure shapes and colors all the institutions of the early culture - and in a less degree the later phases of culture. Under the guidance of this habit of thought, the relation of any individual to his personal effects is conceived to be of a more intimate kind than that of ownership simply.

Ownership is too external and colorless a term to describe the fact. In the apprehension of the savage and the barbarian the limits of his person do not coincide with the limits which modern biological science would recognize. His individuality is conceived to cover, somewhat vaguely and uncertainly, a pretty wide fringe of facts and objects that pertain to him more or less immediately. To our sense of the matter these items lie outside the limits of his person, and to many of them we would conceive him to stand in an economic rather than in an organic relation. This quasi-personal fringe of facts and objects commonly comprises the man's shadow; the reflection of his image in water or any similar surface; his name; his peculiar tattoo marks; his totem, if he has one; his glance; his breath, especially when it is visible; the print of his hand and foot; the sound of his voice; any image or representation of his person; any excretions or exhalations from his person; parings of his nails; cuttings of his hair; his ornaments and amulets; clothing that is in daily use, especially what has been shaped to his person, and more particularly if there is wrought into it any totemic or other design peculiar to him; his weapons, especially his favorite weapons and those which he habitually carries.

Beyond these there is a great number of other, remoter things which may or may not be included in the quasi-personal fringe. As regards this entire range of facts and objects, it is to be said that the "zone of influence" of the individual's personality is not conceived to cover them all with the same degree of potency; his individuality shades off by insensible, penumbral gradations into the external world. The objects and facts that fall within the quasi-personal fringe figure in the habits of thought of the savage as personal to him in a vital sense. They are not a congeries of things to which he stands in an economic relation and to which he has an equitable, legal claim. These articles are conceived to be his in much the same sense as his hands and feet are his, or his pulse-beat, or his digestion, or the heat of his body, or the motions of his limbs or brain. For the satisfaction of any who may be inclined to question this view, appeal may be taken to the usages of almost any people. Some such notion of a pervasive personality, or a penumbra of personality, is implied, for instance, in the giving and keeping of presents and mementos. It is more indubitably present in the working of charms; in all sorcery; in the sacraments and similar devout observances; in such practices as the Tibetan prayer-wheel; in the adoration of relics, images, and symbols; in the almost universal veneration of consecrated places and structures; in astrology; in divination by means of hair-cuttings, nail-parings, photographs, etc. Perhaps the least debatable evidence of belief in such a quasi-personal fringe is afforded by the practices of sympathetic magic; and the practices are strikingly similar in substance the world over from the love-charm to the sacrament. Their substantial ground is the belief that a desired effect can be wrought upon a given person through the means of some object lying within his quasi-personal fringe.

The person who is approached in this way may be a fellow-mortal, or it may be some potent spiritual agent whose intercession is sought for good or ill. If the sorcerer or anyone who works a charm can in any way get at the "penumbra" of a person's individuality, as embodied in his fringe of quasi-personal facts, he will be able to work good or ill to the person to whom the fact or object pertains; and the magic rites performed to this end will work their effect with greater force and precision in proportion as the object which affords the point of attack is more intimately related to the person upon whom the effect is to be wrought. An economic relation, simply, does not afford a handle for sorcery. It may be set down that whenever the relation of a person to a given object is made use of for the purposes of sympathetic magic, the relation is conceived to be something more vital than simple legal ownership.

Such meager belongings of the primitive savage as would under the nomenclature of a later day be classed as personal property are not thought of by him as his property at all; they pertain organically to his person. Of the things comprised in his quasi-personal fringe all do not pertain to him with the same degree of intimacy or persistency; but those articles which are more remotely or more doubtfully included under his individuality are not therefore conceived to be partly organic to him and partly his property simply. The alternative does not lie between this organic relation and ownership. It may easily happen that a given article lying along the margin of the quasi-personal fringe is eliminated from it and is alienated, either by default through lapse of time or by voluntary severance of the relation. But when this happens the article is not conceived to escape from the organic relation into a remoter category of things that are owned by and external to the person in question. If an object escapes in this way from the organic sphere of one person, it may pass into the sphere of another; or, if it is an article that lends itself to common use, it may pass into the common stock of the community.

As regards this common stock, no concept of ownership, either communal or individual, applies in the primitive community. The idea of a communal ownership is of relatively late growth, and must by psychological necessity have been preceded by the idea of individual ownership. Ownership is an accredited discretionary power over an object on the ground of a conventional claim; it implies that the owner is a personal agent who takes thought for the disposal of the object owned.

A personal agent is an individual, and it is only by an eventual refinement - of the nature of a legal fiction - that any group of men is conceived to exercise a corporate discretion over objects. Ownership implies an individual owner. It is only by reflection, and by extending the scope of a concept which is already familiar, that a quasi-personal corporate discretion and control of this kind comes to be imputed to a group of persons. Corporate ownership is quasi-ownership only; it is therefore necessarily a derivative concept, and cannot have preceded the concept of individual ownership of which it is a counterfeit.

After the idea of ownership has been elaborated and has gained some consistency, it is not unusual to find the notion of pervasion by the user's personality applied to articles owned by him. At the same time a given article may also be recognized as lying within the quasi-personal fringe of one person while it is owned by another - as, for instance, ornaments and other articles of daily use which in a personal sense belong to a slave or to an inferior member of a patriarchal household, but which as property belong to the master or head of the household. The two categories, (a) things to which one's personality extends by way of pervasion and (b) things owned, by no means coincide; nor does the one supplant the other. The two ideas are so far from identical that the same object may belong to one person under the one concept and to another person under the other; and, on the other hand, the same person may stand in both relations to a given object without the one concept being lost in the other.

A given article may change owners without passing out of the quasi-personal fringe of the person under whose "self" it has belonged, as, for instance, a photograph or any other memento. A familiar instance is the mundane ownership of any consecrated place or structure which in the personal sense belongs to the saint or deity to whom it is sacred. The two concepts are so far distinct, or even disparate, as to make it extremely improbable that the one has been developed out of the other by a process of growth. A transition involving such a substitution of ideas could scarcely take place except on some notable impulse from without. Such a step would amount to the construction of a new category and a reclassification of certain selected facts under the new head. The impulse to reclassify the facts and things that are comprised in the quasi-personal fringe, so as to place some of them, together with certain other things, under the new category of ownership, must come from some constraining exigency of later growth than the concept whose province it invades. The new category is not simply an amplified form of the old.

Not every item that was originally conceived to belong to an individual by way of pervasion comes to be counted as an item of his wealth after the idea of wealth has come into vogue. Such items, for instance, as a person's footprint, or his image or effigy, or his name, are very tardily included under the head of articles owned by him, if they are eventually included at all. It is a fortuitous circumstance if they come to be owned by him, but they long continue to hold their place in his quasi-personal fringe. The disparity of the two concepts is well brought out by the case of the domestic animals. These non-human individuals are incapable of ownership, but there is imputed to them the attribute of a pervasive individuality, which extends to such items as their footprints, their stalls, clippings of hair, and the like.

These items are made use of for the purposes of sympathetic magic even in modern civilized communities. An illustration that may show this disparity between ownership and pervasion in a still stronger light is afforded by the vulgar belief that the moon's phases may have a propitious or sinister effect on human affairs. The inconstant moon is conceived to work good or ill through a sympathetic influence or spiritual infection which suggests a quasi-personal fringe, but which assuredly does not imply ownership on her part. Ownership is not a simple and instinctive notion that is naively included under the notion of productive effort on the one hand, nor under that of habitual use on the other.

It is not something given to begin with, as an item of the isolated individual's mental furniture; something which has to be unlearned in part when men come to co-operate in production and make working arrangements and mutual renunciations under the stress of associated life - after the manner imputed by the social-contract theory. It is a conventional fact and has to be learned; it is a cultural fact which has grown into an institution in the past through a long course of habituation, and which is transmitted from generation to generation as all cultural facts are. On going back a little way into the cultural history of our own past, we come upon a situation which says that the fact of a person's being engaged in industry was prima facie evidence that he could own nothing. Under serfdom and slavery those who work cannot own, and those who own cannot work. Even very recently - culturally speaking - there was no suspicion that a woman's work, in the patriarchal household, should entitle her to own the products of her work.

Farther back in the barbarian culture, while the patriarchal household was in better preservation than it is now, this position was accepted with more unquestioning faith. The head of the household alone could hold property; and even the scope of his ownership was greatly qualified if he had a feudal superior. The tenure of property is a tenure by prowess, on the one hand, and a tenure by sufferance at the hands of a superior, on the other hand. The recourse to prowess as the definitive basis of tenure becomes more immediate and more habitual the farther the development is traced back into the early barbarian culture; until, on the lower levels of barbarism or the upper levels of savagery, "the good old plan" prevails with but little mitigation. There are always certain conventions, a certain understanding as to what are the legitimate conditions and circumstances that surround ownership and its transmission, chief among which is the fact of habitual acceptance.

What has been currently accepted as the status quo-vested interest - is right and good so long as it does not meet a challenge backed by irresistible force. Property rights sanctioned by immemorial usage are inviolable, as all immemorial usage is, except in the face of forcible dispossession. But seizure and forcible retention very shortly gain the legitimation of usage, and the resulting tenure becomes inviolable through habituation. *Beati possidentes.* Throughout the barbarian culture, where this tenure by prowess prevails, the population falls into two economic classes: those engaged in industrial employments, and those engaged in such non-industrial pursuits as war, government, sports, and religious observances. In the earlier and more naive stages of barbarism the former, in the normal case, own nothing; the latter own such property as they have seized, or such as has, under the sanction of usage, descended upon them from their forebears who seized and held it. At a still lower level of culture, in the primitive savage horde, the population is not similarly divided into economic classes. There is no leisure class resting its prerogative on coercion, prowess, and immemorial status; and there is also no ownership.

It will hold as a rough generalization that in communities where there is no invidious distinction between employments, as exploit, on the one hand, and drudgery, on the other, there is also no tenure of property. In the cultural sequence, ownership does not begin before the rise of a canon of exploit; but it is to be added that it also does not seem to begin with the first beginning of exploit as a manly occupation. In these very rude early communities, especially in the unpropertied hordes of peaceable savages, the rule is that the product of any member's effort is consumed by the group to which he belongs; and it is consumed collectively or indiscriminately, without question of individual right or ownership. The question of ownership is not brought up by the fact that an article has been produced or is at hand in finished form for consumption.

The earliest occurrence of ownership seems to fall in the early stages of barbarism, and the emergence of the institution of ownership is apparently a concomitant of the transition from a peaceable to a predatory habit of life. It is a prerogative of that class in the barbarian culture which leads a life of exploit rather than of industry. The pervading characteristic of the barbarian culture, as distinguished from the peaceable phase of life that precedes it, is the element of exploit, coercion, and seizure. In its earlier phases ownership is this habit of coercion and seizure reduced to system and consistency under the surveillance of usage. The practice of seizing and accumulating goods on individual account could not have come into vogue to the extent of founding a new institution under the peaceable communistic regime of primitive savagery; for the distensions arising from any such resort to mutual force and fraud among its members would have been fatal to the group. For a similar reason individual ownership of consumable goods could not come in with the first beginnings of predatory life; for the primitive fighting horde still needs to consume its scanty means of subsistence in common, in order to give the collective horde its full fighting efficiency.

Otherwise it would succumb before any rival horde that had not yet given up collective consumption. With the advent of predatory life comes the practice of plundering - of seizing goods from the enemy. But in order that the plundering habit should give rise to individual ownership of the things seized, these things must be goods of a somewhat lasting kind, and not immediately consumable means of subsistence. Under the primitive culture the means of subsistence are habitually consumed in common by the group, and the manner in which such goods are consumed is fixed according to an elaborate system of usage. This usage is not readily broken over, for it is a substantial part of the habits of life of every individual member. The practice of collective consumption is at the same time necessary to the survival of the group, and this necessity is present in men's minds and exercises a surveillance over the formation of habits of thought as to what is right and seemly. Any propensity to aggression at this early stage will, therefore, not assert itself in the seizure and retention of consumable goods; nor does the temptation to do so readily present itself, since the idea of individual appropriation of a store of goods is alien to the archaic man's general habits of thought.

The idea of property is not readily attached to anything but tangible and lasting articles. It is only where commercial development is well advanced - where bargain and sale is a large feature in the community's life - that the more perishable articles of consumption are thought of as items of wealth at all. The still more evanescent results of personal service are still more difficult to bring in under the idea of wealth. So much so that the attempt to classify services as wealth is meaningless to laymen, and even the adept economists hold a divided opinion as to the intelligibility of such a classification. In the common-sense apprehension the idea of property is not currently attached to any but tangible, vendible goods of some durability. This is true even in modern civilized communities, where pecuniary ideas and the pecuniary point of view prevail. In a like manner and for a like reason, in an earlier, non-commercial phase of culture there is less occasion for and greater difficulty in applying the concept of ownership to anything but obviously durable articles. But durable articles of use and consumption which are seized in the raids of a predatory horde are either articles of general use or they are articles of immediate and continued personal use to the person who has seized them.

In the former case the goods are consumed in common by the group, without giving rise to a notion of ownership; in the latter case they fall into the class of things that pertain organically to the person of their user, and they would, therefore, not figure as items of property or make up a store of wealth. It is difficult to see how an institution of ownership could have arisen in the early days of predatory life through the seizure of goods, but the case is different with the seizure of persons. Captives are items that do not fit into the scheme of communal consumption, and their appropriation by their individual captor works no manifest detriment to the group.

At the same time these captives continue to be obviously distinct from their captor in point of individuality, and so are not readily brought in under the quasi-personal fringe. The captives taken under rude conditions are chiefly women. There are good reasons for this. Except where there is a slave class of men, the women are more useful, as well as more easily controlled, in the primitive group. Their labor is worth more to the group than their maintenance, and as they do not carry weapons, they are less formidable than men captives would be. They serve the purpose of trophies very effectually, and it is therefore worthwhile for their captor to trace and keep in evidence his relation to them as their captor. To this end he maintains an attitude of dominance and coercion toward women captured by him; and, as being the insignia of his prowess, he does not suffer them to stand at the beck and call of rival warriors. They are fit subjects for command and constraint; it ministers to both his honor and his vanity to domineer over them, and their utility in this respect is very great. But his domineering over them is the evidence of his prowess, and it is incompatible with their utility as trophies that other men should take the liberties with his women which serve as evidence of the coercive relation of captor.

When the practice hardens into custom, the captor comes to exercise a customary right to exclusive use and abuse over the women he has seized; and this customary right of use and abuse over an object which is obviously not an organic part of his person constitutes the relation of ownership, as naively apprehended. After this usage of capture has found its way into the habits of the community, the women so held in constraint and in evidence will commonly fall into a conventionally recognized marriage relation with their captor. The result is a new form of marriage, in which the man is master. This ownership-marriage seems to be the original both of private property and of the patriarchal household. Both of these great institutions are, accordingly, of an emulative origin. The varying details of the development whereby owner ship extends to other persons than captured women cannot be taken up here; neither can the further growth of the marriage institution that came into vogue at the same time with ownership.

Probably at a point in the economic evolution not far subsequent to the definitive installation of the institution of ownership-marriage comes, as its consequence, the ownership of consumable goods. The women held in servile marriage not only render personal service to their master, but they are also employed in the production of articles of use. All the non-combatant or ignoble members of the community are habitually so employed. And when the habit of looking upon and claiming the persons identified with my invidious interest, or subservient to me, as "mine" has become an accepted and integral part of men's habits of thought, it becomes a relatively easy matter to extend this newly achieved concept of ownership to the products of the labor performed by the persons so held in ownership. And the same propensity for emulation which bears so great a part in shaping the original institution of ownership extends its action to the new category of things owned.

Not only are the products of the women's labor claimed and valued for their serviceability in furthering the comfort and fullness of life of the master, but they are valuable also as a conspicuous evidence of his possessing many and efficient servants, and they are therefore useful as an evidence of his superior force. The appropriation and accumulation of consumable goods could scarcely have come into vogue as a direct outgrowth of the primitive horde-communism, but it comes in as an easy and unobtrusive consequence of the ownership of persons.

Chapter 4

The Instinct of Workmanship
and the Irksomeness of Labor

It is one of the commonplaces of the received economic theory that work is irksome. Many a discussion proceeds on this axiom that, so far as regards economic matters, men desire above all things to get the goods produced by labor and to avoid the labor by which the goods are produced. In a general way the common-sense opinion is well in accord with current theory on this head. According to the common-sense-ideal, the economic beatitude lies in an unrestrained consumption of goods, without work; whereas the perfect economic affliction is unremunerated labor. Man instinctively revolts at effort that goes to supply the means of life.

No one will accept the proposition when stated in this bald fashion, but even as it stands it is scarcely an overstatement of what is implied in the writings of eminent economists. If such an aversion to useful effort is an integral part of human nature, then the trail of the Edenic serpent should be plain to all men, for this is a unique distinction of the human species. A consistent aversion to whatever activity goes to maintain the life of the species is assuredly found in no other species of animal. Under the selective process through which species are held to have emerged and gained their stability there is no chance for the survival of a species gifted with such an aversion to the furtherance of its own life process.

If man alone is an exception from the selective norm, then the alien propensity in question must have been intruded into his make-up by some malevolent *deus ex machina*. Yet, for all the apparent absurdity of the thing, there is the fact. With more or less sincerity, people currently avow an aversion to useful effort. The avowal does not cover all effort, but only such as is of some use; it is, more particularly, such effort as is vulgarly recognized to be useful labor.

Less repugnance is expressed as regards effort which brings gain without giving a product that is of human use, as, for example, the effort that goes into war, politics, or other employments of a similar nature. And there is commonly no avowed aversion to sports or other similar employments that yield neither a pecuniary gain nor a useful product. Still, the fact that a given line of effort is useless does not of itself save it from being odious, as is shown by the case of menial service; much of this work serves no useful end, but it is none the less repugnant to all people of sensibility. "The economic man," whose lineaments were traced in outline by the classical economists and filled in by their caricaturists, is an anomaly in the animal world; and yet, to judge by everyday popular expressions of inclination, the portrait is not seriously overdrawn.

But if this economic man is to serve as a lay figure upon which to fit the garment of economic doctrines, it is incumbent upon the science to explain what are his limitations and how he has achieved his emancipation from the law of natural selection. His emancipation from the law is, indeed, more apparent than substantial. The difference in this respect between man and his sometime competitors in the struggle for survival lies not in a slighter but in a fuller adjustment of his propensities to the purposes of the life of the species. He distanced them all in this respect long ago, and by so wide an interval that he is now able, without jeopardy to the life of the species, to play fast and loose with the spiritual basis of its survival.

Like other animals, man is an agent that acts in response to stimuli afforded by the environment in which he lives. Like other species, he is a creature of habit and propensity. But in a higher degree than other species, man mentally digests the content of the habits under whose guidance he acts, and appreciates the trend of these habits and propensities. He is in an eminent sense an intelligent agent. By selective necessity he is endowed with a proclivity for purposeful action. He is possessed of a discriminating sense of purpose, by force of which all futility of life or of action is distasteful to him. There may be a wide divergence between individuals as regards the form and the direction in which this impulse expresses itself, but the impulse itself is not a matter of idiosyncrasy, it is a generic feature of human nature. It is not a trait that occurs sporadically in a few individuals.

Cases occur in which this proclivity for purposeful action is wanting or is present in obviously scant measure, but persons endowed in this stepmotherly fashion are classed as "defective subjects." Lines of descent which carry this defective human nature dwindle and decay even under the propitious circumstances of modern life. The history of hereditarily dependent or defective families is evidence to this effect. Man's great advantage over other species in the struggle for survival has been his superior facility in turning the forces of the environment to account. It is to his proclivity for turning the material means of life to account that he owes his position as lord of creation. It is not a proclivity to effort, but to achievement - to the compassing of an end. His primacy is in the last resort an industrial or economic primacy.

In his economic life man is an agent, not an absorbent; he is an agent seeking in every act the accomplishment of some concrete, objective, impersonal end. As this pervading norm of action guides the life of men in all the use they make of material things, so it must also serve as the point of departure and afford the guiding principle for any science that aims to be a theory of the economic life process. Within the purview of economic theory, the last analysis of any given phenomenon must run back to this ubiquitous human impulse to do the next thing.

All this seems to contradict what has just been said of the conventional aversion to labor. But the contradiction is not so sheer in fact as it appears to be at first sight. Its solution lies in the fact that the aversion to labor is in great part a conventional aversion only. In the intervals of sober reflection, when not harassed with the strain of overwork, men's common sense speaks unequivocally under the guidance of the instinct of workmanship.

They like to see others spend their life to some purpose, and they like to reflect that their own life is of some use. All men have this quasi-aesthetic sense of economic or industrial merit, and to this sense of economic merit futility and inefficiency are distasteful. In its positive expression it is an impulse or instinct of workmanship; negatively it expresses itself in a deprecation of waste. This sense of merit and demerit with respect to the material furtherance or hindrance of life approves, the economically effective act and deprecates economic futility. It is needless to point out in detail the close relation between this norm of economic merit and the ethical norm of conduct, on the one hand, and the aesthetic norm of taste, on the other.

It is very closely related to both of these, both as regards its biological ground and as regards the scope and method of its award. This instinct of workmanship apparently stands in sheer conflict with the conventional antipathy to useful effort. The two are found together in full discord in the common run of men; but whenever a deliberate judgment is passed on conduct or on events, the former asserts its primacy in a pervasive way which suggests that it is altogether the more generic, more abiding trait of human nature. There can scarcely be a serious question of precedence between the two. The former is a human trait necessary to the survival of the species; the latter is a habit of thought possible only in a species which has distanced all competitors, and then it prevails only by sufferance and within limits set by the former.

The question between them is, Is the aversion to labor a derivative of the instinct of workmanship? and, How has it arisen and gained consistency in spite of its being at variance with that instinct? Until recently there has been something of a consensus among those who have written on early culture, to the effect that man, as he first emerged upon the properly human plane, was of a contentious disposition, inclined to isolate his own interest and purposes from those of his fellows, and with a penchant for feuds and brawls. Accordingly, even where the view is met with that men are by native proclivity inclined to action, there is still evident a presumption that this native proclivity to action is a proclivity to action of a destructive kind. It is held that men are inclined to fight, not to work - that the end of action in the normal case is damage rather than repair.

This view would make the proclivity to purposeful action an impulse to sportsmanship rather than to workmanship. In any attempt to fit this view into an evolutionary scheme of culture it would carry the implication that in the pre-human or proto-anthropoid phase of its life the race was a predaceous species, and that the initial phase of human culture, as well as the later cultural development, has been substantially of a predatory kind.

There is much to be said for this view. If mankind is by derivation a race not of workmen but of sportsmen, then there is no need of explaining the conventional aversion to work. Work is unsportsmanlike and therefore distasteful, and perplexity then arises in explaining how men have in any degree become reconciled to any but a predaceous life. Apart from the immediate convenience of this view, it is also enforced by much evidence. Most peoples at a lower stage of culture than our own are of a more predatory habit than our people. The history of mankind, as conventionally written, has been a narrative of predatory exploits, and this history is not commonly felt to be one-sided or misinformed. And a sportsmanlike inclination to warfare is also to be found in nearly all modern communities. Similarly, the sense of honor, so-called, whether it is individual or national honor, is also an expression of sportsmanship. The prevalence of notions of honor may, therefore, be taken as evidence going in the same direction. And as if to further fortify the claim of sportsmanship to antiquity and prescriptive standing, the sense of honor is also noticeably more vivid in communities of a somewhat more archaic culture than our own. Yet there is a considerable body of evidence, both from cultural history and from the present-day phenomena of human life, which traverses this conventionally accepted view that makes man generically a sportsman.

Obscurely but persistently, throughout the history of human culture, the great body of the people have almost everywhere, in their everyday life, been at work to turn things to human use. The proximate aim of all industrial improvement has been the better performance of some workmanlike task. Necessarily this work has, on the one hand, proceeded on the basis of an appreciative interest in the work to be done; for there is no other ground on which to obtain anything better than the aimless performance of a task. And necessarily also, on the other hand, the discipline of work has acted to develop a workmanlike attitude.

It will not do to say that the work accomplished is entirely due to compulsion under a predatory regime, for the most striking advances in this respect have been wrought where the coercive force of a sportsmanlike exploitation has been least. The same view is borne out by the expressions of common sense. As has already been remarked, whenever they dispassionately take thought and pass a judgment on the value of human conduct, the common run of mature men approve workmanship rather than sportsmanship. At the best, they take an apologetic attitude toward the latter. This is well seen in the present (May, 1898) disturbance of the popular temper.

While it may well be granted that the warlike raid upon which this community is entering is substantially an access of sportsmanlike exaltation, it is to be noticed that nearly all those who speak for war are at pains to find some colorable motive of another kind. Predatory exploit, simply as such, is not felt to carry its own legitimation, as it should in the apprehension of any species that is primarily of a predaceous character. What meets unreserved approval is such conduct as furthers human life on the whole, rather than such as furthers the invidious or predatory interest of one as against another.

The most ancient and most consistent habits of the race will best assert themselves when men are not speaking under the stress of instant irritation. Under such circumstances the ancient bent may even bear down the immediate conventional canons of conduct. The archaic turn of mind that inclines men to commend workmanlike serviceability is the outcome of long and consistent habituation to a course of life of such a character as is reflected by this inclination. Man's life is activity; and as he acts, so he thinks and feels. This is necessarily so, since it is the agent man that does the thinking and feeling. Like other species, man is a creature of habits and propensities. He acts under the guidance of propensities which have been imposed upon him by the process of selection to which he owes his differentiation from other species. He is a social animal; and the selective process whereby he has acquired the spiritual make-up of a social animal has at the same time made him substantially a peaceful animal. The race may have wandered far from the ancient position of peacefulness, but even now the traces of a peaceful trend in men's everyday habits of thought and feeling are plain enough.

The sight of blood and the presence of death, even of the blood or death of the lower animals, commonly strike inexperienced persons with a sickening revulsion. In the common run of cases, the habit of complacency with slaughter comes only as the result of discipline. In this respect man differs from the beasts of prey. He differs, of course, most widely in this respect from the solitary beasts, but even among the gregarious animals his nearest spiritual relatives are not found among the carnivora. In his unarmed frame and in the slight degree to which his muscular force is specialized for fighting, as well as in his instinctive aversion to hostile contact with the ferocious beasts, man is to be classed with those animals that owe their survival to an aptitude, for avoiding direct conflict with their competitors, rather than with those which survive by virtue of overcoming and eating their rivals. "Man is the weakest and most defenseless of all living things," and, according to the Law of the Jungle, it is his part to take advice and contrive and turn divers things to account in ways that are incomprehensible to the rest. Without tools he is not a dangerous animal, as animals go. And he did not become a formidable animal until he had made some considerable advance in the contrivance of implements for combat. In the days before tools had been brought into effective use - that is to say, during by far the greater part of the period of human evolution - man could not be primarily an agent of destruction or a disturber of the peace.

He was of a peaceable and retiring disposition by force of circumstances. With the use of tools the possibility of his acquiring a different disposition gradually began, but even then the circumstances favoring the growth of a contentious disposition supervened only gradually and partially. The habits of life of the race were still perforce of a peaceful and industrial character, rather than contentious and destructive. Tools and implements, in the early days, must have served chiefly to shape facts and objects for human use, rather than for inflicting damage and discomfort. Industry would have to develop far before it became possible for one group of men to live at the cost of another; and during the protracted evolution of industry before this point had been reached the discipline of associated life still consistently ran in the direction of industrial efficiency, both as regards men's physical and mental traits and as regards their spiritual attitude.

By selection and by training, the life of man, before a predaceous life became possible, would act to develop and to conserve in him instinct for workmanship. The adaptation to the environment which the situation enforced was of an industrial kind; it required men to acquire facility in shaping things and situations for human use. This does not mean the shaping of things by the individual to his own individual use simply; for archaic man was necessarily a member of a group, and during this early stage, when industrial efficiency was still inconsiderable, no group could have survived except on the basis of a sense of solidarity strong enough to throw self-interest into the background. Self-interest, as an accepted guide of action, is possible only as the concomitant of a predatory life, and a predatory life is possible only after the use of tools has developed so far as to leave a large surplus of product over what is required for the sustenance of the producers. Subsistence by predation implies something substantial to prey upon.

Early man was a member of a group which depended for its survival on the industrial efficiency of its members and on their singleness of purpose in making use of the material means at hand. Some competition between groups for the possession of the fruits of the earth and for advantageous locations there would be even at a relatively early stage, but much hostile contact between groups there could not be; not enough to shape the dominant habits of thought.

What men can do easily is what they do habitually, and this decides what they can think and know easily. They feel at home in the range of ideas which is familiar through their everyday line of action. A habitual line of action constitutes a habitual line of thought, and gives the point of view from which facts and events are apprehended and reduced to a body of knowledge. What is consistent with the habitual course of action is consistent with the habitual line of thought, and gives the definitive ground of knowledge as well as the conventional standard of complacency or approval in any community.

Conversely, a processor method of life, once understood, assimilated in thought works into the scheme of life and becomes a norm of conduct, simply because the thinking, knowing agent is also the acting agent. What is apprehended with facility and is consistent with the process of life and knowledge is thereby apprehended as right and good. All this applies with added force where the habituation is not simply individual and sporadic, but is enforced upon the group or the race by a selective elimination of those individuals and lines of descent that do not conform to the required canon of knowledge and conduct. Where this takes place, the acquired proclivity passes from the status of habit to that of aptitude or propensity. It becomes a transmissible trait, and action under its guidance becomes right and good, and the longer and more consistent the selective adaptation through which the aptitude arises, the more firmly is the resulting aptitude settled upon the race, and the more unquestioned becomes the sanction of the resulting canon of conduct.

So far as regards his relation to the material means of life, the canon of thought and of conduct which was in this way enforced upon early man was what is here called the instinct of workmanship. The interest which men took in economic facts on the basis of this propensity, in the days before spoliation came into vogue, was not primarily of a self-regarding character. The necessary dominance of a sense of group solidarity would preclude that. The selective process must eliminate lines of descent unduly gifted with a self-regarding bias. Still, there was some emulation between individuals, even in the most indigent and most peaceable groups. From the readiness with which a scheme of emulation is entered upon where late circumstances favor its development, it seems probable that the proclivity to emulation must have been present also in the earlier days in sufficient force to assert itself to the extent to which the exigencies of the earlier life of the group would permit. But this emulation could not run in the direction of an individual, acquisition or accumulation of goods, or of a life consistently given to raids and tumults.

It would be emulation such as is found among the peaceable gregarious animals generally; that is to say, it was primarily and chiefly sexual emulation, recurring with more or less regularity. Beyond this there must also have been some wrangling in the distribution of goods on hand, but neither this nor the rivalry for subsistence could have been the dominant note of life. Under the canon of conduct imposed by the instinct of workmanship, efficiency, serviceability, commends itself, and inefficiency or futility is odious. Man contemplates his own conduct and that of his neighbors, and passes a judgment of complacency or of dispraise. The degree of effectiveness with which he lives up to the accepted standard of efficiency in great measure determines his contentment with himself and his situation. A wide or persistent discrepancy in this respect is a source of abounding spiritual discomfort.

Judgment may in this way be passed on the intention of the agent or on the serviceability of the act. In the former case the award of merit or demerit is to be classed as moral; and with award of merit of this kind this paper is not concerned. As regards serviceability or efficiency, men do not only take thought at first hand of the facts of their own conduct; they are also sensitive to rebuke or approval from others. Not only is the immediate consciousness of the achievement of a purpose gratifying and stimulating, but the imputation of efficiency by one's fellows is perhaps no less gratifying or stimulating. Sensitiveness to rebuke or approval is a matter of selective necessity under the circumstances of associated life. Without it no group of men could carry on a collective life in a material environment that requires shaping to the ends of man. In this respect, again, man shows a spiritual relationship with the gregarious animals rather than with the solitary beasts of prey.

Under the guidance of this taste for good work, men are compared with one another and with the accepted ideals of efficiency, and are rated and graded by the common sense of their fellows according to a conventional scheme of merit and demerit. The imputation of efficiency necessarily proceeds on evidence of efficiency. The visible achievement of one man is, therefore, compared with that of another, and the award of esteem comes habitually to rest on an invidious comparison of persons instead of on the immediate bearing of the given line of conduct upon the approved end of action. The ground of esteem in this way shifts from a direct appreciation of the expediency of conduct to a comparison of the abilities of different agents.

Instead of a valuation of serviceability, there is a gauging of capability on the ground of visible success. And what comes to be compared in an invidious comparison of this kind between agents is the force which the agent is able to put forth, rather than the serviceability of the agent's conduct. So soon, therefore, and in so far, as the esteem awarded to serviceability passes into an invidious esteem of one agent as compared with another, the end sought in action will tend to change from naive expediency to the manifestation of capacity or force. It becomes the proximate end of effort to put forth evidence of power, rather than to achieve an impersonal end for its own sake, simply as an item of human use. So that, while in its more immediate expression the norm of economic taste stands out as an impulse to workmanship or a taste for serviceability and a distaste for futility, under given circumstances of associated life it comes in some degree to take on the character of an emulative demonstration of force.

Since the imputation of efficiency and of invidious merit goes on the evidence afforded by visible success, the appearance of evil must be avoided in order to escape dispraise. In the early savage culture, while the group is small and while the conditions favorable to a predatory life are still wanting, the resulting emulation between the members of the group runs chiefly to industrial efficiency. It comes to be the appearance of industrial incapacity that is to be avoided. It is in this direction that force or capacity can be put in evidence most consistently and with the best effect for the good name of the individual. It is, therefore, in this direction that a standard of merit and a canon of meritorious conduct will develop. But even for a growth of emulation in the productive use of brain and muscle, the small, rude, peaceable group of savages is not fertile ground. The situation does not favor a vigorous emulative spirit. The conditions favorable to the growth of a habit of emulative demonstration of force are

(1) the frequent recurrence of conjunctures that call for a great and sudden strain, and

(2) exposure of the individual to a large, and especially to a shifting, human environment whose approval is sought. These conditions are not effectually met on the lower levels of savagery, such as human culture must have been during the early days of the use of tools. Accordingly, relatively little of the emulative spirit is seen in communities that have retained the archaic, peaceable constitution, or that have reverted to it from a higher culture. In such communities a low standard of culture and comfort goes along with an absence of strenuous application to the work in hand, as well as a relative absence of jealousy and gradations of rank. Notions of economic rank and discrimination between persons, whether in point of possessions or in point of comfort, are almost, if not altogether, in abeyance.

With a further development of the use of tools and of human command over the forces of the environment, the habits of life of the savage group change. There is likely to be more of aggression, both in the way of a pursuit of large game and in the way of conflict between groups. As the industrial efficiency of the group increases, and as weapons are brought to greater perfection, the incentives to aggression and the opportunities for achievement along this line increase. The conditions favorable to emulation are more fully met. With the increasing density of population that follows from a heightened industrial efficiency, the group passes, by force of circumstances, from the archaic condition of poverty-stricken peace to a stage of predatory life. This fighting stage - the beginning of barbarism - may involve aggressive predation, or the group may simply be placed on the defensive.

One or the other, or both the lines of activity - and commonly both, no doubt - will be forced upon the group, on pain of extermination. This has apparently been the usual course of early social evolution. When a group emerges into this predatory phase of its development, the employments which most occupy men's attention are employments that involve exploit.

The most serious concern of the group, and at the same time the direction in which the most spectacular effect may be achieved by the individual, is conflict with men and beasts. It becomes easy to make a telling comparison between men when their work is a series of exploits carried out against these difficult adversaries or against the formidable movements of the elements. The assertion of the strong hand, successful aggression, usually of a destructive character, becomes the accepted basis of repute. The dominant life interest of the group throws its strong light upon this creditable employment of force and sagacity, and the other, obscurer ways of serving the group's life fall into the background. The guiding animus of the group becomes a militant one, and men's actions are judged from the standpoint of the fighting man.

What is recognized, without reflection and without misgiving, as serviceable and effective in such a group is fighting capacity. Exploit becomes the conventional ground of invidious comparison between individuals, and repute comes to rest on prowess. As the predatory culture reaches a fuller development, there comes a distinction between employments. The tradition of prowess, as the virtue par excellence, gains in scope and consistency until prowess comes near being recognized as the sole virtue. Those employments alone are then worthy and reputable which involve the exercise of this virtue. Other employments, in which men are occupied with tamely shaping inert materials to human use, become unworthy and end with becoming debasing.

The honorable man must not only show capacity for predatory exploit, but he must also avoid entanglement with the occupations that do not involve exploit. The tame employments, those that involve no obvious destruction of life and no spectacular coercion of refractory antagonists, fall into disrepute and are relegated to those members of the community who are defective in predatory capacity; that is to say, those who are lacking in massiveness, agility, or ferocity. Occupation in these employments argues that the person so occupied falls short of that decent modicum of prowess which would entitle him to be graded as a man in good standing. In order to an unsullied reputation, the appearance of evil must be avoided. Therefore the able-bodied barbarian of the predatory culture, who is at all mindful of his good name, severely leaves all uneventful drudgery to the women and minors of the group.

He puts in his time in the manly arts of war and devotes his talents to devising ways and means of disturbing the peace. That way lies honor. In the barbarian scheme of life the peaceable, industrial employments are women's work. They imply defective force, incapacity for aggression or devastation, and are therefore not of good report. But whatever is accepted as a conventional mark of a shortcoming or a vice comes presently to be accounted intrinsically base. In this way industrial occupations fall under a polite odium and are apprehended to be substantially ignoble. They are unsportsmanlike. Labor carries a taint, and all contamination from vulgar employments must be shunned by self-respecting men.

Where the predatory culture has developed in full consistency, the common-sense apprehension that labor is ignoble has developed into the further refinement that labor is wrong - for those who are not already beneath reproach. Hence certain well-known features of caste and tabu. In the further cultural development, when some wealth has been accumulated and the members of the community fall into a servile class on the one hand and a leisure class on the other, the tradition that labor is ignoble gains an added significance. It is not only a mark of inferior force, but it is also a perquisite of the poor.

This is the situation today. Labor is morally impossible by force of the ancient tradition that has come down from early barbarism, and it is shameful by force of its evil association with poverty. It is indecorous. The irksomeness of labor is a spiritual fact; it lies in the indignity of the thing. The fact of its irksomeness is, of course, none the less real and cogent for its being of a spiritual kind. Indeed, it is all the more substantial and irremediable on that account. Physical irksomeness and distastefulness can be borne, if only the spiritual incentive is present. Witness the attractiveness of warfare, both to the barbarian and to the civilized youth. The most common-place recital of a campaigner's experience carries a sweeping suggestion of privation, exposure, fatigue, vermin, squalor, sickness, and loathsome death; the incidents and accessories of war are said to be unsavory, unsightly, unwholesome beyond the power of words; yet warfare is an attractive employment if one only is gifted with a suitable habit of mind. Most sports, and many other polite employments that are distressing but creditable, are evidence to the same effect.

Physical irksomeness is an incommodity which men habitually make light of if it is not reinforced by the sanction of decorum; but it is otherwise with the spiritual irksomeness of such labor as is condemned by polite usage. That is a cultural fact. There is no remedy for this kind of irksomeness, short of a subversion of that cultural structure on which our canons of decency rest. Appeal may of course be made to taste and conscience to set aside the conventional aversion to labor; such an appeal is made from time to time by well-meaning and sanguine persons, and some fitful results have been achieved in that way. But the commonplace, common-sense man is bound by the deliverances of common-sense decorum on this head - the heritage of an unbroken cultural line of descent that runs back to the beginning.

INSTITUTIONS,
SOCIAL ORGANIZATION
AND ECONOMIC PERFORMANCE

Chapter 1

Christian Morals
and the Competitive System

In the light of the current materialistic outlook and the current skepticism touching supernatural matters, some question may fairly be entertained as to the religious cult of Christianity. Its fortunes in the proximate future, as well as its intrinsic value for the current scheme of civilisation, may be subject to doubt. But a similar doubt is not readily entertained as regards the morals of Christianity.

In some of its elements this morality is so intimately and organically connected with the scheme of western civilisation that its elimination would signify a cultural revolution whereby occidental culture would lose its occidental characteristics and fall into the ranks of ethnic civilisations at large. Much the same may be said of that pecuniary competition which today rules the economic life of Christendom and in large measure guides western civilisation in much else than the economic respect.

Both are institutional factors of first-rate importance in this culture, and as such it might be difficult or impracticable to assign the primacy to the one or the other, since each appears to be in a dominant position. Western civilisation is both Christian and competitive (pecuniary); and it seems bootless to ask whether its course is more substantially under the guidance of the one than of the other of these two institutional norms. Hence, if it should appear, as is sometimes contended, that there is an irreconcilable discrepancy between the two, the student of this culture might have to face the question: Will western civilisation dwindle and decay if one or the other, the morals of competition or the morals of Christianity, definitively fall into abeyance?

In a question between the two codes, or systems of conduct, each must be taken at its best and simplest. That is to say, it is a question of agreement or discrepancy in the larger elementary principles of each, not a question of the variegated details, nor of the practice of the common run of Christians, on the one hand, and of competitive business men, on the other. The variety of detailed elaboration and sophistication is fairly endless in both codes; at the same time many Christians are engaged in competitive business, and conversely. Under the diversified exigencies of daily life neither the accepted principles of morality nor those of business competition work out in an untroubled or untempered course of conduct. Circumstances constrain men unremittingly to shrewd adaptations, if not to some degree of compromise, in their endeavors to live up to their accustomed principles of conduct. Yet both of these principles, or codes of conduct, are actively present throughout life in any modern community.

For all the shrewd adaptation to which they may be subject in the casuistry of individual practice, they will not have fallen into abeyance so long as the current scheme of life is not radically altered. Both the Christian morality and the morality of pecuniary competition are intimately involved in this occidental scheme of life; for it is out of these and the like habits of thought that the scheme of life is made up. Taken at their best, do the two further and fortify one another? do they work together without mutual help or hindrance? or do they mutually inhibit and defeat each other?

In the light of modern science the principles of Christian morality or of pecuniary competition must, like any other principles of conduct, be taken simply as prevalent habits of thought. And in this light no question can be entertained as to the intrinsic merit, the eternal validity, of either. They are, humanly speaking, institutions which have arisen in the growth of the western civilisation. Their genesis and growth are incidents, or possibly episodes, in the life-history of this culture - habits of thought induced by the discipline of life in the course of this culture's growth, and more or less intrinsic and essential to its character as a phase of civilisation. Therefore, the question of their consistency with one another, or with the cultural scheme in which they are involved, turns into a question as to the conditions to which they owe their rise and continued force as institutions - as to the discipline of experience in the past, out of which each of them has come and to which, therefore, each is (presumably) suited. The exigencies of life and the discipline of experience in a complex cultural situation are many and diverse, and it is always possible that any given phase of culture may give rise to divergent lines of institutional growth, to habits of conduct which are mutually incompatible, and which may at the same time be incompatible with the continued life of that cultural situation which has brought them to pass.

The dead civilisations of history, particularly the greater ones, seem commonly to have died of some such malady. If Christian morality and pecuniary competition are the outgrowth of the same or similar lines of habituation, there should presumably be no incompatibility or discrepancy between them; otherwise it is an open question. Leaving on one side, then, all question of its divine or supernatural origin, force, and warrant, as well as of its truth and its intrinsic merit or demerit, it may be feasible to trace the human line of derivation of this spirit of Christianity, considered as a spiritual attitude habitual to civilised mankind. The details and mutations of the many variants of the cult and creed might likewise be traced back, by shrewd analysis, to their origins in the habits enforced by past civilised life, and might on this ground be appraised in respect of their fitness to survive under the changing conditions of later culture; but such a work of detailed inquiry is neither practicable nor necessary here. The variants are many and diverse, but for all the diversity and discord among them, they have certain large features in common, by which they are identified as Christian and are contrasted with the ethnic cults and creeds.

There is a certain Christian animus which pervades most of them, and marks them off against the non-Christian spiritual world. This is, perhaps, more particularly true of the moral principles of Christianity than of the general fabric of its many creeds and cults. Certain elemental features of this Christian animus stand forth obtrusively in its beginnings, and have, with varying fortunes of dominance and decay, persisted or survived unbroken, on the whole, to the present day. These are non-resistance (humility) and brotherly love. Something further might be added, perhaps, but this much is common, in some degree, to the several variants of Christianity, late or early; and the inclusion of other common principles besides these would be debatable and precarious, except in case of such moral principles as are also common to certain of the ethnic cults as well as to Christianity.

Even with respect to the two principles named, there might be some debate as to their belonging peculiarly and characteristically to the Christian spirit, exclusive of all other spiritual habits of mind. But it is at least a tenable position that these principles are intrinsic to the Christian spirit, and that they habitually serve as competent marks of identification. With the exclusion or final obsolescence of either of these, the cult would no longer be Christian, in the current acceptation of the term; though much else, chiefly not of an ethical character, would have to be added to make up a passably complete characterisation of the Christian system, as, e.g., monotheism, sin and atonement, eschatological retribution, and the like. But the two principles named bear immediately on the morals of Christianity; they are, indeed, the spiritual capital with which the Christian movement started out, and they are still the characteristics by force of which it survives. It is commonly held that these principles are not inherent traits of human nature as such, congenital and hereditary traits of the species which assert themselves instinctively, impulsively, by force of the mere absence of repression. Such, at least, in effect, is the teaching of the Christian creeds, in that they hold these spiritual qualities to be a gift of divine grace, not a heritage of sinful human nature.

Such an account of their origin and their acquirement by the successive generations of men does not fit these two main supports of Christian morality in the same degree. It may fairly be questioned as regards the principle of brotherly love, or the impulse to mutual service. While this seems to be a characteristic trait of Christian morals and may serve as a specific mark by which to distinguish this morality from the greater non-Christian cults, it is apparently a trait which Christendom shares with many of the obscurer cultures, and which does not in any higher degree characterise Christendom than it does these other, lower cultures. In the lower, non-Christian cultures, particularly among the more peaceable communities of savages, something of the kind appears to prevail by mere force of hereditary propensity; at least it appears, in some degree, to belong in these lower civilisations without being traceable to special teaching or to a visible interposition of divine grace. And in an obscure and dubious fashion, perhaps sporadically, it recurs throughout the life of human society with such an air of ubiquity as would argue that it is an elemental trait of the species, rather than a cultural product of Christendom. It may not be an overstatement to say that this principle is, in its elements, in some sort an atavistic trait, and that Christendom comes by it through a cultural reversion to the animus of the lower (peaceable) savage culture. But even if such an account be admitted as substantially sound, it does not account for that cultural reversion to which

Christendom owes its peculiar partiality for this principle; nor is its association with its fellow principle, non-resistance, thereby accounted for. The two come into play together in the beginnings of Christianity, and are thenceforward associated together, more or less inseparably, throughout the later vicissitudes of the cult and its moral code.

The second-named principle, of non-resistance and renunciation, is placed first in order of importance in the earlier formulations of Christian conduct. This is not similarly to be traced back as a culturally atavistic trait, as the outgrowth of such an archaic cultural situation as if offered by the lower savagery. Non-resistance has no such air of ubiquity and spontaneous recrudescence, and does not show itself, even sporadically, as a matter of course in cultures that are otherwise apparently unrelated; particularly not in the lower cultures, where the hereditary traits of the species should presumably assert themselves, on occasion, in a less sophisticated expression than on the more highly conventionalised levels of civilisation.

On the contrary, it belongs almost wholly to the more highly developed, more coercively organised civilisations, that are possessed of a consistent monotheistic religion and a somewhat arbitrary secular authority; and it is not always, indeed not commonly, present in these. Christianity at its inception did not take over this moral principle, ready-made, from any of the older cults or cultures from which the Christian movement was in a position to draw. It is not found, at least not in appreciable force, in the received Judaism; nor can it be derived from the classical (Graeco-Roman) cultures, which had none of it; nor is it to be found among the pagan antiquities of these barbarians whose descendants make up the great body of Christendom today.

Yet Christianity sets out with the principle of non-resistance full-blown, in the days of its early diffusion, and finds assent and acceptance for it with such readiness as seems to argue that mankind was prepared beforehand for just such a principle of conduct. Mankind, particularly the populace, within the confines of that Roman dominion within which the early diffusion of Christianity took place, was apparently in a frame of mind to accept such a principle of morality, or such a maxim of conduct; and the same is progressively true for the outlying populations to which Christianity spread in the next four centuries .To any modern student of human culture, this ready acceptance of such a principle (habit of thought) gives evidence that the section of mankind which had thus shifted its moral footing to a new and revolutionary moral principle must have been trained, by recently past experience, by the discipline of daily life in the immediate past, into such a frame of mind as predisposed them for its acceptance; that is to say, they must have been disciplined into a spiritual attitude to which such a new principle of conduct would commend itself as reasonable, if not as a matter of course.

And in due process, as this suitable attitude was enforced upon the other, outlying populations by suitable disciplinary means, Christianity with its gospel of renunciation tended to spread and supplant the outworn cults that no longer fitted the altered cultural situation. But in its later diffusion, among peoples not securely under Roman rule and not reduced to such a frame of mind by a protracted experience of Roman discipline, Christianity makes less capital of the morality of non-resistance. It was among the peoples subject to the Roman rule that Christianity first arose and spread; among the lower orders of the populace especially, who had been beaten to a pulp by the hard-handed, systematic, inexorable power of the imperial city; who had no rights which the Roman master was bound to respect; who were aliens and practically outlaws under the sway of the Caesars; and who had acquired, under high pressure, the conviction that non-resistance was the chief of virtues if not the whole duty of man. They had learned to render unto Caesar that which is Caesar's, and were in a frame of mind to render unto God that which is God's.

It is a notable fact also that, as a general rule, in its subsequent diffusion to regions and peoples not benefited by the Roman discipline, Christianity spread in proportion to the more or less protracted experience of defeat and helpless submission undergone by these peoples; and that it was the subject populace rather than the master classes that took kindly to the doctrine of non-resistance. In the outlying corners of the western world, such as the Scandinavian and British countries, where subjection to arbitrary rule in temporal matters had been less consistently and less enduringly enforced, the principle of non-resistance took less firm root. And in the days when the peoples of Christendom were sharply differentiated into ruling and subject classes, non-resistance was accepted by the lower rather than by the upper classes.

Much the same, indeed, is true of the companion principle of mutual succor. On the whole, it is not too bold a generalisation to say that these elements of the moral code which distinguish Christianity from the ethnic cults are elements of the morals of low life, of the subject populace. There is, in point of practical morality, not much to choose, e.g., between the upper-class mediaeval Christianity and the contemporary Mohammedan morality. It is only in later times, after the western culture had lost its aristocratic-feudalistic character and had become, in its typical form, though not in all its ramifications, a kind of universalised low-life culture - it is only at this later period that these principles of low-life morality also became in some degree universalised principles of Christian duty; and it still remains true that these principles are most at home in the more vulgar divisions of the Christian cult.

The higher-class variants of Christianity still differ little in the substance of their morality from Judaism or Islam. The morality of the upper class is in a less degree the morality of non-resistance and brotherly love, and is in a greater degree the morality of coercive control and kindly tutelage, which are in no degree distinctive traits of Christianity, as contrasted with the other great religious systems.

In their experience of Roman devastation and punishment-at-large, which predisposed the populace for this principle of non-resistance, the subject peoples commonly also lost such class distinctions and differential rights and privileges as they had previously enjoyed. They were leveled down to a passably homogeneous state of subjection, in which one class or individual had little to gain at the cost of another, and in which, also, each and all palpably needed the succor of all the rest. The institutional fabric had crumbled, very much as it does in an earthquake. The conventional differentiations, handed down out of the past, had proved vain and meaningless in the face of the current situation.

The pride of caste and all the principles of differential dignity and honor fell away, and left mankind naked and unashamed and free to follow the promptings of hereditary savage human nature which make for fellowship and Christian charity. Barring repressive conventionalities, reversion to the spiritual state of savagery is always easy; for human nature is still substantially savage. The discipline of savage life, selective and adaptive, has been by far the most protracted and probably the most exacting of any phase of culture in all the life-history of the race; so that by heredity human nature still is, and must indefinitely continue to be, savage human nature. This savage spiritual heritage that "springs eternal" when the pressure of conventionality is removed or relieved, seems highly conducive to the two main traits of Christian morality, though more so to the principle of brotherly love than to that of renunciation. And this may well be the chief circumstance that has contributed to the persistence of these principles of conduct even in later times, when the external conditions have not visibly favored or called for their continued exercise.

The principles of conduct underlying pecuniary competition are the principles of Natural Rights, and as such date from the eighteenth century. In respect of their acceptance into the body of commonplace morality and practice and the constraining force which they exercise, they are apparently an outgrowth of modern civilisation-whatever older antiquity may be assigned them in respect of their documentary pedigree. Comparatively speaking, they are absent from the scheme of life and from the common-sense apprehension of rights and duties in mediaeval times. They derive their warrant as moral principles from the discipline of life under the cultural situation of early modern times. They are accordingly of relatively recent date as prevalent habits of thought, at least in their fuller and freer development; even though the underlying traits of human nature which have lent themselves to the formation of these habits of thought may be as ancient as any other.

The period of their growth coincides somewhat closely with that of the philosophy of egoism, self-interest, or "individualism," as it is less aptly called. This egoistic outlook gradually assumes a dominant place in the occidental scheme of thought during and after the transition from mediaeval to modern times; it appears to be a result of the habituation to those new conditions of life which characterise the modern, as contrasted with the mediaeval, situation. Assuming, as is now commonly done, that the fundamental and controlling changes which shape and guide the transition from the institutional situation of the mediaeval to that of the modern world are economic changes, one may with fair confidence trace a connection between these economic changes and the concomitant growth of modern business principles.

The vulgar element, held cheap, kept under, hut massive, in the mediaeval order of society, comes gradually into the foreground and into the controlling position in economic life; so that the aristocratic or chivalric standards and ideals are gradually supplanted or displaced by the vulgar apprehension of what is right and best in the conduct of life. The chivalric canons of destructive exploit and of status give place to the more sordid canons of workmanlike efficiency and pecuniary strength. The economic changes which thus gave a new and hitherto impotent element of society the primacy in the social order and in the common-sense apprehensions of what is worth while, are, in the main and characteristically, the growth of handicraft and petty trade; giving rise to the industrial towns, to the growth of markets, to a pecuniary field of individual enterprise and initiative, and to a valuation of men, things, and events in pecuniary terms. It is impossible here to go narrowly into the traits of culture and of human nature which were evolved in the rise and progress of handicraft and the petty trade, and brought about the decay of mediaevalism and the rise of the modern cultural scheme. But so much seems plain on the face of things: there is at work in all this growth of the new, pecuniary culture, a large element of emulation, both in the acquisition of goods and in their conspicuous consumption. Pecuniary exploit in a degree supplies the place of chivalric exploit.

But emulation is not the whole of the motive force of the new order, nor does it supply all the canons of conduct and standards of merit under the new order. In its earlier stages, while dominated by the exigencies of handicraft and the petty trade, the modern culture is fully as much shaped and guided by considerations of livelihood, as by the ideals of differential gain. The material conditions of the new economic situation would not tolerate the institutional conditions of the old situation. There was being enforced upon the community, primarily upon that workday element into whose hands the new industrial exigencies were shifting the directive force, a new range of habitual notions as to what was needful and what was right. In both of the characteristically modern lines of occupation-handicraft and the petty trade-the individual, the workman or trader, is the central and efficient factor, on whose initiative, force, diligence, and discretion his own economic fortunes and those of the community visibly turn. It is an economic situation in which, necessarily, individual deals with individual on a footing of pecuniary efficiency; where the ties of group solidarity, which control the individual's economic (and social) relations, are themselves of a pecuniary character, and are made or broken more or less at the individual's discretion and in pecuniary terms; and it is, moreover, a cultural situation in which the social and civil relations binding the individual are prevailingly and increasingly formed for pecuniary ends, 'and enforced by pecuniary sanctions.

The individualism of the modern era sets out with industrial aims and makes its way by force of industrial efficiency. And since the individual relations under this system take the pecuniary form, the individualism thus worked out and incorporated in the modern institutional fabric is a pecuniary individualism, and is therefore also typically egoistic. The principles governing right conduct according to the habits of thought native to this individualistic era are the egoistic principles of natural rights and natural liberty. These rights and this liberty are egoistic rights and liberty of the individual. They are to be summed up as freedom and security of person and of pecuniary transactions. It is a curious fact, significant of the extreme preponderance of the vulgar element in this cultural revolution, that among these natural rights there are included no remnants of those prerogatives and disabilities of birth, office, or station, which seemed matters of course and of common-sense to the earlier generations of men who had grown up under the influence of the mediaeval social order. Nor, curiously, are there remnants of the more ancient rights and duties of the bond of kinship, the blood feud, or clan allegiance, such as were once also matters of course and of common-sense in the cultural eras and areas in which the social order of the kinship group or the clan organisation had prevailed.

On the other hand, while these institutional elements have (in theory) lost all standing, the analogous institution of property has become an element of the natural order of things. The system of natural rights is natural in the sense of being consonant with the nature of handicraft and petty trade. Meanwhile, times have changed since the eighteenth century, when this system of pecuniary egoism reached its mature development. That is to say, the material circumstances, the economic exigencies, have changed, and the discipline of habit resulting from the changed situation has, as a consequence, tended to a somewhat different effect - as is evidenced by the fact that the sanctity and sole efficacy of the principles of natural rights are beginning to be called in question. The excellence and sufficiency of an enlightened pecuniary egoism are no longer a matter of course and of common-sense to the mind of this generation, which has experienced the current era of machine industry, credit, delegated corporation management, and distant markets.

What fortune may overtake these business principles, these habits of thought native to the handicraft era, in the further sequence of economic changes can, of course, not be foretold; but it is at least certain that they cannot remain standing and effective, in the long run, unless the modern community should return to an economic regime equivalent to the era of handicraft and petty trade. For the business principles in question are of the nature of habits of thought, and habits of thought are made by habits of life; and the habits of life necessary to maintain these principles and to give them their effective sanction in the common-sense convictions of the community are the habits of life enforced by the system of handicraft and petty trade.

It appears, then, that these two codes of conduct, Christian morals and business principles, are the institutional by-products of two different cultural situations. The former, in so far as they are typically Christian, arose out of the abjectly and precariously servile relations in which the populace stood to their masters in late Roman times, as also, in a great, though perhaps less, degree, during the "Dark" and the Middle Ages. The latter, the morals of pecuniary competition, on the other hand, are habits of thought induced by the exigencies of vulgar life under the rule of handicraft and petty trade, out of which has come the peculiar system of rights and duties characteristic of modern Christendom. Yet there is something in common between the two. The Christian principles inculcate brotherly love, mutual succor: Love thy neighbor as thyself; *Mutuum date, nihil inde sperantes.* This principle seems, in its elements at least, to be a culturally atavistic trait, belonging to the ancient, not to say primordial, peaceable culture of the lower savagery. The natural-rights analogue of this principle of solidarity and mutual succor is the principle of fair play, which appears to be the nearest approach to the golden rule that the pecuniary civilisation will admit. There is no reach of ingenuity or of ingenuousness by which the one of these may be converted into the other; nor does the regime of fair play - essentially a regime of emulation - conduce to the reinforcement of the golden rule. Yet throughout all the vicissitudes of cultural change, the golden rule of the peaceable savage has never lost the respect of occidental mankind, and its hold on men's convictions is, perhaps, stronger now than at any earlier period of the modern time. It seems incompatible with business principles, but appreciably less so than with the principles of conduct that ruled the western world in the days before the Grace of God was supplanted by the Rights of Man. The distaste for the spectacle of contemporary life seldom rises to the pitch of renunciation of the world" under the new dispensation.

While one half of the Christian moral code, that pious principle which inculcates humility, submission to irresponsible authority, found easier lodgment in the mediaeval culture, the more humane moral element of mutual succor seems less alien to the modern culture of pecuniary self-help. The presumptive degree of compatibility between the two codes of morality may be shown by a comparison of the cultural setting, out of which each has arisen and in which each should be at home. In the most general outline, and neglecting details as far as may be, we may describe the upshot of this growth of occidental principles as follows: The ancient Christian principle of humility, renunciation, abnegation, or non-resistance has been virtually eliminated from the moral scheme of Christendom; nothing better than a sophisticated affectation of it has any extensive currency in modern life. The conditions to which it owes its rise - bare-handed despotism and servile helplessness - are, for the immediate present and the recent past, no longer effectual elements in the cultural situation; and it is, of course, in the recent past that the conditions must be sought which have shaped the habits of thought of the immediate present.

Its companion principle, brotherly love or mutual service, appears, in its elements at least, to be a very deep rooted and ancient cultural trait, due to an extremely protracted experience of the race in the early stages of human culture, reinforced and defined by the social conditions prevalent in the early days of Christianity. In the naive and particular formulation given it by the early Christians, this habit of thought has also lost much of

its force, or has fallen somewhat into abeyance; being currently represented by a thrifty charity, and, perhaps, by the negative principle of fair play,
neither of which can fairly be rated as a competent expression of the
Christian spirit. Yet this principle is forever reasserting itself in economic
matters, in the impulsive approval of whatever conduct is serviceable to
the common good and in the disapproval of disserviceable conduct even
within the limits of legality and natural right. It seems, indeed, to be nothing else than a somewhat specialised manifestation of the instinct of
workmanship, and as such it has the indefeasible vitality that belongs to
the hereditary traits of human nature.

The pecuniary scheme of right conduct is of recent growth, but it is an
outcome of a recently past phase of modern culture rather than of the
immediate present. This system of natural rights, including the right of
ownership and the principles of pecuniary good and evil that go with it, no
longer has the consistent support of current events. Under the conditions
prevalent in the era of handicraft, the rights of ownership made for equality rather than the reverse, so that their exercise was in effect not notably
inconsistent with the ancient bias in favor of mutual aid and human
brotherhood. This is more particularly apparent if the particular form of
organisation and the spirit of the regulations then ruling in vulgar life be
kept in mind. The technology of handicraft, as well as the market relations
of the system of petty trade, pushed the individual workman into the foreground and led men to think of economic interests in terms of this workman and his work; the situation emphasised his creative relation to his
product, as well as his responsibility for this product and for its serviceability to the common welfare. It was a situation in which the acquisition of
property depended, in the main, on the workmanlike serviceability of the
man who acquired it, and in which, on the whole, honesty was the best
policy.

Under such conditions the principles of fair play and the inviolability of
ownership would be somewhat closely in touch with the ancient human
instinct of workmanship, which approves mutual aid and serviceability to
the common good. On the other hand, the current experience of men in
the communities of Christendom, now no longer acts to reinforce these
habits of thought embodied in the system of natural rights; and it is
scarcely conceivable that a conviction of the goodness, sufficiency, and
inviolability of the rights of ownership could arise out of such a condition
of things, technological and pecuniary, as now prevails.

Hence there are indications in current events that these principles - habits of thought - are in process of disintegration rather than otherwise. With
the revolutionary changes that have supervened in technology and in pecuniary relations, there is no longer such a close and visible touch between the workman and his product as would persuade men that the
product belongs to him by force of an extension of his personality; nor is
there a visible relation between serviceability and acquisition; nor between the discretionary use of wealth and the common welfare. The principles of fair play and pecuniary discretion have, in great measure, lost the
sanction once afforded them by the human propensity for serviceability to

the common good, neutral as that sanction has been at its best. Particularly is this true since business has taken on the character of an impersonal, dispassionate, not to say graceless, investment for profit. There is little in the current situation to keep the natural right of pecuniary discretion in touch with the impulsive bias of brotherly love, and there is in the spiritual discipline of this situation much that makes for an effectual discrepancy between the two.

Except for a possible reversion to a cultural situation strongly characterised by ideals of emulation and status, the ancient racial bias embodied in the Christian principle of brotherhood should logically continue to gain ground at the expense of the pecuniary morals of competitive business.

Chapter 2

The Intellectual Pre-Eminence
of Jews in Modern Europe

Among all the clamorous projects of national self-determination which surround the return of peace, the proposal of the Zionists is notable for sobriety, good will, and a poise of self-assurance. More confidently and perspicuously than all the others, the Zionists propose a rehabilitation of their national integrity under a regime of live and let live, "with charity for all, with malice toward none." Yet it is always a project for withdrawal up- on themselves, a scheme of national demarcation between Jew and gen- tile; indeed, it is a scheme of territorial demarcation and national frontiers of the conventional sort, within which Jews and Jewish traits, traditions, and aspirations are to find scope and breathing space for a home-bred culture and a free unfolding of all that is best and most characteristic in the endowment of the race.

There runs through it all a dominant bias of isolation and inbreeding, and a confident persuasion that this isolation and inbreeding will bring great and good results for all concerned. The Zionists aspire to bring to full fruition all that massive endowment of spiritual and intellectual capacities of which their people have given evidence throughout their troubled his- tory, and not least during these concluding centuries of their exile. The whole project has an idyllic and engaging air. And any disinterested by- stander will be greatly moved to wish them godspeed. Yet there comes in a regret that this experiment in isolation and inbreeding could not have been put to the test at an earlier date, before the new order of large-scale industry and universal intercourse had made any conclusive degree of such national isolation impracticable, before this same new order had so shaped the run of things that any nation or community drawn on this small scale would necessarily be dependent on and subsidiary to the run of things at large. It is now, unhappily, true that any "nation" of the size and geographical emplacement of the projected Zion will, for the present and the calculable future, necessarily be something of a national make- believe. The current state of the industrial arts will necessarily deny it a rounded and self-balanced national integrity in any substantial sense.

The days of Solomon and the caravan trade which underlay the glory of Solomon are long past. Yet much can doubtless be done by taking thought and making the most of that spirit of stubborn clannishness which has never been the least among the traits of this people. But again, to any dis- interested bystander there will come the question: What is the use of it all? It is not so much a question of what is aimed at, as of the chances of its working-out. The logic of the Zionist project plainly runs to the effect that, whereas this people have achieved great things while living under condi- tions of great adversity, scattered piecemeal among the gentiles of Europe, they are due to achieve much greater things and to reach an unexampled prosperity so soon as they shall have a chance to follow their own devices untroubled within the shelter of their own frontiers. But the doubt presents itself that the conditioning circumstances are not the same or of the same kind in the occidental twentieth century A. D. as in the oriental twelfth century B. C.; nor need it follow that those things which scattered Jews have achieved during their dispersion among the gentiles of Europe are a safe index of what things may be expected of a nation of Jews turned in upon themselves within the insulating frontiers of the Holy Land. It is on this latter point that a question is raised here as to the nature and causes of Jewish achievement in gentile Europe; and the contrast of the conditions offered by the projected Zion will present itself without argument.

It is a fact which must strike any dispassionate observer that the Jewish people have contributed much more than an even share to the intellectual life of modern Europe. So also it is plain that the civilisation of Christendom continues today to draw heavily on the Jews for men devoted to science and scholarly pursuits. It is not only that men of Jewish extraction continue to supply more than a proportionate quota to the rank and file engaged in scientific and scholarly work, but a disproportionate number of the men to whom modern science and scholarship look for guidance and leadership are of the same derivation. Particularly is this true of the modern sciences, and it applies perhaps especially in the field of scientific theory, even beyond the extent of its application in the domain of workday detail. So much is notorious. This notable and indeed highly creditable showing has, of course, not escaped the attention of those men of Jewish race who interest themselves in the fortune of their own people.

Not unusually it is set down as a national trait, as evidence of a peculiarly fortunate intellectual endowment, native and hereditary, in the Jewish people. There is much to be said for such a view, but it should not follow that any inquiry into the place and value of the Jewish people in western civilisation should come to rest with this broad assertion of pre-eminence in point of native endowment. It is true that the history of the Chosen People, late and early, throws them into a position of distinction among the nations with which they have been associated; and it will commonly be accepted without much argument that they have, both late and early, shown distinctive traits of temperament and aptitude, such as to mark them off more or less sharply from all the gentiles among whom it has been their lot to be thrown.

So general is the recognition of special Jewish traits, of character and of capacity, that any refusal to recognise something which may be called a Jewish type of hereditary endowment would come to nothing much better than a borrowing of trouble. That there should be such a tenacious spiritual and intellectual heritage transmissible within the Jewish community and marking that people off in any perceptible degree from their gentile neighbors is all the more notable in view of the known life-history of the children of Israel. No unbiased ethnologist will question the fact that the Jewish people are a nation of hybrids; that gentile blood of many kinds has been infused into the people in large proportions in the course of time.

Indeed none of the peoples of Christendom has been more unremittingly exposed to hybridisation, in spite of all the stiff conventional precautions that have been taken to keep the breed pure. It is not a question of a surreptitious hybrid strain, such as would show itself in sporadic reversions to an alien type; but rather it is a question whether the Jewish strain itself, racially speaking, can at all reasonably be held to account for one half of the pedigree of the Jewish nation as it stands. The hybrid antecedents of the Children of Israel are not a mere matter of bookish record. Evidence of their hybrid descent is written all over them, wherever they are to be met with, so that in this respect the Jews of Europe are in the same case as the other Europeans, who are also universally cross-bred. It would perplex any anthropologist to identify a single individual among them all who could safely be set down as embodying the Jewish racial type without abatement.

The variations in all the measurable traits that go to identify any individual in the schedules of the anthropologists are wide and ubiquitous as regards both their physical and their spiritual traits, in respect of anthropometric measurements as well as in temperament and capacities. And yet, when all is said in abatement of it, the Jewish type, it must be admitted, asserts itself with amazing persistence through all the disguises with which it has been overlaid in the course of age-long hybridisation. Whatever may be found true elsewhere, in their contact with other racial types than those of Europe, it still appears that within this European racial environment the outcome given by any infusion of Jewish blood in these cross-bred individuals is something which can be identified as Jewish.

Cross-breeding commonly results in a gain to the Jewish community rather than conversely; and the hybrid offspring is a child of Israel rather than of the gentiles. In effect, therefore, it is the contribution of this Jewish-hybrid people to the culture of modern Europe that is in question. The men of this Jewish extraction count for more than their proportionate share in the intellectual life of western civilisation; and they count particularly among the vanguard, the pioneers, the uneasy guild of pathfinders and iconoclasts, in science, scholarship, and institutional change and growth. On its face it appears as if an infusion of Jewish blood, even in some degree of hybrid attenuation, were the one decisive factor in the case; and something of that sort may be well allowed, to avoid argument if for no more substantial reason. But even a casual survey of the available evidence will leave so broad a claim in doubt.

Of course, there is the fact to be allowed for at the outset, so far as need be, that these intellectuals of Jewish extraction are, after all, of hybrid extraction as well; but this feature of the case need be given no undue weight. It is of consequence in its bearing on the case of the Jews only in the same manner and degree as it is of consequence for any other hybrid people. Cross-breeding gives a wider range of variation and a greater diversity of individual endowment than can be had in any passably pure-bred population; from which results a greater effectual flexibility of aptitudes and capacities in such a people when exposed to conditions that make for change. In this respect the Jews are neither more nor less fortunate than their gentile compatriots. It may be more to the purpose to note that this intellectual pre-eminence of the Jews has come into bearing within the gentile community of peoples, not from the outside; that the men who have been its bearers have been men immersed in this gentile culture in which they have played their part of guidance and incitement, not bearers of a compelling message from afar or proselytisers of enlightenment conjuring with a ready formula worked out in the ghetto and carried over into the gentile community for its mental regeneration. In point of fact, neither these nor other Jews have done effectual missionary work, in any ordinary sense of that term, in this or any other connection; nor have they entertained a design to do so. Indeed, the Chosen People have quite characteristically never been addicted to missionary enterprise; nor does the Jewish scheme of right and honest living comprise anything of the kind.

This, too, is notorious fact; so much so that this allusion to it may well strike any Jew as foolish insistence on a commonplace matter of course. In their character of a Chosen People, it is not for them to take thought of their unblest neighbors and seek to dispel the darkness that overlies the soul of the gentiles. The cultural heritage of the Jewish people is large and rich, and it is of ancient and honorable lineage. And from time immemorial this people has shown aptitude for such work as will tax the powers of thought and imagination Their home-bred achievements of the ancient time, before the Diaspora, are among the secure cultural monuments of mankind; but these achievements of the Jewish ancients neither touch the frontiers of modern science nor do they fall in the lines of modern scholarship. So also the later achievements of the Jewish scholars and savants, in so far as their intellectual enterprise has gone forward on what may be called distinctively Jewish lines, within the confines of their own community and by the leading of their own home-bred interest, untouched by that peculiar drift of inquiry that characterises the speculations of the modern gentile world - is learning of the later generations of home-bred Jewish scholars is also reputed to have run into lucubrations that have no significance for contemporary science or scholarship at large.

It appears to be only when the gifted Jew escapes from the cultural environment created and fed by the particular genius of his own people, only when he falls into the alien lines of gentile inquiry and becomes a naturalised, though hyphenate, citizen in the gentile republic of learning, that he comes into his own as a creative leader in the world's intellectual enterprise. It is by loss of allegiance, or at the best by force of a divided allegiance to the people of his origin, that he finds himself in the vanguard of modern inquiry. It will not do to say that none but renegade Jews count effectually in the modern sciences. Such a statement would be too broad; but, for all its excessive breadth, it exceeds the fact only by a margin. The margin may seem wide, so wide as to vitiate the general statement, perhaps, or at least wide enough materially to reduce its cogency. But it would be wider of the mark to claim that the renegades are to be counted only as sporadic exceptions among a body of unmitigated Jews who make up the virtual total of that muster of creative men of science which the Jewish people have thrown into the intellectual advance of Christendom. The first requisite for constructive work in modern science, and indeed for any work of inquiry that shall bring enduring results, is a skeptical frame of mind. The enterprising skeptic alone can be counted on to further the increase of knowledge in any substantial fashion. This will be found true both in the modern sciences and in the field of scholarship at large. Much good and serviceable workmanship of a workday character goes into the grand total of modern scientific achievement; but that pioneering and engineering work of guidance, design, and theoretical correlation, without which the most painstaking collection and canvass of information is irrelevant, incompetent, and impertinent - this intellectual enterprise that goes forward presupposes a degree of exemption from hard-and-fast preconceptions, a skeptical animus, *Unbefangenheit*, release from the dead hand of conventional finality. The intellectually gifted Jew is in a peculiarly fortunate position in respect of this requisite immunity from the inhibitions of intellectual quietism. But he can come in for such immunity only at the cost of losing his secure place in the scheme of conventions into which he has been born, and at the cost, also, of finding no similarly secure place in that scheme of gentile conventions into which he is thrown. For him as for other men in the like case, the skepticism that goes to make him an effectual factor in the increase and diffusion of knowledge among men involves a loss of that peace of mind that is the birthright of the safe and sane quietist. He becomes a disturber of the intellectual peace, but only at the cost of becoming an intellectual wayfaring man, a wanderer in the intellectual no-man's-land, seeking another place to rest, farther along the road, somewhere over the horizon. They are neither a complaisant nor a contented lot, these aliens of the uneasy feet; but that is, after all, not the point in question.

The young Jew who is at all gifted with a taste for knowledge will unavoidably go afield into that domain of learning where the gentile interests dominate and the gentile orientation gives the outcome. There is nowhere else to go on this quest. He comes forthwith to realise that the scheme of traditions and conventional verities handed down within the pale of his own people are matters of habit handed down by tradition, that they have only such force as belongs to matters of habit and convention, and that they lose their binding force so soon as the habitually accepted outlook is given up or seriously deranged. These nationally binding convictions of what is true, good, and beautiful in the world of the human spirit are forthwith seen to be only contingently good and true; to be binding only so far as the habitual will to believe in them and to seek the truth along their lines remains intact.

That is to say, only so long as no scheme of habituation alien to the man's traditional outlook has broken in on him, and has forced him to see that those convictions and verities which hold their place as fundamentally and eternally good and right within the balanced scheme of received traditions prove to be, after all, only an ephemeral web of habits of thought; so soon as his current habits of life no longer continue to fall in those traditional fines that keep these habits of thought in countenance.

Now it happens that the home-bred Jewish scheme of things, human and divine, and the ways and means of knowledge that go with such a scheme, are of an archaic fashion, good and true, perhaps, beyond all praise, for the time and conditions that gave rise to it all, that wove that web of habituation and bound its close-knit tissue of traditional verities and conventions. But it all bears the date-mark, "B.C." It is of a divine complexion, monotheistic even, and perhaps intrinsically thearchic; it is ritualistic, with an exceedingly and beautifully magical efficacy of ritual necessity. It is imperiously self-balanced and self-sufficient, to the point of sanctity; and as is always true of such schemes of sanctity and magical sufficiency, it runs on a logic of personal and spiritual traits, qualities and relations, a class of imponderables which are no longer of the substance of those things that are inquired into by men to whom the ever increasingly mechanistic orientation of the modern time becomes habitual.

When the gifted young Jew, still flexible in respect of his mental habits, is set loose among the iron pots of this mechanistic orientation, the clay vessel of Jewish archaism suffers that fortune which is due and coming to clay vessels among the iron pots. His beautifully rounded heirloom, trade-marked "B.C.," goes to pieces between his hands, and they are left empty. He is divested of those archaic conventional preconceptions which will not comport with the intellectual environment in which he finds himself. But he is not thereby invested with the gentile's peculiar heritage of conventional preconceptions which have stood over, by inertia of habit, out of the gentile past, which go, on the one hand, to make the safe and sane gentile, conservative and complacent, and which conduce also, on the other hand, to blur the safe and sane gentile's intellectual vision, and to leave him intellectually sessile.

The young Jew finds his own heritage of usage and outlook untenable; but this does not mean that he therefore will take over and inwardly assimilate the traditions of usage and outlook which the gentile world has to offer; or at the most he does not uncritically take over all the intellectual prepossessions that are always standing over among the substantial citizens of the republic of learning. The idols of his own tribe have crumbled in decay and no longer cumber the ground, but that release does not induce him to set up a new line of idols borrowed from an alien tribe to do the same disservice. By consequence he is in a peculiar degree exposed to the unmediated facts of the current situation; and in a peculiar degree, therefore, he takes his orientation from the run of the facts as he finds them, rather than from the traditional interpretation of analogous facts in the past. In short, he is a skeptic by force of circumstances over which he has no control. Which comes to saying that he is in line to become a guide and leader of men in that intellectual enterprise out of which comes the increase and diffusion of knowledge among men, provided always that he is by native gift endowed with that net modicum of intelligence which takes effect in the play of the idle curiosity.

Intellectually he is likely to become an alien; spiritually he is more than likely to remain a Jew; for the heart-strings of affection and consuetude are tied early, and they are not readily retied in after life. Nor does the animus with which the community of safe and sane gentiles is wont to meet him conduce at all to his personal incorporation in that community, whatever may befall the intellectual assets which he brings. Their people need not become his people nor their gods his gods, and indeed the provocation is forever and irritably present all over the place to turn back from following after them. The most amiable share in the gentile community's life that is likely to fall to his lot is that of being interned. One who goes away from home will come to see many unfamiliar things, and to take note of them; but it does not follow that he will swear by all the strange gods whom he meets along the road.

As bearing on the Zionist's enterprise in isolation and nationality, this fable appears to teach a two-fold moral: If the adventure is carried to that consummate outcome which seems to be aimed at, it should apparently be due to be crowned with a large national complacency and, possibly, a profound and self-sufficient content on the part of the Chosen People domiciled once more in the Chosen Land; and when and in so far as the Jewish people in this way turn inward on themselves, their prospective contribution to the world's intellectual output should, in the light of the historical evidence, fairly be expected to take on the complexion of Talmudic lore, rather than that character of free-swung skeptical initiative which their renegades have habitually infused into the pursuit of the modern sciences abroad among the nations. Doubtless, even so the supply of Jewish renegades would not altogether cease, though it should presumably fall off to a relatively inconsiderable residue. And not all renegades are fit guides and leaders of men on the quest of knowledge, nor is their dominant incentive always or ordinarily the quest of the idle curiosity.

There should be some loss to Christendom at large, and there might be some gain to the repatriated Children of Israel. It is a sufficiently difficult choice between a life of complacent futility at home and a thankless quest of unprofitable knowledge abroad. It is, after all, a matter of the drift of circumstance; and behind that lies a question of taste, about which there is no disputing.

Chapter 3
The Opportunity of Japan

What is here intended by "the opportunity of Japan" is not so much an outlook of prospective gain for the Japanese people as of aggrandizement for the Japanese State. It will hold true in this instance as in so many others that the advantage of the country's population does not in any sensible degree coincide with that of its directorate, except it be in point of sentiment.

For any modern people imbued with a sense of loyalty to their rulers as is eminently the case with the Japanese people, the dynastic ambitions of their masters are necessarily an object of veneration, and any political success scored by their rulers is of course a source of gratification. And it may fairly be left an open question whether this sentimental value which the people so attach to the political gains achieved by their government is to be rated as a sufficiently substantial matter to admit speaking of these political successes as a substantial gain for the people at large. To speak of any more substantial gain presumed to accrue to the common man from these manoeuvres of political aggrandizement anything like a material advantage, e.g. would be out of the question, except, of course, in a patriotic harangue. The cost of such dynastic aggrandizement falls, of course, on the people at large; and equally of course except in patriotic harangues such material gains as may accrue from these political successes fall, equally of course, directly to the personnel of the governing class, together with a certain contingent of enterprising business men who are under modern conditions necessary to the conduct of any national enterprise and are in a position to profit by that trade that is said to "follow the flag." This will necessarily hold true with less qualification the more the country's government partakes of that character of absolute and irresponsible mastery that has been exemplified in medieval and early modern Europe as, e.g., the Ancient Regime under the Grand Monarch, or, again, the Imperial Regime in Germany under William II; and it holds true in an eminent degree for Japan, where absolute and irresponsible rule is more securely established than it has been in any European power of the first class, barring Turkey perhaps. To the Japanese government, or "State," the country, with its human denizens, is an estate to be husbanded and exploited for the State's ends; which comes near saying, for the prestige of the Mikado's government. In the material respect, therefore, the division of interest as between the people at large and the governing class is particularly well marked and well maintained; being, indeed, a division after the same fashion as that which holds between servant and master in any community that is organised on a servile footing. So that the people at large, the common man, has no appreciable share and no substantial concern in the measures taken by the governmental agencies, or even in the deliberations of that advisory board of nobility and gentry that has, under the constitution, been installed under the rubric, "Parliament." In effect, the people at large are the government's chattels, to be bred, fed, trained and consumed as the shrewd econ my of dynastic politics may best require. All this is well enough known, though it is not commonly spoken of in such naive terms. The government established by the revolution, or "restoration," of Meiji is of the nature of an autonomous co-optative bureaucracy, made up out of certain lines and cliques of the nobility (to some extent of a bureaucratic origin), backed by the loyal adhesion of a large body of gentry which differs from the displaced Samurai in its workday avocations rather than in its spirit of aristocratic fealty or its substantially parasitic livelihood. In point of its substantial powers, as in point of substantial accountability, the current bureaucratic organisation that does business in the name of the Mikado apparently differs in no sensible degree from the Shogunate which it displaced.

The emperor is now paraded instead of being retired behind the screen, and there is much ceremonial dust thrown up about his ostensible share in the measures taken by the bureaucratic directorate; all of which is, doubtless, good management. The powers of the crown except as they are construed to be identical with the powers of the cabinet are apparently of much the same fainantise nature as they were under the earlier dispensation, prior to 1868.

Of course, none of this characterisation is intended in the least to question or deprecate that peculiar and well-authenticated emanation of virtuous influence whereby this divine ruler magically or preternaturally animates his official servants and, at a farther remove, his subjects more at large; but it is to be noted that apart from such magical control, after the pattern of "absent treatment," it is not evident that the incumbent of the throne exerts any initiative, choice, impulse, guidance or check in the affairs of state. Power vests in a self-appointed, self-authenticating aristocratic cabinet under the mask of a piously nourished monarchical fiction with the advice, but without the consent, of a "parliament" endowed with advisory power.

This bureaucratic organ of control is still animated with the "Spirit of Old Japan," and it still rests on and draws its force from a population animated with the same feudalistic spirit. It is, hitherto, only in respect of its material ways and means, its technological equipment and information, that the "New Japan" differs from the old. That superficial reorganisation and amelioration of its civil and political institutions that went into effect in the Restoration has not yet had time to remove the spiritual landmarks of feudalism or appreciably to weaken the servile-aristocratic bias that still guides the intrigues of the court circle, the policies of state, and the larger manoeuvres of diplomacy. It is in this unique combination of a high-wrought spirit of feudalistic fealty and chivalric honor with the material efficiency given by the modern technology that the strength of the Japanese nation lies. In this respect in being able anachronistically to combine the use of modern technical ways and means with the medieval spirit of servile solidarity the position of the Japanese government is not unique except in the eminent degree of its successful operation.

The several governments of Europe are also, and with a varying measure of success, endeavoring similarly to exploit the modern state of the industrial arts by recourse to the servile patriotism of the common man, and for the purposes of a dynastic politics that is substantially of a medieval character; but in respect of the measure of success which this anachronistic enterprise meets with, these European powers, while differing greatly among themselves, each and several fall short of the Japanese pattern by a long interval. With great, perhaps with exceptional facility, the Japanese have been taking over and assimilating the industrial ways and means offered by the technological knowledge and the material sciences of the Western peoples. But, except in the most superficial fashion, their habituation to these technological ways and means and to this matter-of fact insight in the domain of the material sciences has not yet had its effect on the spiritual outlook and sentimental convictions of the people; nor have these borrowed achievements in the field of matter-of-fact seriously begun to dismantle and reshape those matters of imputation that make up the working specifications of the institutional fabric, the ethical (sentimental) values and conventional principles of conduct by force of which it holds true that "man lives not by bread alone."

The Japanese people are learning to gain their "bread" (their fish and rice) by use of the modern, Western state of the industrial arts, but they still conduct their life and spend their endeavor in the light of those principles and with an untroubled view to those values that have been handed down from a now obsolescent state of industry and economic organisation in their own recent medieval past. In a measure their case is paralleled by that of the German people, e.g., who have recently made an analogous but less immoderate and less precipitate move out of medieval ism into the modern system of industry and science; and in the like analogous way the German people, carrying over much of the servile-aristocratic spirit of medievalism into their bureaucratic and irresponsible imperial present, have allowed their new-found technological efficiency to be turned to the service of dynastic politics; though herein, again, the rate and ratio of enhanced achievement on the part of the Germans fall short of the spectacular sweep of the Japanese.

And by the way, it should be something more than a blind historical accident when the Japanese committee of bureaucrats have found it to their account to draw so largely as they have done from the example of German bureaucratic imperialism, both in their constitutional reorganisation and in the excessively devious and irresponsible ways of their diplomacy. An analogy farther afield and to a different effect, and yet perhaps even more suggestive in its way, may be found in the case of the English people and their history, both in the industrial and the political respect; but here the analogy is more valuable for its contrasts than for any direct parallelism it may afford. Taking their case over the long run it will be found that, like the Japanese, the English have been a nation of borrowers, particularly borrowers of technological elements. But their borrowings have been extended over an incomparably longer interval of history and have in no case involved so abrupt a break with the people's own cultural past, having commonly been drawn from neighbors occupying a technological plane not conspicuously more advanced than the state of the industrial arts already previously at the command of the English community. And the technological borrowing of the English virtually ceased at a date so far in the past as already to have allowed all borrowed elements not only to be fully assimilated in a virtually home-bred technological system, but also to have so far worked out their secondary, institutional, consequences as to afford an object lesson of what the cultural consequences of any such technological borrowing should necessarily be.

Down through the middle ages and early modern times the English were, culturally speaking, and particularly in the technological respect, constantly and cumulatively indebted to their Continental neighbors, in a fashion resembling that in which the Japanese throughout their long medieval experience were, culturally, followers and dependents of China and Korea. But there is in the English case this striking feature of contrast as against the current Japanese situation, that while the English borrowed unremittingly, until such time as the course of events threw them into the lead in Europe's industrial advance, their borrowing took effect at so moderate a pace that the consequently changing state of the industrial arts among them had time and scope concomitantly to work out its effect upon the habits of thought of the community, and so to bring about a state of the institutional conventions answering to the altered state of the industrial arts. It should, then, confidently be presumed that as Japan has with great facility and effect taken over the Occidental state of the industrial arts, so should its population be due, presently and expeditiously, to fall in with the peculiar habits of thought that make the faults and qualities of the Western culture - the spiritual outlook and the principles of conduct and ethical values that have been induced by the exacting discipline of this same state of the industrial arts among the technologically more advanced and mature of the Western peoples.

For good or ill, life under the conditions imposed by the modern industrial system, and by that economic system of price, business enterprise, and competitive earning and spending that always goes with it, is in the long run incompatible with the prepossessions of medievalism. So that as soon as her people shall have digested the Western state of science and technology and have assimilated its spiritual contents, the Spirit of Old Japan will, in effect, have been dissipated. Ravelings of its genial tradition will still trail at the skirts of the new era, but as an asset available for the enterprise in dynastic politics the Spirit of Old Japan will have little more than the value of a tale that is told. There will doubtless continue to float through the adolescent brains of Young Japan some yellow vapor of truculence, such as would under other skies be called *el valor español,* and such as may give rise to occasional exploits of abandon, but the joy of living in obscure privation and contumely for the sake of the Emperor's politics and posthumous fame will be lost to the common man.

The opportunity of imperial Japan as a fearsome power in the world's concert of dynastic politics may by consequence confidently be expected to lie within the historical interval that so intervenes between Japan's acquirement of the Western state of the industrial arts and its consequent, slower but inevitable, falling into line with those materialistic, commercial and spendthrift conceptions of right and honest living that make the outcome among the (Christian) peoples that have gone before along the road of industrial dominion and individual self-help. The "Spirit of Old Japan" is an institutional matter; that is to say it is a matter of acquired habits of thought, of tradition and training, rather than of native endowment peculiar to the race. As such it is necessarily of a transitory, not to say transient, nature, depending for its maintenance on the continued maintenance of those workday habits of life out of which it has arisen and to which it owes its consistency.

Barring such retardation as necessarily attached to the growth of new principles and values induced by new circumstances, a radical change in the material ways and means by which the people live must, here as elsewhere, work a consequent change in the people's scheme of life in the accepted rule of rights and duties. Ideals, ethical values, principles (habits of thought) induced by the conditions of life in the past must presently give place to a different range of ideals, values and principles, so soon as the range of habituation to which they owe their force has ceased to be operative. The fact that, in the case of the Japanese as in other similar cases, the popular and romantic faith holds the received scheme of habits to be an innate and irreducible specific character peculiar to this people, and therefore holds it to be a national heritage unalterable and indefeasible through the ages "as it was in the beginning, is now, and ever shall be," etc.; this romantic prejudice need of course not detain us, since it is itself an integral part in that scheme of habits of thought that comes and goes under the compulsion of shifting circumstance.

The Japanese people should be no exception to the common rule in this respect. The elements engaged in their case are of much the same character as those that have been seen at work in the history of the Western nations, and they should be amendable to the same discipline of those material circumstances that are now coming to condition the national life. So, in point of their racial make-up the Japanese are in very much the same case as the Occidental nations from whom they are now borrowing ways and means and into the midst of whom they are driving their way by help of these borrowed ways and means. It is, of course, not intended to claim that there subsists anything like an identity of race, as between the Japanese and the Christian nations, nor even a particularly near or intimate ethnic relationship ; but the run of the well known facts is sufficiently convincing to the effect that the Japanese people readily fall into the same ways of thinking and reasoning, that they readily assimilate the same manner of theoretical constructions in science and technology, that the same scheme of conceptual values and logical sequence carries conviction in Japan as in the Occident.

Their intellectual perspective is so nearly the same that the same facts, seen in the same connection, are convincing to the same effect. It need by no means imply an inclusive psychological identity or duplication, but the facility and effect with which the Japanese are taking to Western habits of

thought in matters of technology and scientific knowledge shows a sufficiently convincing equality or equivalence between them and their Western fellow men in respect of their intellectual make-up. This intellectual
similarity or psychological equivalence will stand out in relief when the
Japanese case is contrasted with what has befallen certain other peoples,
racially alien to the bearers of the Western culture, such as the Negro, Pol-
ynesian, or East Indian. These others have been exposed to the Occidental
technological system the system of the machine industry but they have
been brought to no effectual comprehension of the logic and efficiency of
the Western technological equipment, have not acquired or assimilated
the drift and bias of the material science of the West, and have, even under
hard compulsion, been unable to effect anything like a practicable working arrangement with the Occidental system of mechanical efficiency and
economic control. And even as the Japanese show this facile apprehension
of

Occidental methods and values in the domain of material knowledge, so
also is there apparently a close resemblance in point of emotional complexion, suggested, e.g., by the close similarity between the feudal system
as it has prevailed in Japan and, in its time, in Western Europe. Similar material circumstances, particularly in respect of the industrial arts, appear
to have induced similar institutional results and a parallel range of ideals
and ethical values, such as would presume a somewhat closely similar run
of human nature in the two cases. This similarity in point of native traits, if
so it can be called, is due not to an identity of race but rather to a parallelism in racial composition. Like the peoples of Christendom, and more
particularly like that group of peoples that cluster about the North Sea,
and that make up the center of diffusion of the Western culture, the Japanese are, racially, a hybrid population.

The several racial elements that go to make up the hybrid mixture are, of
course, not the same in the two cases under comparison, nor are they,
perhaps, at all nearly related in point of racial derivation. But both of these
two contrasted populations alike show that wide-ranging variability of
individuals that is characteristic of hybrid peoples, both in the absence of
uniformity in respect of physical type and in their relatively great variety of
intellectual and spiritual endowment, both in degree and in kind. This
variability of these hybrid peoples becomes more obvious when they are
contrasted with peoples of relatively unmixed stock, or even with the average run of mankind at large. Indeed, it may be set down as an earmark of
hybridism. It is a factor of serious consequence for the cultural scheme of
any such population, particularly for its stability; since such a wide-
fluctuating variability of individuals within any given community will give,
in effect, a large available flexibility of type, and so will afford a wide and
facile susceptibility to new ideas and new grounds of action.

Such being the character of the human raw material in and by which the
Japanese situation is to be worked out, it should presumably follow that,
just as the material and matter-of-fact elements of Western civilisation are
finding ready lodgment and fertile ground among them, so should these
intrusive matter-of-fact conceptions presently, and with celerity, induce

the working out of a corresponding fabric of matters of imputation principles of conduct, articles of faith, social conventions, ethical values. The impersonal and materialistic bias of modern science and technology has among the Western peoples, already gone far to dissipate those putative values on which any feudal and autocratic regime must necessarily rest. And since the same impersonal and materialistic frame of mind proves, to all appearance, to be characteristic of the Japanese, they should also expect presently to experience its spiritual, and therefore its institutional consequences. Hitherto and for the immediate future, therefore, Japan has the usufruct of the modern state of science and the industrial arts, without the faults of its qualities. But in the long run its faults are as inseparable from this system as its structure. How far these faults or infirmities are to be rated as such at large is a question that need not be argued here. They are infirmities for the imperialistic purposes of Great Nippon, and it should be a matter of no great difficulty to see how and why, or even to see that they are already incipiently in process of realisation. This may be better appreciated on calling to mind certain features of the change that is going forward in the economic circumstances of Japan.

Effectually to turn its usufruct of the Western science and technology to account, it will be necessary for Japan, in all essential respects, to follow the lead given by the Western peoples. Such a course is prescribed by the circumstances of the case; partly in that the modern state of the industrial arts involves a certain kind and degree of popular education and a certain impersonal, mechanistic organisation and coordination of the material equipment (mechanical and human) and of the processes employed; partly because nothing like the full advantage of the methods employed can be had except by entering into close relations of give and take, commercially and otherwise, with the other nations that have adopted the scope and method of the mechanical industry. In its full scope this industrial system is necessarily of an international or cosmopolitan character, and any attempt to work it on narrower than international lines must fall short of that highest efficiency which alone can satisfy the imperialistic needs or the national pride of Japan. It is only by way of commerce and a commercialised industry that Japan can get a footing among the commercial nations of the West; and in this necessary commercialisation of its industry and its economic institutions Japan must in all essential respects accept the scheme as it is already in force among the nations of the West. But the unintended consequences of such a course must also follow.

So, a competent system of communication, internal and external, is of the essence of the case, and in this matter the Japanese are already far on their way, with steamships, railway, telegraph, telephone, postal service and newspapers, as well as an improved and extended system of highways; from which it follows that the isolation, parcelment and consequent homebred animus of the people is already beginning to disappear, and the corresponding clan nishness and adhesive loyalty to their hereditary local masters is also in process of decay. The feudal organisation, and the spirit of fealty, rests on an industrial system of self-sufficient local units and on discrepancies of usage and convention as between self-sufficient local organisations.

Again, the modern (Western) state of the industrial arts requires, in order to its efficient working, a relatively high degree of "intelligence," so-called, among the workmen, it should more accurately be spoken of as a large volume of relatively exact information within the peculiar lines of the material sciences. This involves schooling, of a set and special character, extended far beyond the bounds of what was needed in that way under the earlier industrial system, and specifically it involves, as an imperative requirement, the familiar use of printed matter. (It may be noted by the way that the percentage of illiteracy among the Japanese has fallen off since the Restoration at a rate that is fairly alarming for the stability of the established order.) It is particularly for the sake of matter-of-fact information, serviceable in the mechanically organised system of industry and communication, that this high rate of literacy is indispensable, and the effect of this industrial system and of life organised on these mechanical lines is unavoidably to extend and diffuse information of this kind.

At the same time the workday training of the routine of life under this industrial system, and of its ubiquitous and exacting system of communication, goes in a pronouncedly one-sided way to inculcate a matter-of-fact, and especially a materialistic, habit of mind; such as comports ill with those elusive putative verities of occult personal excellence in which the Spirit of Old Japan is grounded. So, e.g., the spread of such matter-of-fact information and such mechanistic conceptions must unavoidably act to dissipate all substantial belief in that opra bouffe mythology that makes up the state religion and supplies the foundation of the Japanese faith in the Emperor's divine pedigree and occult virtues; for these time-worn elements of Shinto are even less viable under the exacting mechanistic discipline of modern industry than are the frayed remnants of the faith that conventionally serve as articles of belief among the Christian peoples.

Under the given conditions, brought on throughout the Western world by the machine industry itself and by the antecedent institutional situation out of which it arose, this modern state of the industrial arts can be turned to account for the purposes of any national or dynastic ambitions only by the help or through the mediation of a business organisation of the modern kind. No other method of control or exploitation would serve, because no other system of control will articulate with the industrial organisation of those commercial nations with whom coordination and intercourse is requisite to bring the industry of the Japanese people to its best (pecuniary) efficiency.

Within the comprehensive community of nations that lies under the dominion of the machine process any degree of isolation counts as a disability. It is a system of interlocking processes; and the mechanism of coordination and commutation in the case is the commercial traffic in which all these communities are engaged. Incompetent, or even puerile, as this commercial enterprise may seem when seen in the large and taken as a means of the international coordination of industry, it still affords the sole method available for the purpose under the given conditions, because it is one of the chief of the given conditions. This business enterprise under whose tutelage the industrial system is placed does not directly contemplate or concern itself with serviceability to national, dynastic, or collective ends of any kind. It is a matter of individual enterprise, animated by motives of pecuniary gain and carried on a competitive basis.

Wherever it reaches it carries a "commercialisation" of human relations and social standards, and effects a displacement of such aims and values as can not be stated in terms of pecuniary gain; and so it throws pecuniary solvency into that position of first consideration that has once been occupied by pedigree and putative excellences of character. This pecuniary enterprise that so comes necessarily to take the oversight of the industrial system has certain specific consequences, secondary but essential, which the Japanese community has not yet experienced in full, because the secondary effects of the industrial revolution in Japan have not yet had time to come to a head. The most obvious of these, or at least the one most readily to be stated and appreciated in concrete (material) terms, is what might be called the "sabotage" of capitalism the competitive working at cross purposes of rival business concerns and the control of industrial processes by considerations of net gain to the managers rather than of material serviceability.

By virtue of this pecuniary control it has come about, in all countries in which the modern industrial system has had time to fall into settled lines, that the equipment is rarely, if ever, worked to its capacity often, over long intervals, at less than one-half its capacity and that the products, whether goods or services, are turned out with a view, in respect of kind, time, place and sophistication, to their profitable sale rather than to their serviceable consumption. It is presumably well within the mark to say that by force of this unavoidable capitalistic "sabotage" the industries in the maturer commercial countries fall short of their theoretically normal efficiency by something more than fifty per cent. The new era in Japan has not yet reached this stage of economic maturity, but there is no reason to presume a different outcome for Japan in this respect, given the necessary time for adjustment. With competitive gain as the legitimate end of endeavor comes also competitive spending as its legitimate counter foil, leading to a ubiquitous system of "conspicuous waste."

With this canon of right pecuniary living, reinforced by the new ethical principles of self-help and commercial solvency, comes in as a benchmark in public fife the well-worn principle of modern politics that "public office is a means of private gain." Hence the comprehensive system of "graft" that envelops all civilised affairs of state, and that once, e.g., allowed the great organisation of Russian officials to be defeated by the Japanese. This phase of civilisation must also of right come to the Japanese in due course of maturity So, again, through the competitive wage system, as well as by other channels of commercial indoctrination, the same principle of competitive consumption comes to permeate the industrial population and presently induces a higher standard of living, or more accurately of expenditure; which cuts into the disposable margin of production above cost, that might otherwise be drawn to the service of imperial politics. It would of course be hazardous to guess how long an interval must necessarily elapse between Japan's acquirement of the Western state of the industrial arts and the consequent disintegration of that Spirit of Old Japan that still is the chief asset of the state as a warlike power; but it may be accepted without hazard that such must be the event, sooner or later. And it is within this interval that Japan's opportunity lies.

The spiritual disintegration has already visibly set in, under all the several forms of modernisation spoken of above, but it is presumably still safe to say that hitherto the rate of gross gain in material efficiency due to the new scientific and technological knowledge is more than sufficient to offset this incipient spiritual deterioration; so that while the climax of the nation's net efficiency as a political or warlike force lies yet in the future, it would seem at least to lie in the calculable future. When this critical point in the country's growing maturity under the new economic dispensation shall be passed, when Japan shall have reached the plane of materialism and commercialisation occupied by the Christian nations, in respect of pecuniary ideals and self-help as well as of technological efficiency; then the advantage that now visibly inures to the government of Japan from the anomalous cultural situation of that country should be at an end, and the efficiency of the Japanese national organization should then presumably fall to the same level of efficiency per unit of men and of expenditure as is now occupied by the older peoples within the European community of nations. It is the present high efficiency of the Japanese, an efficiency which may be formulated as an exceptionally wide margin between cost of production and output of military force it is this that makes Japan formidable in the eyes of her Western competitors for imperial honors, and in substance it is this on which the Japanese masters of political intrigue rest their sanguine hopes of empire.

As already implied in what has been said above, the Japanese, statesmen and subjects, seeing the rapid rate of gain already made in material efficiency, and failing to see what their own experience has not taught them, that the new industrial era carries the faults of its own qualities; seeing the coefficient of gain, and not discounting the yet incipiently operative coefficient of loss, they count on the present rate of gross gain as a secure basis of prospective net gain. But from the considerations set forth above it follows that if this new-found efficiency is to serve the turn for the dynastic aggrandizement of Japan, it must be turned to account before the cumulatively accelerating rate of institutional deterioration overtakes and neutralises the cumulatively declining rate of gain in material efficiency; which should, humanly speaking, mean that Japan must strike, if at all, within the effective lifetime of the generation that is now coming to maturity. For, facile as the Japanese people have shown themselves to be, there is no reason to doubt that the commercialisation of Japan should be passably complete within that period. It is, therefore, also contained in the premises that, in order to an (imperialistically) successful issue, the imperial government must throw all its available force, without reservation, into one headlong rush; since in the nature of the case no second opportunity of the kind is to be looked for.

Index

www.ingramcontent.com/pod-product-compliance
Lightning Source LLC
Chambersburg PA
CBHW061209220326
41599CB00025B/4581